Praise for *Success*

"At a time when we need more support as individuals, Scott provides very helpful suggestions for strengthening our resolve to thrive. It's refreshing to see a young professional focusing on such important questions and on the challenges that all of us face each day. It's clear that he has drawn wisdom from his evolution as a human being."

—Dr. Freeman A. Hrabowski III, President Emeritus of the University of Maryland, Baltimore Country (UMBC), named one of America's Best Leaders by U.S. News & World Report

"Are you ready to challenge yourself to be your best self? Are you ready to be real with yourself? Chazz is the real deal. What he's telling you is what he practices. As a science communicator, I am amazed at how Chazz provides easy to follow science-based principles to help individuals live better lives!"

—Hakeem Oluseyi, American NASA astrophysicist, cosmologist, and author of *A Quantum Life: My Unlikely Journey from the Street to the Stars*

"As a social entrepreneur and small business advocate, I strongly believe that outer wealth begins with inner success. Scott offers a unique perspective to enlighten the minds of the next generation and a scientific approach to achieving true personal and professional actualization. This book feels a lot like the modern day *Think & Grow Rich*!"

—Johnny Bailey, CEO of ShineHard Network

"What a breath of fresh air! Chazz offers a timely, unique, and practical approach to redefining how to reach and sustain real success. Packed with tips and step-by-step exercises, *Success Starts Within* will help readers unlock their inner strength, break through limiting beliefs, and achieve a prosperous life."

—Dr. Joe Vitale, author of *The Attractor Factor* and appeared in the movie *The Secret*

"As burnout, stress, and anxiety continue to increase in our communities, this book offers an essential guide for anyone ready to elevate their life."
    —Jay Barnett, mental health expert, author of *Just Heal, Bro*

"In a culture where it's considered cool to overwork and 'chase the next biggest thing,' my man Chazz provides a powerful guide for a better path to lasting success without forgoing essential wellness needs"
    —Brandon McEachern, cofounder of Broccoli City

"In a world where mental health is at the forefront of everyone's minds right now, this book offers an easy-to-follow, transformational approach to changing behaviors and habits that can affect the overall well-being of an individual."
    —Jonathan Shepherd, MD, board-certified child, adolescent, and adult psychiatrist, Chief Medical Director, Hope Health Systems, Inc.

"We have learned two things from our twenty-first century, post-pandemic experience as human beings: success without wellness is fool's gold, and wellness cannot be maintained without a regimen of consistent self-care—of mind, body, and spirit. In *Success Starts Within*, Chazz Scott provides such a regimen, and in doing so, delivers a blueprint for authentic fulfillment and resilience despite turbulent times and circumstances. If you want results, follow this regimen."
    —Alfred Edmond Jr., Senior Vice President and Executive Editor, Black Enterprise

"*Success Starts Within* is a truly inspiring and insightful book that has the power to transform the lives of its readers. Chazz's approach to regular radical self-care is a game-changer, and his strategies for creating the internal conditions necessary for success are both practical and powerful. This book is a must-read for anyone looking to achieve their full potential and live their best life."
    —Karen Allen, author of *Stop & Shift: The Mindset Reset that Changes Everything*

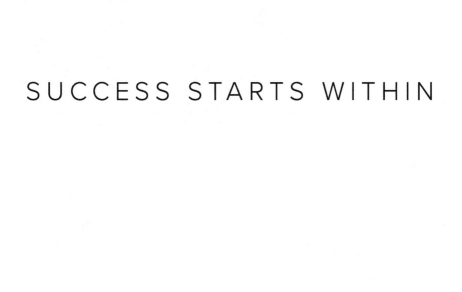

SUCCESS STARTS WITHIN

SUCCESS STARTS WITHIN

ACHIEVE
YOUR POTENTIAL
THROUGH RADICAL
SELF-CARE

CHAZZ SCOTT

Central Recovery Press (CRP) is committed to publishing exceptional materials addressing addiction treatment, recovery, and behavioral healthcare topics.

For more information, visit www.centralrecoverypress.com.

Publisher: Central Recovery Press
       3321 N. Buffalo Drive
       Las Vegas, NV 89129

28 27 26 25 24 23   1 2 3 4 5

Library of Congress Cataloging-in-Publication Data
Names: Scott, Chazz, author.
Title: Success starts within : achieve your potential through radical
   self-care / Chazz Scott.
Description: Las Vegas, NV : Central Recovery Press, [2023] | Includes
   bibliographical references.
Identifiers: LCCN 2023003493 (print) | LCCN 2023003494 (ebook) | ISBN
   9781949481839 (paperback) | ISBN 9781949481846 (ebook)
Subjects: LCSH: Self-realization. | Self-care, Health. | Mental health. |
   Well-being. | Success.
Classification: LCC BF637.S4 S393 2023 (print) | LCC BF637.S4 (ebook) |
   DDC 158.1--dc23/eng/20230415
LC record available at https://lccn.loc.gov/2023003493
LC ebook record available at https://lccn.loc.gov/2023003494
Photo of Chazz Scott by Cameron Evans.

Every attempt has been made to contact copyright holders. If copyright holders have not been properly acknowledged please contact us. Central Recovery Press will be happy to rectify the omission in future printings of this book.

Publisher's Note
This book contains general information about practical strategies for self-care, how to transcend negative thinking, gain inner confidence, improve focus, and develop meaningful relationships. The information contained herein is not medical advice. This book is not an alternative to medical advice from your doctor or other professional healthcare provider.

Our books represent the experiences and opinions of their authors only. Every effort has been made to ensure that events, institutions, and statistics presented in our books as facts are accurate and up to date. To protect their privacy, the names of some of the people, places, and institutions in this book may have been changed.

Cover design by The Book Designers. Interior design by Deb Tremper, Six Penny Graphics.

For Chris and Tyler.
Thank you for showing me what it means to be a friend.
You will be missed.

TABLE OF CONTENTS

When you don't go within, you go without.

Yogi Bhajan

INTRODUCTION

Growing up I always heard, "get good grades," "be successful," do what's necessary to "achieve your goals," do the "hard work," and when that doesn't work, "put in more hours." While nothing is inherently wrong with these statements, it forces you to believe the only route to a happy, fulfilled, and successful life is through overworking and putting in long hours, even at the expense of your health, happiness, and peace of mind. Thus, promoting the toxic hustle culture of burnout, stress, and the continual mental health crisis. As a result, many of us are striving harder but are thriving less in our lives. We continue to work out of external necessity rather than for inner well-being.

This mindset drives employees to unconsciously sacrifice everything—if it means rising to the next level in their career. It urges entrepreneurs to put in eighty-hour weeks. We sacrifice so much of our *now* for a better tomorrow. The sacrifices may pay off for short-term victories but can be detrimental to true long-term success and well-being. And many times, we don't gain the traction we are seeking. Striving and overworking may have their place as a societal norm, but a more effective and sustainable route is necessary.

As we continue our journey toward success and a satisfying life, we unconsciously assume that the progress and happiness we innately yearn for will somehow be found through this human-built construct. It almost feels like we are always chasing but never arriving. And even if success and happiness do come, it can be challenging and elusive to sustain. If we believe life is not working in our favor, we automatically resort to striving and working harder. In fact, it unconsciously forces us to believe that success and happiness are constantly in the distant future when, in actuality, they can be experienced *now*. What we will learn is that success, happiness, and living out our potential cannot be pursued. It ensues as a by-product of well-being.

This is a process of becoming, rather than just arriving. *Success Starts Within* is based on a sustaining principle that inward and outward success can be cultivated in the here and now, not by overworking or burning out but through continual and regular *radical self-care* that can be integrated into your daily routine.

Our hyperactive lifestyles are making it difficult to reach our potential professionally and personally. From the constant pings, overstimulation, distractions, and social media binges, our current environment elicits our body's fight-or-flight responses that stop us from achieving who we desire to become. Over time, without consciously realizing it, this increased demand externally has become detrimental to our internal needs to foster a full and exuberant life. Many of us are living in constant survival mode—"just trying to make it through the day"—which depletes the energy our bodies need to access higher mental functions for creativity, problem-solving, and joy. Ultimately, this makes it nearly impossible to embrace our soul's potential and carry out our true calling.

We must return to a way of life that allows us to thrive no matter what capacity or environment we find ourselves in.

This book came to fruition because I knew there was something more for me, but I didn't know how to cultivate it. I worked harder externally, but inner growth never came. After engaging in hours of personal study that included studying scientific research about the human brain, conducting countless youth mental wellness workshops with our nonprofit, Positively Caviar, Inc., and providing corporate seminars—I experienced a paradigm shift that altered my outlook on how to successfully approach life.

True personal growth and progress didn't come by putting in longer hours; it came when I stopped and became conscious, still, and integrated the daily principles found in this book. From this journey, I realized it came back to the fundamentals of what we desire and who we all innately yearn to become—taking care of our pure intrinsic core self to live and reach our highest self. And to live the highest expression of our self, we must create the proper conditions internally so our minds and bodies can yield the capacity, creativity, energy, and vibrancy to carry out the growth and progress we are seeking. Continual cultivation of your inner wealth is the central goal of this book.

This is your manual for your mind, body, and soul to counter the environment that is becoming seemingly unconducive for your desired unfoldment toward your potential.

This is your guide to cultivating the inner conditions within yourself, therefore transforming your external day-to-day life that will allow you to express your full self in your career, creative work, and relationships and create a life you are proud of and enjoy. This book will show you how to use your mind and body more effectively to teach you how to *slow down to speed up*, to improve your performance, boost creativity, build resilience, and manifest your desires.

Let me be clear and say this is not a book full of hacks and tricks for short-term achievement. These are proven principles and science-backed integrative daily techniques that have stood the test of time and can radically enhance the quality of your life, thereby improving your results.

There are new rules being written for what true success means, and a central component of this goal is cultivating and maintaining your inner wealth. Society has glorified the word success and attached it to overworking, skipping meals, and sacrificing our body's health to achieve the results we want in our lives. This is just unsustainable and, quite frankly, an unenjoyable experience. The demanding hustle culture combined with our always-on, frazzled lifestyles are unconsciously undermining the natural progression toward humans' deepest desires and our ever-expanding potential.

Success Starts Within is your guide to not only success but to successful living. This is your catalyst to sustaining success and attaining a joyful life experience. This book is about tapping into the deep reservoirs of talent and ability that already exist inside you so that you can effectively expand toward your desires. And it all starts with taking care of your internal self first. Success is linked to well-being. This is where true success begins and is sustained.

CHAPTER ONE

THE INTERSECTION OF WELLNESS AND SUCCESS

*Every organism has one and only one central
need in life, to fulfill its own potentialities.*
Rollo May

The True You Craves Expansion

Let's do some self-reflection. Think about a time in your life when you truly felt happy or fulfilled. You may have felt grateful, expansive, empowered, joyful, or even worthy. Or maybe you felt like you were "in the flow" and time stood still. You may have even felt a sense of completeness within yourself and with life in that moment.

For many of us, examples of these moments shouldn't take very long to bubble up to the surface of our mind. They could have come as a result of accomplishing a worthwhile endeavor, progressing toward a goal, enjoying a hobby, expressing a talent, or even helping someone in need. Such moments of joy may have even stirred up so much emotion that you wanted nothing more than to share it with the people closest to you.

We've all had events like these in our lives. Why? Because it's what our souls desperately crave.

**A basic desire of the human soul is to grow,
create, and expand creatively.**

This desire can be expressed through our workplace, our relationships, or even our hobbies. We yearn to do our best in our profession to advance ourselves in our career. We immerse ourselves in our hobbies to express ourselves creatively. We desire to provide more for our loved ones, emotionally and financially, to let them know we are there for them. We set New Year's resolutions and dream about a future vision for our lives because we aspire to be the best that we can possibly be. We purchase new books to provide us with inspiration and help us learn more about ourselves so we can show up to life more effectively. This inner longing and desire to consistently strive to reach our potential seems to never leave us. No matter where you are or what you have achieved, you always desire for a little more.

You'll notice this work has less to do with **what you do** and more to do with **who you become** as a result of expanding yourself toward your potential. The "what" is just a tool to be able to express and demonstrate your full authentic self.

The reason these moments are so powerful is because they reflect back to us who we really are. Happiness, joy, health, radiant living, and success are within us. And this desire is craving to seek expression through us.

Unfortunately, if we're not consciously paying attention, our twenty-first century always-on lifestyle that is full of distractions, social constructs, demands, and stress can stifle our basic human desire to reach true success and sustainable well-being in our personal and professional lives.

Many of us run around feeling as though we simultaneously have *one foot on the gas and one on the brake.* You know what this would look like if you tried it in an actual car. You'd end up going nowhere and creating a lot of avoidable damage to your car in the process. In life this can look like the following: working hard but not seeing the progress or success that you want. Setting a goal but somehow never accomplishing it. Having the persistent sense that you are not truly tapping into your potential but not knowing where to start. Feeling discontent in your life but not knowing how to approach lasting change.

It is hard to express happiness and revel in success if you are feeling burned out, unproductive, lacking in motivation and vibrancy, stuck in a mental rut, or unfulfilled. These experiences can further spill over into your career, health, relationships, and overall vitality.

In addition, our society has forced us to believe the only route to success is through "chasing the next big thing," working sixty-hour weeks, and forcefully using our physical powers to get the things we want. Ironically, this way of life undermines our mind, body, and soul's basic needs to adequately expand and reach our potential. In essence, our potential to bring our full self to life can be stifled by following this false path to success. We've prioritized "doing well" over "being well."

As a result, many of us are working hard to chase our dreams but failing to cultivate the needs of our mind, body, and soul. To some, these needs are almost considered secondary to achieving success, but in fact, they are *essential*. When we put our mind, body, and soul's needs first, this sets us on the true path to achieving success and a satisfying life. Even since the pandemic, Fortune 500 companies have made it clear that well-being isn't just a nice-to-have employee perk but an essential business strategy for success. It's time for us to stop hustling and start aligning.

Achieving our potential can be likened to a seed or plant growing. When the conditions are adequate—enough water, food, sunlight—the plant will simply grow to become what it's supposed to be. No force is required for the plant to reach its potential. In fact, force will only hinder it. Same with us. Once the proper conditions, which can include our beliefs, mindset, habits, and patterns of thinking are cultivated consistently, our mind, body, and soul are able to unfold and expand. Thus, realizing our full potential requires no force or anxious effort; given the proper conditions, we become who we were meant to be.

Let me digress a bit. A better way to depict this path and what I mean when I use the term "needs" or "core needs" throughout the book is by using renowned psychologist Abraham Maslow's Hierarchy of Needs. This hierarchy (shown below in Figure 1) has been used to show the needs, in order of priority, of a human being to help us understand human motivation and fulfill our innate potential.

According to Maslow, there are five categories of need: physiological, safety, love and belonging, esteem, and finally culminating in self-actualization. The hierarchy serves as a guiding model to show that once a lower need is met, the next need will become the focus of our attention. For example, it can be quite difficult for someone who is extremely hungry, which is a physiological need, to focus on anything but food. Or let's take esteem, for instance; if this need is not met, you may experience what psychologists refer to as feelings of inferiority or inadequacy.

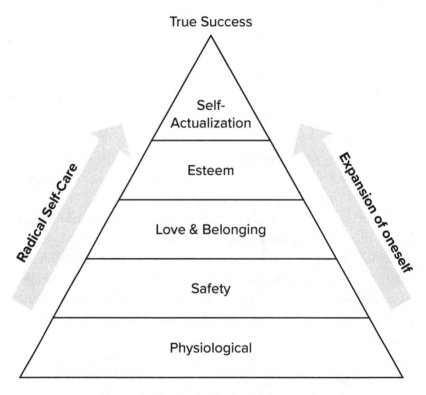

Figure 1: Maslow's Hierarchy of Needs
This hierarchy structure is meant to serve as a model to depict the expansion of oneself toward their potential and what I define as true success. When the needs of a human are properly addressed continuously, using radical self-care techniques, this results in self-actualization and feelings of fulfillment that lead to unshakable success.

When the needs of food, safety, social connection, and self-esteem are met, you can advance up the hierarchy toward self-actualization, which refers to feeling fulfilled and achieving your potential. This is considered the highest of human needs and is an integral piece of the expansion of who you are. You can think of it like this: as you start to move up the hierarchy, you are expanding yourself. And to adequately expand and ultimately fulfill your potential, these core needs should be met consistently.

In the context of radical self-care and building success from within, if you are not getting enough sleep or rest—a physiological need—it can be difficult to realize your potential; the brain and body need adequate time to recharge so you can solve problems effectively and think creatively. Or suppose your dietary patterns are full of ultra-processed foods and lack a healthy balance of fruits and veggies. In this case, your body will not yield you the capacity or energy to biochemically enable you to execute your dreams and respond to stressful events appropriately.

Ultimately, the mindset to achieve success that society continues to foster has caused us to think that success in life derives from external factors, such as a certain job position, material items, or letters behind our names, when, ironically, real success and growth come *from within*. In other words, what your soul is seeking is not related to what you want or what you hope to accomplish; it's about who you become as a result of these things.

This is where *radical self-care* comes into play.

In order to adequately meet your soul's root desire for expansion toward self-actualization and rise above the demands of life, you must address the depths of who you are. What makes you, you. Importantly, you must look at taking care of what I like to call your "intrinsic core self," which is your mind, body, and soul's basic impulse. When you can nurture your intrinsic core self, you are able to effortlessly be guided and led to the opportunities, synchronicities, fulfillment, and happiness that your soul craves—even in the midst of distractions and the demands of life. As you nurture your intrinsic core self through seeking therapy, letting go of habits that don't serve you, forgiving, becoming mindful of your self-talk, and taking a deep look at your beliefs of self-worth, amazing things begin to occur in your life.

When you become aligned with yourself and take care of your core needs, your success will come faster than you expect.

When you are out of alignment with yourself, it can feel as though you are blocking yourself from your own greatness, as I mentioned previously, like you have your foot on the gas and the brakes at the same time. Radical self-care is about adopting an effective approach to achieving your success in life so you can keep your foot comfortably on the gas while taking care of yourself in the process. Consistently restoring balance and rhythm in your soul is the goal here.

Interestingly, when you can continuously take care of your intrinsic core self internally by using the radical self-care techniques presented in this book, your success, happiness, and fulfillment become streamlined externally. This experience will be demystified and expressed through you as you take your radical self-care journey.

What Is Radical Self-Care?

We live in a society that demands so much from us that we rarely create the space we need to take care of ourselves. To truly achieve our potential, we must demand the time and space to pay attention to our mind, body, and soul. Radical self-care is about taking care of our intrinsic core self—the part that makes us human. So rather than just managing symptoms or sugarcoating problems, hoping for a quick fix, we take care of things at the source. This process is about addressing the causes, not the effects.

The source of who you are extends from these crucial interconnected domains:

- Patterns of thinking
- Core purpose of living
- Habits
- Mental conditioning
- Self-image
- Mindset
- Beliefs

And because this is your core self, it never leaves you and is difficult to change without developing a proper understanding of who you are and taking intelligent action. For example, if you don't understand how your patterns of thinking influence your outcomes in life (health, wealth, happiness), it can feel like you're taking one step forward and two steps back when trying to make any sustainable changes. This is because these integral domains of who you are influence every decision you make or don't make, which ultimately plays a vital role in the overall success in all areas of your life. Practically speaking, a person may change their home, profession, or friends, but that person will not find lasting satisfaction until a change *within* occurs. This is your core self.

As American author and motivational speaker Tony Robbins would say, "80 percent of success is psychology and 20 percent is mechanics." Meaning that no matter how many books you read, strategies you implement, podcasts you listen to, or coaches you see, your success is unlikely unless you have the right mindset and beliefs. This book will address these core areas of who you are that are essential to wellness and, therefore, to success.

This isn't a one-and-done exercise, either. It's not just practiced when emergencies happen, like losing a job or experiencing dissatisfaction or a sense of emptiness. Although this approach to life can be used during these situations, it works best when it is cultivated day in and day out to address your core intrinsic self—because there are always new levels to discover within yourself. If you think you've reached a plateau, know that there is always more to experience and enjoy.

Radical self-care addresses your core self so true change and proper unfoldment continuously emanate from you and overflow into every aspect of your life. This is a proactive rather than reactive approach to life, to better prepare you and help you effortlessly manage the demands that life may throw at you. I am not suggesting that things will be easy, but continuous cultivation of the strategies presented in this book will allow you to rise above life's adversities so you can consistently activate potential.

How do I know this? Because I've been there! One morning in the winter of 2017, I awoke in puddles of my own sweat drenching my sheets. The mental conflicts and confusion gripping me seeped from my pores as I slept. Every morning I would rise feeling unfulfilled and fearful. It felt like I was at the mercy of my circumstances leaving me feeling vulnerable and not in control of my life. Every day at work I felt like I was going through the motions, just waiting for the weekend to come. I was unhappy and empty. I felt stuck. I sensed there was something more for me in my life but didn't know what that could be nor where to start. I had lost my passion for life.

Everything felt like a chore—from going to the grocery store, gym, and work to hanging out with friends. The things I used to enjoy were no longer feeding my inner soul like they used to. The lack of joy and growth in my life soon was reflected in how I spoke (to myself and others), walked, and even how I treated my friends and family. Now don't get me wrong, I had a "nice job" and steady pay, and I did all the things I thought I was supposed to do to be "successful." But something was off, and I couldn't make sense of it.

Then one day it hit me like a freight train. As I sat in my room, unhappy, discouraged, and quite frankly lost, I realized that I wasn't the best son, friend, big brother, significant other, coworker, or community member I knew I could be. My unhappiness was affecting others, and the worst part of it was that I didn't know how to stop the negative thoughts and emotions that were bubbling up nonstop throughout the day.

After engaging in personal study, trying all the techniques presented in this book (and more not included here), and meditating a few minutes each day, I slowly began to feel a shift in my internal experience, which begin to change my external reality. My zest for life began to gradually come back, and I started to experience fulfillment again. This was when I experienced my first taste of what would truly change my paradigm of life.

Many of us live in a constant state of stress, and it can feel like we are running on empty. This emptiness can lead to discontent, poor health, a pervasive state of melancholy, and a lack of passion for life. The care, nourishment, and proper understanding of how to take care of one's mind, body, and soul remain paramount for anyone seeking a full life. In my case, I started to realize I was not consistently taking care of my intrinsic core self—my mind, body, and soul.

When most people think of self-care, they think of journaling or keeping a list of things they're grateful for. There is nothing wrong with these activities. In fact, I encourage them. But we must take the work a step further to address the source of who you are. True change and growth are much deeper. Radical self-care takes everyday self-care to another level to reveal the core of who you are so that lasting shifts can manifest in your life. Again, this stems from becoming aware of your patterns of thinking and beliefs that may be holding you back, and also letting go of habits that may not be serving you. It's considered "radical" because when this approach to life is practiced, it fundamentally alters every aspect of your life.

When practiced consistently, radical self-care can help you uncover and focus on the needs you must address in order to activate your potential and obtain new levels of your authentic self.

Once your core self is addressed continuously, you are able to bring your full self to life, no matter the setting—whether it be the workplace, the classroom, in friendships, or in intimate relationships. Radical self-care gives you back to yourself. Ultimately, your core intrinsic self is able to be fully expressed through allowing yourself to grow, create, and expand creatively so that you can achieve the fulfillment and happiness you naturally seek. Radical self-care is about more than health: It is about living fully.

How Does Radical Self-Care Lead to Success?

Happiness, achievement of one's desires, and wellness all play integral roles in one's overall success in life, but they are often viewed as being separate from one another. In fact, they feed off one another throughout our journey in life.

Someone who is taking care of their core intrinsic self—mind, body, and soul—is in the proper condition to allow themselves to expand appropriately toward their potential, which I addressed earlier as an essential human desire that can be stifled in today's society. When our core needs are properly addressed, it often leads to states of fulfillment and achievement of one's goals and desires. Now, understand that this process is not linear in nature; it's a feedback loop that will need to be addressed continuously.

This is how some celebrities can have millions of dollars and reach the pinnacle of "success" and remain unhappy. Many of them fail to clearly see that external material items are useless substitutes for inner success and well-being.

Or maybe you've finally made it to your dream job but still feel unfulfilled. Or you're constantly overworking yourself hoping to achieve success but are growing physically, emotionally, and mentally distressed in the process. These examples can represent situations where your core intrinsic self is not being attended to properly.

And it doesn't help that our society glamorizes quick fixes, such as "6-minute 6-pack abs" or "how to get rich quickly." Overnight success programs like these rarely address the depths of our being in order to bring about true change and everlasting success. In addition, we are constantly being told that nonstop work with rarely any rest is the only way to achieve success. As a result, many of us forgo the wellness of our mind, body, and soul, thinking it's the only way to achieve the goals we desire. We now live in a society that makes us feel guilty for resting and being still when ironically, these conditions revitalize our brains and bodies and help propel us toward our goals and dreams.

Often, high achievers are persuaded by concepts like the "10,000-hour rule," which suggests that in order to achieve extraordinary success, you must put in at least 10,000 hours of practice. Discipline and continuous repetition are necessary, but what happens when you put in 10,000 hours to master your skill and your body breaks down in the process, leaving you feeling depleted and unfulfilled? Or maybe you finally reach your ideal level of success but don't know how to properly sustain it to truly relish the fruits of your labor. You don't have to exhaust your body's vital resources to achieve superior success in your chosen field. Maintaining a healthy body and mastering your craft are not mutually exclusive. You can have both with the proper guidance to not only ensure your success but also maintain a successful life worth living.

It almost seems like society is trying to speed us up while new research is concluding that real success and lasting fulfillment in life come from what I like to call mastering the art of *slowing down to speed up*. For example, psychologists Ken Sheldon and Tim Kasser discovered in their research that people who are joyful and mentally and physically healthy have a higher degree of "vertical coherence" among their goals, which exists "when lower-level goals are consistent with or regulated by higher level goals." In other words, when you take time to care for your being first, whether through meditation or becoming centered on a future vision of yourself, your brain and body seem to accelerate you toward your success faster. I'm going to teach you how to get twice as much done in half the time. It's all about increasing your personal effectiveness so you can feel better, do better, and live better. That is what you will learn in this book!

We are constantly moving our bodies, thinking we need to "make things happen" in order to achieve success, when, in reality, real massive growth is found from slowing down, taking time for introspection, getting intentional rest, and deepening your understanding of yourself. This can seem counterintuitive in a society that recognizes movement and activity for progress.

When you consistently stabilize who you are and what you have (your body, mind, and soul), your success and desires tend to multiply. And when you take care of yourself, this also frees up mental capacity to think creatively to solve problems and fulfill your potential. The strategies in this book may encourage you to take a break to meditate in order to come up with the best solution when solving a professional or personal problem instead of using your willpower to force your way through intensive grunt work.

A quote from renowned psychologist Dr. Susan Jeffers, from her book *Feel the Fear and Do It Anyway*, further explains this concept: "We get some of our most inspired ideas when we are relaxing or doing something other than the task that needs a solution."

This may feel like an unorthodox way to streamline your path to success in life, but the science provided in this book will show you how radical self-care will help you upgrade your mental capacities to achieve success.

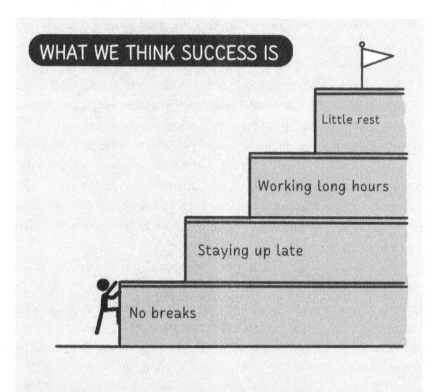

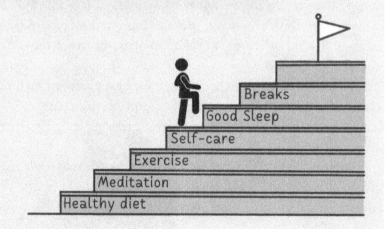

Now here's what you should know: Whether or not you realize this, you already possess the talents, abilities, and creative potential to achieve the success and fulfillment you yearn for.

Radical self-care helps to uncover your potential so you can activate it to achieve your desires.

Here's a story to help put this concept in perspective:

In 1957, a monastery in Thailand, along with a giant clay Buddha, was being relocated by a group of monks. As they began moving the giant Buddha, one of the monks noticed a large crack in the clay. To make matters worse, it began to rain. The head monk covered the crack with a piece of cloth to protect it from the rain.

Later that evening, the head monk went to check on the giant Buddha. While he held his torch under the cloth, he noticed a golden glow emanating from the crack. He wondered if there was something underneath the clay that covered the Buddha. The monk got his hammer and chisel and begin to chip away the clay. After many hours of work, the strange glow grew bigger and brighter. It was finally revealed that the statue was in fact made of solid gold. Historians believe the Buddha had been covered with clay by the Thai monks hundreds of years ago to protect it from an attack by the Burmese army, who were interested in invading Thailand, formally known as Siam. Today it's believed the Buddha statue is valued at over 200 million dollars. As you might imagine, the monks were determined to protect the statue because of its tremendous meaning to its people and, of course, it's monetary value if the Burmese army found it.

This story eloquently shows us that inside each of us lies a golden Buddha waiting to be expressed. Unfortunately, throughout life, many of us pile on layers of clay—whether it be due to societal expectations, limited thinking, unconscious conditioning, or external influences (which you will learn to overcome)—forcing us to slowly bury our deep reservoirs of talent and ability. Over time, with so much clay piled on, we can eventually forget that the golden Buddha has been within us the entire time just waiting to be revealed and properly expressed.

By using the radical self-care strategies presented in this book, you will be able to effectively chip away at this clay so you are not hindered on your path to expressing your full potential and achieving your dreams. This is a process of getting back to the fundamentals of who you are.

Earlier in the chapter, I invited you to remember those moments in life that brought you true joy, that made you feel expansive or worthy—this was your golden Buddha shining through! This book is here to help you reconnect to that part of yourself on a continual basis.

You will start to uncover the deep capacities of your being to bring forth what you truly want from life as you engage in this process. As you will see, attending to your core intrinsic self—physically, mentally, emotionally, spiritually—contributes to being able to fulfill your purpose with vitality and a certain aliveness, which leads to true success and fulfillment.

RADICAL SELF-CARE TIP:
Stop Hustling, Start Aligning

Have you ever felt stressed about all the items on your to-do list or anxious about an upcoming presentation? Ever felt overwhelmed and frazzled by the sensory overload of information and pings? Or maybe you want to improve your focus on a task that requires your full attention. And many of us, without even knowing it, are suffering from a case of email apnea (or screen apnea), which involves shallow breathing or holding your breath unconsciously when responding to an email or viewing a screen. Taking control of your breath using a simple breathing technique may be the simplest way to calm your nervous system, boost your mental clarity, bring coherence to your body, and instantly lower stress levels.

Here's the insanely simple technique: make your exhalations longer than your inhalations. When your exhale is a few seconds longer than your inhale, the vagus nerve, which runs down your neck through the diaphragm, sends a signal to turn on your parasympathetic nervous system, simultaneously turning down your sympathetic nervous system. When we feel stressed or anxious, our body's sympathetic nervous system is in full gear, thus activating our body's fight-or-flight response. As a result, your heart rate speeds up, and stress hormones like cortisol are released into your body. Essentially, the body knows it's not safe, so it wants to protect itself as if it's running from a physical threat. But when your exhale is longer than your inhale, your parasympathetic nervous system, also known as the rest and digest system, is activated, which drops your heart rate, lowers your blood pressure, and puts you in a state of calm for improved cognition. By doing this exercise, you signal to your body that you are safe so you can fully utilize your mental resources to activate your potential more efficiently.

Try the popular 4-7-8 technique, which involves the following steps:

1. Find a comfortable place to sit or lie down.
2. Inhale for a count of four seconds through your nose.
3. Now, hold your breath and count for seven seconds.
4. Finally, exhale through your mouth for a count of eight seconds.
5. Repeat the steps above for four more cycles.

If you need to maintain grace under pressure, improve your sleep, or calm your mind, try this simple breathing technique. It may not make all your jitters or stress symptoms disappear, but I can guarantee that you will feel more relaxed, focused, and calm afterward. If you can manage your nervous system, you can master your destiny.

Will Radical Self-Care Make Me Happy or Rich?

Radical self-care is a process that will help you uncover your potential so you can bring your full self to life. Now, tangentially, as you become more aware of your capabilities by expressing your natural talents, deepening your belief within yourself, and continuously engaging in your personal growth, happiness and wealth *internally* will ensue. It's possible that your "inner wealth" may lead to an accumulation of *external* wealth over time.

Let's look at an example of how radical self-care might increase your earning potential. Let's say you hate your drive to work, your work environment can be dysfunctional a lot of the time, and you're not as productive as you know you can be, but you can't figure out why since the job is actually a good fit. After doing some of the radical self-care work outlined in this book, you realize your negative self-talk is off the charts, especially during your morning commute. Once you implement self-care strategies, your drive becomes bearable, your less-agitated demeanor makes it easier to function within the office environment, and you become far more productive. You might even get that well-deserved bonus or salary increase at the end of the year! Internal wealth *can* equal external wealth. Money flows toward stability and positive emotions, while negative emotions repel it.

But external wealth isn't necessarily the goal of this book. As I've discussed, your true self—or your golden Buddha—is just waiting to shine through you. When you engage in this process and begin to chip away at the clay, you will realize that "you were born rich," as self-help author and speaker Bob Proctor would say. Not rich just in the sense of money or material items, but rich in experiences, relationships, happiness, and satisfaction with life itself.

When you begin to care for yourself and learn more about who you are, you are able to make wise decisions in your life—decisions that are in alignment with your purpose and goals. And when better decisions can be made consistently, the results tend to show up in your life. In this case, the results are your happiness, more fulfilling relationships, better health, internal (and maybe external) wealth, and overall life satisfaction.

When you become aware of your beliefs, patterns of thinking, and mindset, you can take the appropriate action so your life is producing the results you want. I will discuss this later, and I've included an exercise in the book that may help you.

We often don't realize how much subtle negative or limiting beliefs and mindsets can influence our lives, whether it's our happiness or earning potential. But when you discover "what makes you tick," by engaging in your radical self-care journey, you start to unmask the potential that is waiting to be expressed through you. When this happens, your talents, natural abilities, and gifts are able to shine through, thus creating the life you desire.

As it is written in the Bible, your gifts will make room for you. And when you begin to uncover and utilize those gifts, this puts you on the path toward the happiness and riches you seek that already lie within you. This is what "health is wealth" really means.

Is Radical Self-Care Selfish?

Many people associate radical self-care with selfishness when in fact it's the complete opposite. Indiana State University defines radical self-care as the "assertion that you have the responsibility to take care of yourself first before attempting to take care of others. It's necessary to fill your cup first, then to give to others from the overflow." The simple truth is that prioritizing self-care does not exhibit a lack of love or care for others; instead, it shows care and love for yourself, so you are able to adequately take care of others.

To put differently, when you properly focus on your needs first, the highest form of yourself is able to shine through, enabling you to give to others more abundantly. Many of us regularly deplete our souls at the expense of others. When this happens, we don't perform at our best and we don't feel our best; this depletion can also stifle our success and hinder our ability to care for others. Simply put, only when you give yourself the attention you need and invest in your personal growth can you then give to others.

For example, when I meditate and exercise consistently I have much more patience and understanding when my wife and I get into a disagreement. My mind feels at ease, which allows my wife to get me at my best so I can see her side much more clearly and adequately. Thus, allowing us to reach a common understanding much more quickly than if I were agitated, stressed, or not feeling at peace with myself. When you invest in yourself, everyone benefits. This is what it means when the Bible says, "Love your neighbor as yourself." As author and American Minister

Catherine Ponder stated in her book *Open Your Mind to Receive*, "You cannot possibly give to others unless you first have something to give."

If you have ever been on a plane, you've likely heard a flight attendant instruct passengers to put on their oxygen mask first, before assisting others, in the event of an emergency. This is not selfish; this is lifesaving. So, yes, you must put on your mask before helping your sibling, partner, or even child! After all, how do you intend to help a loved one if you run out of oxygen? In the case of self-care, your "mask" can be any number of things—physical, emotional, intellectual, or spiritual—in order to get your basic needs met.

Ironically, to fully give yourself to anything in life, whether it be your significant other, your career, or a close friend, it's imperative to learn how to consistently fill up your cup first. How can you abundantly give to another if you don't have the discipline to manage your finances? How can you teach a child about compassion if you have difficulty forgiving yourself for your own mistakes? How do you expect to wholeheartedly love your significant other when you're not taking the time to love and care for yourself? How can you be the best father, mother, businessperson, or community member without learning how to help yourself first?

We must not over-give to others and under-give to ourselves. In essence, we should be exceptional stewards of the mind and body that we were given and even of the money we earn. It's much harder to serve others effectively with a shaky foundation. As author and speaker, Michael Beckwith said, "You can't be the light of the world if you can't pay your light bill."

We must be great stewards of what we have been given
first before we can adequately give to others.

And when you make yourself a priority and become a great steward of your resources: Your friends' successes will make you happy. You will express love to your significant other without the expectation of receiving anything in return. You will tip more at restaurants because you know there is enough to go around. You will feel compelled to help people climb their ladder to success in business or workplace. You will do more for your family and friends. You will feel emotions of abundance and opportunity instead of lack and hindrance. You will realize that giving selflessly is an act of courage, knowing that everything will be returned to you tenfold. And at the end of the day, you will feel like you've won because you know the real prize is helping and inspiring others to live courageously and abundantly.

Now that's a feedback loop worth experiencing. This is sustainable for everyone because you are not depleting your own soul at the expense of others.

Here's another situation you may have faced. Have you ever noticed how harmonious it feels to be genuinely happy for someone else when you feel like your life is on the right path? But then when things are just not going right in your life, it takes much more of a conscious effort to feel genuinely happy for another person? This is simply because what you do for yourself, you do for others. When you think of yourself in the highest form, you also think of others in that way. But if you marginalize yourself, you begin to marginalize the people around you. And when you marginalize your gifts and abilities, you marginalize the talents of those closest to you—whether in your career or personal relationships. As American self-help author, Wayne Dyer would say, "You can't give away what you don't have."

If what you have in your heart is jealousy, fear, scarcity, or contempt, that is also what tends to be expressed to others whether you consciously realize it or not. And this harms your relationships with coworkers, loved ones, and friends. However, through radical self-care, you can counter these limiting emotions and, in turn, repair valued relationships with others.

To bring this closer to home, have you ever heard the tale of the two wolves? Well, it goes a little something like this:

One evening a Cherokee elder was teaching his grandson about life. He told his grandson, "There is a battle between two wolves inside us all. One is evil. It is anger, jealousy, greed, resentment, inferiority, lies, and ego. The other is good. It is joy, peace, love, hope, humility, kindness, empathy, and truth." The boy thought about it and asked, "Grandfather, which wolf wins?" The grandfather quietly replied, "The one you feed."

This tale represents the inner turmoil many of us face throughout life: Each day we wake up with a choice—a choice to consciously choose which wolf we want to feed. It's critical to continue to focus on the care of our inner core selves to strengthen compassion, kindness, and love, which will simultaneously restrain and reduce anger, competition, and envy in our lives. By cultivating care and personal growth for ourselves, these things naturally overflow into every other area of our lives.

A New Definition of Success

Success is commonly understood to be connected to material items, to a certain position, or to making a lot of money. While there is nothing wrong with wanting these things, this understanding, spurred by society, has led to many of us resorting to overworking, popping Adderall, burning out, getting little sleep, and becoming emotionally drained. We are forced into thinking this is the only path to achieving success, happiness, and fulfillment in life. We need to change our definition of what genuine success really is.

We have misunderstood where true success lies and the path it takes to get there. The crown jewels we seek are already within us. Remember the golden Buddha! I'm not just talking "woo-woo" spiritual stuff here. This is a practical fact. There is nothing that you have to go out and get for success to come to you. According to self-help author U.S. Andersen, "Nobody achieves anything by 'going out and getting it.' The very premise insinuates at the outset that he believes whatever he is after belongs to somebody else and he has 'to take it away.'"

Our culture has masked success, happiness, and fulfillment as something you have to attain—when it's always been about the constant unfoldment and expansion of who you are. The true path of your success is not "out there"; it is in the process of expanding toward who you are becoming.

So, while some will say success is the progressive realization of a worthy goal, this statement is only partly true. It's much deeper than that. **Success is the progressive expansion of oneself.**

And in order to enable this process and set you along the proper path, your core intrinsic self needs to be consistently taken care of. In other words:

Your soul craves expansion and growth, and in order to meet this demand consistently and adequately, you must first know how to take care of your core intrinsic self. Once you understand how to do this, you can consistently progress toward the highest form of yourself.

At the center of a happy, successful, and fulfilled life is the ability to govern your internal self. If you can do this, everything external—whether it be stress, fear, or disappointment—will feel much more manageable; you can face these things head-on and bounce back from the experiences. And you will find that when you take care of your core intrinsic self and allow yourself to properly unfold, you'll learn to tap into a deeper calm within yourself, even in the midst of external adversities. Eventually, you will not only feel a sense of ease with yourself, but you will be able to meet daily challenges calmly and constructively. You will "feel no sense of hurry, yet you accomplish your daily tasks far more effectively," as American author Vernon Howard has stated.

By using the principles and exercises presented in this book, your internal wealth and wholeness will get transmuted into external success. And your inner peace and self-liberation will reflect outwardly to produce external freedom and joy. This is because you've placed your inner wealth first, not second. When this happens, your exterior life can take its proper place. In time, what you will discover, when practiced consistently, is that your ideas will often be realized, synchronicities tend to happen, opportunities frequently show up, and you start to see your dreams more clearly. Things begin to change in your life in ways you never thought possible. This is because your internal needs are consistently being taken care of, which ensures there are no blockages hindering your creative potential.

This is when genuine success is achieved and simultaneously enjoyed.

And when you feel whole within, you will be able to accomplish your goals with effortless ease, knowing that you have everything you need. But not only that—you will learn to never stop growing into who you were meant to become and to fulfill the inner longing for everlasting expansion.

More importantly, you will feel compelled to share your success and joy with others to help them win in life as well.

This is the *true* definition of success.

Deepak Chopra said, "A seed doesn't struggle to become a tree." It simply *becomes* because that's what it's meant to do. You were meant to succeed, not struggle. The seeds of your success lie dormant within you.

The purpose of this book is about allowing something that's naturally within you to come forward to express itself so you can realize your full potential.

RADICAL SELF-CARE EXERCISE:
Ask Yourself Empowering Questions

I first learned this strategy through author and speaker Michael Beckwith (so all credit goes to him), but I've put it into a prescriptive exercise that will be useful in the context of radical self-care.

Your radical self-care journey first starts with asking yourself empowering questions, so you can begin to move the needle from victim to victor. These questions should be asked periodically as a form of radical self-care throughout your life—when you are stressed, facing a big decision, feeling stagnant or in a rut, or looking for a change in your life.

Whether or not we realize it, many of us resort to asking ourselves disempowering questions like "Why me?" or "Why do I always make the same mistakes?" or "Why is life never working in my favor?"

Questions like these send you on a downward spiral instead of an upward one. They should be reframed to allow for expansion and growth to take place in your life.

1.) Take some time, grab a journal and pen, and slowly read over the questions below. Do any of them resonate with you? Do any of them tug at your inner being?
- What is the greatest possible expression of myself?
- What needs to change in my life so that I can be the fullest expression of myself?
- How do I want to live my life? Am I presently living the life I envisioned for myself a couple of years ago? If not, why?
- What types of experiences do I want to manifest in my life?

- What kinds of elevated emotions do I want to feel?
- What hobby or passion makes me feel excited about life?
- Who or what do I need to let go of to continue to grow?
- What change do I need to make to feel joy and to manifest the life I desire?
- What habit do I need to let go of to show up to life as my authentic self?

2.) Once you've had a chance to read through the questions above, choose the one that speaks to you most in your current situation (or feel free to use them all). As the question tugs at you, write whatever comes to mind. Write down what comes into your heart.

3.) Take a couple of minutes and review what you've written. You might be surprised by the solutions or sudden insights that bubble to the surface of your mind.

4.) The next step is to take small actions toward your solution with what you've written down. If you feel like you don't know what actions to take, don't worry; revisit the question and your written answer daily, and you will be guided to a solution.

Here are some examples to help guide you:
- Are you going to consciously remove yourself from negativity or a negative person in your life?
- Are you going to pick back up a childhood hobby or sport that brings you joy?
- Are you going to start waking up earlier to implement a morning routine to prepare your mind for the day? (I will discuss the importance of a morning routine later in the book.)
- Are you going to monitor how much time you spend unconsciously scrolling on social media?
- Are you going to set a goal to read a good self-help book for ten minutes daily to increase your productivity, sense of fulfillment, or clarity?
- Are you going to listen to inspiring or motivational videos to get your day started?
- Are you going to listen to inspirational or educational podcasts on your way to work to prep your mind for the day?

Asking yourself questions like these is an integral part of radical self-care. These questions are your guiding lights to help you understand where you are, how you want to live, and how you want your future self to be.

The fact that you even have the courage to ask yourself these pivotal questions is promising.

To live an abundant, successful, and fulfilled life, you have to consciously ask yourself empowering questions that send you on an upward spiral toward the solutions you seek.

Always remember the phrase, "Garbage in, garbage out." This means that whatever you feed your mind is what you will become and what you will outwardly express. So, if you feed your mind celebrity gossip and negativity throughout the day, guess what you are going to express day-to-day? You may experience feelings of doubt, discontent, low self-esteem, lack, or competition because of the type of information you are allowing in.

But if you feed your mind with positivity—stories of inspiration, information about ways to increase your productivity, and books on finding fulfillment and purpose in your life—guess what will happen to you? I'll let you find out for yourself!

The same can be said of the types of questions you ask yourself daily. Use questions such as those mentioned previously to allow you to expand and grow—to empower you. When done consistently, the practice of asking yourself these questions will start to edge the needle and guide you toward taking the necessary actions to reach your potential.

Use the hashtags #RadicalSelfCare and #SuccessStartsWithin on social media and share with others to inspire them to join you on your path toward activating your potential.

CHAPTER TWO

GUARD YOUR MIND

Stand guard at the portal of your mind.
Ralph Waldo Emerson

Be Prepared for Whatever May Come

In today's society, we are inundated with so much information that it can influence our minds, both consciously and unconsciously. So it becomes increasingly important to be mindful of what we expose ourselves to. Your brain is conditioning itself (more on this in Chapter Three) whether you realize it or not through your internal dialog and external surroundings. These inputs influence your success, health, relationships, and overall happiness. Whatever you feed your mind and body is what is expressed, so it's necessary to feed it positive inputs to uplift you toward your desired outcomes in life.

A large part of ensuring you are feeding your mind with what you need is consciously standing at the gate of your mind. This is where "guarding your mind" comes into play. You can think of yourself as your own security guard standing at the front of a gate only allowing and disallowing the people, thoughts, and information in that are in alignment with your desires and what serves your future self.

When you learn how to guard your mind, it will become a part of your arsenal of tools to maneuver, escape, and avoid the negativity that can slowly affect your self-esteem, health, career, and relationships. Your radical self-care journey will need to include preparedness to know how to evade negative circumstances and allow positive ones in to ensure your life is progressing toward your soul's desires. When practiced properly your perception will begin to alter and you will start to notice more positive and joyful moments in life.

To be clear: Negativity, negative emotions, bad news, stress, anxiety, and even negative people will inevitably arise in life. The objective of this chapter is to show you how to put yourself in the best position to overcome and adapt to these unfavorable circumstances. With preparation, you can accomplish your desired outcomes *regardless of* adversity, stress, or unfavorable circumstances. It's possible even through life's most challenging moments.

Let's face it; life is not sweet and cheerful all the time, so we need to be prepared with the correct tools to face life head-on to continue to achieve our desires despite adverse or rough conditions. At some point in our lives, we all will face tough circumstances, whether it be losing a family member, a job, a complex business pivot, a challenging personal or career decision, or an unexpected health problem. Unfortunately, we can't avoid them, but there are tools to better manage life's most demanding situations to ease the emotional turmoil. As Martin Seligman, considered to be the father of positive psychology, wrote in *Learned Optimism*: "It is far more important to know how to deal with the negative than to be positive." Turbulence may come in life, but the question that should be asked is: Am I prepared and ready with the right tools?

I'm certainly not saying you need to continue to look over your shoulder, expecting dire circumstances to happen. That's not how anyone should live their life. What I am saying is it's your duty to be prepared, the same way an airplane and its crew is prepared for turbulence or rough air. The pilots and passengers all hope for a smooth flight, but harsh conditions will undoubtedly come every once in and while. And what does the pilot do—he or she is prepared.

The pilot turns on the seat belt sign notification in the cabin and tells the passengers and flight attendants that everyone must sit down and buckle their seatbelts to prepare for a bumpy ride. Once the turbulence is over, the pilot turns off the seat belt sign, and flight attendants are back to serving drinks and snacks. This is a perfect analogy of how life can look.

The problem is many people are not prepared with the proper "internal notifications" so they can be guided toward the most effective corrective actions to swiftly leap over challenging moments in life. They don't have a seat belt nor a pilot in their life to guide them through the turbulence. Many of us go through life and get knocked down without any precautions or preparedness. As a result, we continue to make the same mistakes without understanding how our minds truly work or targeting the real cause that can substantially improve our lives. This chapter will give you the basic framework of how your mind works so you can sustain your well-being and success in life. The goal here is to live an empowered life so you can continue to activate your potential even when challenging moments arise!

Unleash the Power of Your Conscious and Subconscious Mind

Now to be prepared and live a successful life, it's necessary to understand one of the most essential facilities that allows us to be a participant in the game of life—our minds!

Within our minds, there are what's called conscious and subconscious. I'm sure you've heard these terms before but most people don't realize they are not two different minds; they are two spheres of activity within your mind. Each has two distinct goals and objectives. Our conscious minds are involved in everything that we are currently aware of or thinking about. It's your reasoning mind. Sigmund Freud states that our conscious minds are everything inside our awareness. This can include all of your feelings, thoughts, goals, plans, and willpower inside your current state of awareness. Now here is where it gets interesting. Researchers believe our conscious minds make up a tiny portion of who we are daily.

So small, in fact, the estimated percentage is about 5–10 percent of who we are. So, where is the other 90–95 percent? It's hidden in our subconscious minds, which is beyond our awareness. Our minds are like icebergs, in which 95 percent of an iceberg is hidden below the surface of the water, and only 5 percent of the iceberg is visible just above the surface. Most of who we are—our decisions, habits, and behaviors are determined and influenced below the surface in our subconscious minds. Meaning that most of who we are is outside our conscious awareness. Our subconscious minds include our imaginations, identifications, cultural paradigms, habitual thoughts, habits, defense mechanisms, fears, tastes, and even our values.

Let me provide a clear practical example so you can understand how these two spheres of activity influence your life. Say you desire to work four-hour days on the beach somewhere, but your belief is that you have to work exceptionally hard to earn money or maybe deep down inside you feel like you are not deserving enough, which could stem from your parent's beliefs about money or societal conditioning. In this case, it is unlikely you will accomplish your goal because your belief continues to drive your behaviors, actions, and nonactions toward the belief of "I have to work exceptionally hard to earn money."

From a scientific point of view, you have a conscious goal to work four-hour days but your belief of "I have to work exceptionally hard to earn money," which is stored in your subconscious mind overpowers your conscious goal. This can also be as simple as saying negative repetitive mental scripts to yourself like "I'm terrible at remembering names" or "I just don't have enough time in the day." If you continue to say statements like these, you can bet you will never remember names or demonstrate the behaviors to actually carve out time for the things you really want to do. You can bet your subconscious mind on it! It's always listening to you.

In summary, if your conscious thoughts and desires are out of alignment with your subconscious beliefs (or repetitive mental scripts) then it's unlikely you will achieve your goals because your subconscious mind is much more powerful. Your beliefs will continue to override every decision you make or don't make. This is why any change or advancement in any area in life can be difficult without the proper understanding how your mind works. Why is this? *It's because we only manifest what we subconsciously believe we are worthy of receiving.* The key word is "believe." But here's the best part, once you become aware of the beliefs that may be holding you back, you have the ability to change them.

This is the real reason why changing our diets, going to the gym more, developing a positive mindset, modifying our spending habits, and other various New Year resolutions are so hard to change and instill. It's because we haven't taken a clear look at our beliefs and effectively influenced our subconscious minds. This is where lasting change happens. Changing and shaping our beliefs are the root of where all positive change begins. For example, religions and spiritual traditions for thousands of years are exceptional examples of helping to shape our beliefs and empower us, which in turn, influence our behaviors to accomplish feats or overcome challenges we never thought possible.

Understanding how the mind works and using the exercises throughout this book will help create sustainable change toward your well-being and success.

Very often we know what to do to change our lives for the better, but it can feel like our brains or bodies won't let us. Developing daily habits like meditation and exercising are good examples. We know they are good for us, but they can be tough integrate at first. It can feel like we're struggling to roll a heavy rock up a hill only to have it roll back down as we get close to the top! This is why simply obtaining more knowledge is not enough to change behaviors. It's useful but if it's not followed up with intelligent action, well, I think we are all too aware of the futility that ensues. If just having knowledge was the case, many of us would be rich, happy, and healthy.

Many of these behaviors can be obvious; however, some are hidden, such as the four-hour work week example. Often it may be a subconscious belief that we may not even be consciously aware of that is holding us back from change, progress, or the results we desire in our life.

Have you ever wondered what some of your subconscious beliefs are? Try this quick exercise I learned from self-help author and speaker, Dr. Joe Vitale. The next time you are with a friend, listen to yourself describe your situation, goal, or problem. What words are you using to explain your situation or goal? Are they empowering or disempowering? Are they blaming others or taking accountability? We often don't realize that whatever comes out our mouth in dialog with a friend is usually what we believe at a subconscious level. How you speak and the words you select reflects your beliefs. You are revealing yourself every time you open your mouth. Try it, you may uncover a self-limiting belief you didn't even realize you had! The good thing is that once you discover it, your awareness heightens, ultimately putting you in a better position to change it.

Understanding your subconscious mind and how to influence it is a necessary skill that should be adopted for favorable results to manifest in your life.

Our subconscious minds are so powerful that it influences every bodily function and every facet of our lives, and we don't even know it. It helps keep us alive, so we don't have to consciously think about it. It helps us to digest our food and helps regulate our breathing. It remembers and records everything you've ever said, done, or witnessed—even if you felt like you forgot it.

Here's an example that I am sure you've experienced. Have you ever forgotten an important fact, the name of a restaurant you went to recently (this happens to my wife and I a lot!), or someone's name you just met? It's on the tip of your tongue but somehow you still can't bring it forth. You tugged your mind desperately searching for the information, but for some reason can't retrieve it in the moment. And the more you tugged and pulled the further it ran from you. Suddenly when you let it go—for a few minutes or hours—it pops right into your head. This is your subconscious mind working on your behalf. You've set an intention and now your subconscious mind says, "Let me find this information for you." It remembers everything!

It is very mighty indeed, but the most important thing here is that it can be trained to positively influence your life. Unlike the conscious mind, the subconscious mind is subjective, meaning it doesn't act until it is called upon. It does not reason, "think," or care if your ideas are true or false. To put differently, when you think a thought in your conscious mind and believe it to be true, your subconscious mind immediately accepts it. You can think of your subconscious mind as a *brilliant idiot*. It's very powerful but has to be given the right instructions from the conscious mind. And you can think of your conscious mind as a *child who wants to become a king*.

Through the proper use of your conscious mind (with the help of the Radical-Self Care exercise at the end of this chapter), it can be trained to become a *wise king*. Now once the *brilliant idiot* meets the *wise king*, it's been said that the genius of the mind can be established so you can advance confidently toward your desires without any self-sabotaging, hindrances, or doubts.

As Joseph Murphy states in *The Power of Your Subconscious Mind*, "Your subconscious mind is like a bed of soil that accepts any kind of seed, good or bad." So when we have negative or self-destructive thoughts, our subconscious minds will absorb them. Eventually, these negative thoughts will become an outer experience that mirrors the content of those thoughts.

This is good news because the same can be said for positive thoughts and behaviors to improve your thinking patterns, habits, and life. It is why feeding yourself thoughts, ideas, and beliefs that heal, bless your soul, and uplift your spirit is critical. This even comes down to the type of people you surround yourself with and the type of digital content you consume daily. Because "whatever is impressed in your subconscious mind is expressed," whether it's beneficial for you or not. Remember "garbage in garbage out" from the exercise in Chapter One.

It's really the small habits you've instilled over time that make you who you are. How you spend your mornings, how you talk to yourself when no one is around, what you watch, what you read, who you give your energy to, and who you allow into your life. These are the small things that can influence your subconscious mind and profoundly influence the behaviors and results you ultimately experience in life.

It's estimated that our conscious minds, again, everything that we are consciously aware of, can only handle about forty to fifty bits of information per second while our subconscious minds can sense up to eleven million bits of information from our environment.

This means most of the information we are consuming daily through our senses are happening outside of our conscious awareness. Every song, movie, TV series, and every person you ever met influences your subconscious mind—negatively or positively. Your subconscious mind is eavesdropping and is sucking up everything like a vacuum to affirm *who you think you are*.

This is why it is so important to be mindful of the type of digital content you consume while watching TV or on your phone because it can have an unconscious lasting effect on the decisions you make, the goals you wish to accomplish, and what you *believe* to be true about yourself.

If you don't consciously guard your mind appropriately, you'll be wondering your entire life why you haven't taken the actions to reach a particular goal or never can seem to get rid of that bad habit you know is not serving you. So, if you don't like the outcomes or results you are getting out of life, try focusing instead on changing the information going into your mind through your senses (see "Radical Self-Care Exercise: Guard Your Mind (GYM)" later in this chapter.) By standing guard of your mind and not blindly accepting information, you can put yourself in a better position to become who you desire to be.

RADICAL SELF-CARE TIP:
Guard Your Mind (GYM) Before Sleep

Our subconscious minds are highly suggestible through repetition, visualization, and altered states of consciousness. Because of this, it is critical that you are aware of the type of content you consume, especially right before you go to sleep and when you wake up. During these critical states of consciousness, your brain waves move from beta, alpha, theta, and finally delta when you reach deep sleep. In the evening, during this brain wave transition process, your subconscious mind is easily suggestible, which makes more of an impact on who are.

This means you are less analytical to fend off negative ideas and beliefs you may experience externally that may not support your relationships, health, goals, or self-image. Your subconscious mind basically opens up like a superhighway, making it that much easier to "program" or "hack" your brain of who you *think* you are or who you will become. Again, this is happening outside of your conscious awareness, so you don't even realize it. This also occurs when you began to awaken in the morning as well.

An important tip here is to be mindful of what you are doing on your phone, the TV shows you watch, or what you view on the internet. Neuromarketers and advertisers use this to their advantage to manipulate you into spending money on something you may not even need or even influence your beliefs about yourself and the world. Also, constantly viewing pessimistic news on TV or social media, which hijacks your brain's amygdala to activate your fight-or-flight response without any initiative from you, can have lasting effects on your well-being and happiness. Ever watch a scary movie before bed and then have nightmares about the movie all night? This is exactly what I am talking about. As Joe Dispenza said in *Becoming Supernatural*: "Don't watch anything on television or on the internet or participate in any mode of entertainment that you don't want to experience—not only before bed, but ever."

Instead of unconsciously picking up your phone and scrolling on social media or watching TV before bed, better options could be to read a self-help or inspiring book, meditate, or even write down what you need to accomplish the next day.

Some of the most accomplished people in the world, including Barack Obama and Bill Gates, read for at least a half hour every night before bed. In fact, a 2009 study highlighted in the *Daily Telegraph* newspaper by the University of Sussex concluded that reading before bed can reduce stress by 68 percent. In addition, another study has shown a strong link between one's reading skills and the ability to pay attention. This is because the simple act of reading demands your full attention that can carry over to improving your focus in other areas of life, which can catapult your productivity.

Examples like reading or meditation deposit something back into you that help foster who you want to become. You may not be able to try all of these examples at once before bed but try one and see if you notice a change in the quality of your life.

Challenge Your Self-Limiting Beliefs

Having self-limiting beliefs can keep you stagnant and make you feel like your progression is being blocked by something external from you that does not allow you to achieve your desires. We read books, listen to podcasts, work with coaches, see therapists but somehow, change still remains tough. We can't get rid of that bad habit or reach that particular goal. Most of the time, it can come down to an unconscious belief about yourself that you maybe didn't even know you had. To better understand this, let's bring an elephant analogy to help make this crystal clear.

As you know elephants are quite heavy. In fact, the average African elephant weighs between 5,000 to 14,000 pounds. Now here's what's interesting, despite their enormous power and weight, it's been said that when they are held in captivity they can be tied with a thin rope and stake in the ground. Now how on earth can that be? A huge elephant tied to a small rope. Why can't it escape? Well, when the elephants were just babies, they were tied to this same small rope.

As baby elephants, they pulled, tugged, and struggled, but eventually, they realized they couldn't break free from the rope and gave up. Now that the elephants are full grown adults even with their massive power and weight, they still *believe* they can't break free from this tiny rope. This analogy provides a great example for how childhood experiences and traumas can influence our thinking, beliefs, and actions we may want to take to advance ourselves in our lives even though they may not be true.

This can happen either due to an emotional childhood experience or who and what we repetitiously expose ourselves to. For example, when we were young, we quickly learned that touching a hot stove was not a bright idea. This traumatizing experience is programmed into the subconscious mind—letting you know that "if I touch this hot stove again, I will experience pain." As a result, this experience helps protect us for the rest of our lives. Or maybe we were told not to walk out in the middle of the street before looking both ways. Now we look both ways before crossing every intersection without giving it a second thought. These are both great examples of how our subconscious minds tend to swiftly register and store data to help us survive and provide a framework to live our lives in an orderly fashion.

However, the other side to this could be a self-limiting belief that has been programmed into your subconscious mind that is blocking you from not achieving your desires, goals, or the life you desire. Like the elephant analogy, one related example could be growing up hearing from your parents or, sometimes, preachers shouting that "money is the root of all evil." If you subconsciously believe that money is wrong or evil, even though you may desire it, it will cause you nothing but problems as you try to pursue it. Because inherently you believe it's wrong to have money. And as we know our beliefs—which are stored in the subconscious mind—will continue to override and control our actions and behaviors (conscious mind) every time.

Consciously you may be interested in obtaining more income to secure a better future for your family, but subconsciously you've been conditioned that money is inherently bad, and you continue to limit yourself when trying to achieve financial abundance. Subconsciously you will continue to have doubts, resistance, and even self-sabotaging behaviors that push you away from the very thing you desire. To change this, you first have to become aware of this belief and how it may be affecting the desires you are seeking.

Once this happens, you can slowly start to begin to release the resistance through proper self-talk, which I'll discuss in Chapter Four, and start to use visualization so that you can wholeheartedly begin your journey of attaining wealth without having any guilt, blockages, or shame. There are many more subconscious beliefs you have about yourself that you were told as a child and experiences you've encountered that could be limiting your fullest potential. With the help of this book and your own self-investigation it remains your job to uncover them to ensure you are not contributing to a self-fulfilling prophecy that can cause you inner turmoil and impact the people closest to you.

It's clear our subconscious minds can control every action, thought, and belief about ourselves, and we may not even know it. The most important part here is that you now have the knowledge to understand your mind better to effectively achieve the goals and life you desire. Even though it may seem your subconscious mind overrules you, this can be changed with your awareness, knowledge, and understanding of how your mind works. You still have control over who you are and who you want to become.

Meaningful change lies in effectively influencing your subconscious mind through repetition, visualization, and altered states of consciousness— like just before heading to sleep, right after waking up, or during meditation. I will speak more about this in later chapters.

As Reverend Ike would say, "You experience life according to your belief about yourself." So, what is your belief about yourself? And how do you think your beliefs may be unconsciously pushing you away from the health, wealth, and success you wish to foster in your life?

Develop Your Psychological Stability

I tend to think of myself as a positive person, but I wasn't always like this. I was quite the opposite growing up—in fact, I was pretty pessimistic. I remember purposely lowering the bar of my life expectations so I wouldn't be upset with how things turned out. What I didn't realize was that if you expect things to go poorly, your mind will search for evidence to support that expectation. For example, if you think you will have a bad day, your mind will unconsciously search for things that match your internal expectations, even if good things are actually happening. It wasn't until I gained a new understanding of myself and how my harmful internal self-talk was creating the reality I didn't want. Using the many principles in this book, I begin to train my brain to look at life with the glass half-full rather than half-empty.

However, I am certainly not Pollyanna about life where I pretend problems don't exist at all. In order to get life on your side, you must face obstacles. In fact, this is exactly what being an optimist is all about. We don't run from our problems. We run toward them knowing that there is a solution to every problem we face. Adverse events and unfavorable people will always show up in our life. But it's our duty to ensure we properly develop our minds for these situations to increase our odds of well-being and success. Fortunately, guarding one's mind is one way to safeguard against a negative mind invasion. But what about when life throws us the unexpected? Can we catch problems mid-air before they crash down around us? Yes, we can. It's possible with the right mindset.

You can indeed live your life with less fear and more peace internally, knowing that you are prepared for anything that might happen in life. This desired state of what some people call *impermanence* or *equanimity* is achievable, and it is my opinion, one of the most important states of mind a human can ever attain. Impermanence is a philosophy that asserts all existence is temporary. This basically means moments come and go, and you are constantly changing and evolving. You realize that you will go through negative emotions and positive emotions, but nothing is permanent as you continue to grow through life.

It's almost inevitable that many of us will experience states of sadness, pain, discomfort, and anguish deriving from life's experiences that we seem to have no control over. But if you can face these situations in life knowing and fully accepting in your mind that nothing is permanent, you can be more likely to handle and overcome them appropriately. The key here is being able to change your perspective of low moments in life. If you change your perspective, you can virtually change your life.

Better yet, like Wayne Dyer said, "If you change the way you look at things, the things you look at change." And the more you change your perspective during life's challenging moments; the more your brain begins to reconstruct itself through a process called *neuroplasticity*, making it much more manageable for you to overcome similar stressful situations in the future. The science of neuroplasticity states that you can rewire your brain in favor of the activity through repeated behavior or action. This means you are not stuck!

Change is possible with the proper understanding and by taking intelligent action. Think about all the limitations you might be placing on yourself in your life that could be blocking you from the joy, health, and success you wish to experience. Personally, when I first began studying neuroplasticity, it was one of the most gratifying realizations in my life because there was scientific proof that I could improve who I was, and my brain would rewire and grow to support the very change I was seeking.

So, if you think you aren't the most positive person, you can become one. If you currently think you aren't the most disciplined or consistent, you can change. If you think your memory is terrible, it can get better. If you don't think you have the skills or experience to start your dream business, you can learn and develop them. If you don't think you're the most confident, you can improve it. And finally, if you feel you aren't the best at handling stress in your life, you can grow to change your relationship to it. I think you get the picture. The center of all change and the results we seek start within our brains and what we *believe* it can do for us. I will discuss this more later in the book.

In the context of developing your stress-resilient muscles, as you start engaging in the principles in this book, you're essentially "developing psychological muscles to cope with greater and greater levels of stress," as Yongery Mingyur Rinpoche stated in his book, *The Joy of Living*.

Just as negative experiences are not permanent, neither are positive ones. Internalizing and recognizing this psychological balance are necessary to construct a balanced perspective in life. So rather than seeing a situation in life as inevitable or like it's the "end of the world," you can begin to see them for what they are and learn from them.

When I was young, I experienced anxiety and moments in life that indeed threw me off track. I allowed external circumstances to control my internal state of mind. I had no idea that I was allowing my own thoughts and emotions to control me negatively. I was attacking myself and I didn't even know it. Let me be clear and say you don't have to allow your emotions to control you. If you don't train your mind to be stronger than your emotions, you'll lose yourself every time a challenging situation or adversity arises.

One of the main reasons why meditation has completely changed my life and so many others is because it allows you to observe your thoughts and not be pulled by them. It puts you in the position to simply allow yourself to notice your thoughts without being immersed or controlled by them in any given moment. This is a powerful state of mind that can enable you to meet daily challenges calmy and constructively, whether it be in your profession or personal relationships and, most importantly, put you at ease with yourself.

This type of inner clarity is one of the most powerful gifts you can have, and it's available to those who seek it. The gift of peace, tranquility, and serenity within your own mind is undoubtedly a treasure that is already yours, you just have to claim it using the principles in this book.

Adopt a Respond Instead of React Mindset

We know by now we can't always control what happens to us in our lives, but we can absolutely control how we approach and respond to events. Consciously *responding* to life's stressful moments instead of just *reacting* to them is a skill that can be cultivated with intentional practice.

To build this skill, it's important to understand the difference between the two.

Reacting to life is instant. It's a gut reaction mostly driven by fears, insecurities, biases, and even beliefs that have been unconsciously lodged into our subconscious minds. It doesn't require any thought and is based on the external circumstance that arises. It's basically a survival mechanism that could pan out okay initially but often results in something you regret later. This is what I like to call *living in* autopilot mode. In this state, your perception shrinks, and you tend to head down a path of more issues. Living in autopilot mode may sound convenient at first, but it can inevitably lead you toward a downward spiral of regret, shame, and unhappiness.

Responding, on the other hand, is consciously assessing a situation that may arise and then deciding the best course of action to take based upon the circumstance. This option, most of the time, favors better results for your health and success. This is when you shift gears from *living in* autopilot mode and move into *living with mindfulness*. In this state your perception of what's possible for you expands and you begin to see opportunities that guide you toward sustainable solutions. In this mindset you are empowered to make healthy choices that can influence your outcomes. When used in your relationships, career, or health, it can catapult you over your obstacles to more effective solutions to life problems.

For example, let's say you failed a big test, someone makes you upset, you didn't get that job promotion, or just got out of a failed relationship or marriage. After recognizing the feelings of disappointment, you immediately react by getting sad, angry, or frustrated. You even start to feel unworthy and may even foster emotions that may make it feel like you can't get over your adversity. Over an extended period, feelings begin to worsen and slowly feed your subconscious mind of these inaccurate thoughts and beliefs about yourself.

In the future, when faced with a similar challenge in life, you may unconsciously feel timid, fearful, and stuck. You may not feel as though you deserve another job opportunity you are thinking about applying for. You may not take the chance to study for a test or job certification that you know you can pass. You may not believe you deserve another relationship in your life, forcing you to unconsciously push away great potential partners and even self-sabotaging yourself from anyone getting close to you again. And without you even realizing it, this particular adversity starts to bleed over to other critical areas of your life, including your diet, habits, goals, and even could influence the relationships of the people closest to you.

This is a vicious feedback loop that can be self-destructive. In fact, long-term stress and anxiety can contribute to increased cortisol levels that can wear down the brain's ability to function properly. Touro University Worldwide explains that "stress can kill brain cells and even reduce the size of the brain" and "chronic stress has a shrinking effect on the prefrontal cortex, the area of the brain responsible for memory and learning."

You can now see how repetitiously listening to incorrect self-limiting thoughts about yourself based on one moment in your life can be mentally and physically self-destructive if you're not mindful. It's important to exercise awareness to not allow one moment in your life to *define* your life. One moment in life should not define your self-identity. And it becomes your duty to see through the false story you may end up telling yourself. Sometimes, you may not even consciously realize that you are stuck in this limiting loop, and that's okay. As long as you begin to recognize your unconscious self-limiting belief, you are well on your way to a healthier self-image.

Gaining self-awareness is the first big step during those moments between reacting and responding. The rest is corrective action.

Now let's see how this situation might have panned out if you chose to respond. Again, let's say you failed a big test, someone makes you upset, you didn't get the promotion, the job you hoped for, or just got out of a failed relationship. Let's say you begin to notice the emotions bubbling up to the surface. You begin to notice the anger, sadness, and disappointment. You might say to yourself, "Okay, I realize this situation doesn't make me feel good, but I will consciously choose what to do next." You may be upset, but you begin to weigh the pros and cons and consider what might be the next best step for yourself. You've recognized and become self-aware of your emotions bubbling up, but you don't let them drive you toward a path of self-destruction. You remain calm, thoughtful, and aware of the next best approach to take. This does not mean you don't let the emotions come. You let the emotions rise and fall but you do not identify yourself with the emotion.

In this space of mindfulness, you give yourself time to consciously choose a path that may be better for you in the long run. You think long-term instead of short-term. You begin to choose a skillful response that is productive and aligns with your future self. As neurologist Viktor Frankl has said, "Between stimulus and response there is space. In that space is our power to choose our response, in our response lies our growth and freedom." For a better depiction of this, see the chart below:

Living in Autopilot: Reacting	Living in Mindfulness: Responding
Fear-based	Love-based
Short-sighted	Comes from knowledge
Poor communication	Connected communication
Emotions driven	Well thought out
Weakens you	Empowers you
Often something you regret later	Stays in line with core values
Inconsiderate of your well-being and others which could lead to more stress	Takes into consideration the well-being of yourself and others
Perception shrinks to see nothing but challenges.	**Perception widens to see opportunities.**

Leads to more problems   **Leads to solutions**

This respond mindset will put you in a position to challenge the inner critic that may be constantly talking yourself down and out of your goals and future vision. After you had time to process your emotions and choose a skillful response, you can now begin to empower yourself to move toward a place of expansion and continuous self-development.

You may feel thrown off at first, but your mindful response to this adversity allows you to quickly get your head back in the game to where it doesn't bleed over to other areas of your life. Your diet relatively stays the same, you continue to keep on top of your exercise routine, and your closest relationships continue to blossom.

Choosing how we think and respond to life's circumstances instead of unconsciously reacting is an invaluable skill that should be fostered to avoid the destructive loop of negative thinking cycles we can unconsciously put ourselves through. American psychologist, Martin Seligman has potently said, "One of the most significant findings in psychology in the last twenty years is that individuals can choose the way they think."

So, you now may be asking how you can use this technique to deal with negativity and negative people in your life? Let's look at another example I love that David Hooper writes perfectly in *The Rich Switch*. In his book, he clearly states: "When harsh words are spoken toward you, silently make the conscious decision to offer the person who is speaking your compassion and understanding, knowing that hurtful words are only spoken by those who are wounded themselves."

The key here is to consciously respond differently from a new mindset. When you respond to negativity with compassion and understanding, Hooper says you may be surprised to notice a positive shift in negative people as well. But even if you don't see a change in the other person, just know you're developing invaluable skills to build a strong mindset and enhance your well-being. It's necessary to remember that everyone is on their own journey in life; however, it's important not to let the ignorance of others or their own internal suffering hold you back from reaching your potential.

A couple of years ago, I had to use this strategy when my family and I went on a weeklong summer family vacation to Santa Rosa, Florida. We rented a big beach house, which happened to be in a relatively affluent area.

During sundown, my brother and I started playing catch on the beach by the water, and we both noticed what looked to be letters sketched into the sand. As we took a step back, we realized someone had written in big letters, "God hates black people," directly in front of our beach house. I'm no stranger to hearing or seeing comments like these as a Black man living in America. Still, as you might imagine, I was nervous for the safety of my family as this was during a period of heightened racial reckonings in America due to the ongoing injustices related to the rise in police brutality cases and uncovering the deep history of systemic racism reverberating around the country. Would our family be safe to stay in the beach house? Should we call the police just in case? Why can't we just enjoy our summer vacation as thousands of families do? Do I tell my entire family in the house? If I told them, I knew this would be a rude awakening and a tough pill for my family to swallow as we try to enjoy our vacation.

When I first saw the words etched into the sand, I immediately felt a tightness in my chest. I'll be the first to tell you all that compassion and understanding went *right* out the window! I was shocked, disgusted, and then suddenly became angry, but as I gazed out into the ocean searching for answers, I suddenly realized the only thing I was doing was making myself upset and stressed. At that moment, I knew I could choose a better response instead of letting my unconscious reaction and emotions cycle me down a path that wasn't healthy in the long run. I admit it was tough to read, but I silently told myself I would not accept the pain of someone else's suffering. My brother and I agreed only to tell a select few family members so that we wouldn't cause a negative shift in the household's energy but enough so we could exercise caution and be safe for the rest of our weeklong vacation. It was a delicate balance for sure, but one that was needed so we could continue to enjoy the vacation we worked so hard to plan.

Have there been times in your life when someone threw negativity or said harmful words toward you, whether in the workplace, in your relationships, or even with a stranger? Naysayers not believing in your dreams? Are there any haters always trying to tear you down? It may not seem possible at first, but it's essential to remember there is always space for *choice* in your response. And, as Viktor Frankl said, "in that space lies your true power for growth and freedom" to rise above the negativity so you can continue to walk in the direction of your purpose.

This choice may not sound easy initially, but through practice, you begin to develop psychological resilience to recognize the best route to take when confronting life's stressful moments, negative people, or negativity. Again, this is neuroplasticity at its finest, and it can become much more manageable over time. In fact, when you chose to respond instead of reacting, you begin to put yourself in the driver's seat of your life, and you are now engaging in what Dr. Rick Hanson calls "self-directed neuroplasticity." When this happens, you are now in control of your mind, and external circumstances will not perturb you as much.

Dr. Hanson described this perfectly in his book *Resilient* by saying, "You can live more boldly, trusting that you can explore and enjoy the deeper waters of life, and handle any storms that come your way." When you respond to life, you are consciously molding and shaping your brain to become more adaptable and calmer during moments of anxiety, stress, and disappointment. Your brain is becoming an asset, not a liability that is paying hefty dividends.

The Worry and Stress Antidote

Now that we know how to mindfully respond to unexpected moments and negativity in life, it's time to discuss what Buddhism refers to as the "monkey mind." The brain's monkey mind is the never-ending little voice in the back of your head. It continually fears the future and regrets the past. It's almost never focused on the present moment. Sometimes it can feel like a never-ending battle of fighting with yourself. It can make *you* feel anxious, restless, jumpy, and exhausted throughout the day.

But there are ways to pull yourself out of this never-ending loop so that it is not detrimental to your health or personal and professional life. Grasping awareness and understanding of your brain's monkey mind is critical to ensure you have the tools needed to adequately guard your mind from daily unfavorable circumstances.

Here is one thing you might find interesting about the brain and body. Whether you are experiencing stress and worry because of something physically happening to you or you are simply thinking about them, the body doesn't know the difference. (The same can be said for your goals and desires as well, which I will discuss later in the book.)

In other words, if you have thoughts about worrying about the future or regretting the past—your brain releases chemicals, like cortisol or adrenaline, into the body *as if* you were running from an actual physical threat. Humans are capable of turning on the stress response in the body by just thought alone. This is how powerful our thoughts are! This is okay for short periods of time when you may need to run or fight a threat, such as a burglar, but long-term thoughts of stress, worry, anxiety, or guilt literally keep our bodies in survival mode.

This is our primitive fight-or-flight nervous system or what scientists refer to as our sympathetic nervous system in full gear as if a predator is constantly chasing us throughout the day.

When your brain is aroused and living in survival mode all the time, it can be challenging for you to think creatively, have the capacity to express love to those people close to you, obtain a sense of peace, and accomplish your goals. Remember Maslow Hierarchy of Needs in Chapter One? Before you can move up the pyramid to experience higher levels of joy and creativity, your basic needs of safety and security need to be met. In this case, stress signals to your body that you are not safe.

This can also significantly decrease the brain's ability to think clearly, effectively solve problems in life, and lead to memory problems. Our bodies are not made to be in constant fight-or-flight mode every single day. This is what's happening when we put ourselves in a state of worry or stress. And, over long periods of time, stress can feel like a way of life that can have huge ramifications on your body's health long-term.

In addition, as we continue to advance in our cybercentric society, it's only becoming more prevalent as pings, notifications, missing a Zoom call, and negative news unconsciously activate our fight-or-flight response. This results in seemingly *everything being an emergency* from our brain's perspective. It can leave us frantic, fragmented, and increase anxiety levels throughout the day without us even realizing it. This is why setting a few minutes each day for breaks or meditation is so critical.

Research shows how the body can turn on its parasympathetic nervous system by setting aside just a few minutes a day to meditate, spend time in nature, engage in deep breathing exercises, yoga, or my personal favorite, flotation therapy (if you're ever in the Washington D.C. area, check out Soulex Float Spa). Even a technique known as tapping, also known as Emotional Freedom Technique (EFT), is another effective strategy to lower stress and engage the parasympathetic nervous system. Essentially, this is known as the "rest and digest" nervous system, which is basically the opposite of the sympathetic nervous system. When your parasympathetic nervous system is activated, it can slow down your heart rate, lower blood pressure, and produce a calm and relaxed feeling in the mind and body.

To provide you with some more motivation, one study concluded that just fifteen-minute meditations appeared to help people make better decisions. And another study found that twenty-five-minute meditations after just three days help to reduce stress levels in participants. So, if you want to accelerate your health and success, I invite you to integrate meditation for a few minutes a day to calm your body.

When worry does arise, I want you to think of this quote by Michel De Montaigne in which he says, "My life has been full of terrible misfortunes most of which never happened." As it turns out, this quote is *absolutely true* as research has concluded that at least 85 percent of what people worry about never happens. More specifically, the study "looked into how many of our imagined misfortunes never materialized." Participants of the study were asked to write down their worries over a two-week period, and then they were asked to identify which one of their misfortunes did not actually happen. Not only did the study conclude that at least 85 percent of the worries the participants wrote down never came true but with the 15 percent that did happen, 79 percent of the subjects discovered they could actually handle the situation better than expected. In addition, participants even believed the difficulty taught them a valuable lesson.

The significance of this study, as Don Joseph Goewey, author of *The End of Stress* concludes, is that most of our worries are actually not worth worrying about. Most of them are either "misconceptions or exaggerations" that likely won't materialize according to Goewey. Take some time to think about this in your life. Imagine being able to cut out most of your worries about the future, and even in the smallest chance it did happen, it was easier to overcome than you initially thought.

The next time you began to worry, and your body slips into fight-or-flight mode, think about this study and realize that your body is doing what it should be doing to protect you. However, it's your duty to take back your mind to find the space of constructiveness and mindfulness between your thoughts and how your body reacts. Once you find space and realize your body is sending signals to itself to protect you and nothing is actually chasing you (aka the fight-or-flight response), you are more adept to see things clearly thus yielding better responses.

Always remember you are more than prepared to take on future challenges in your life even when your body feels like it tells you the opposite during moments of stress and worry. And, as already discussed, constant worrying can lead to stress that physically disrupts the body. More specifically, studies have concluded that long-term chronic stress can lower your IQ, contribute to premature aging, hypertension, heart disease, predict marital problems, depression, and even lead to cancer. Long-term stress can quite literally make us stupid and make our lives miserable if not addressed properly. My intention in providing all of these studies is not to scare you but to impress upon you the importance of daily intentional rest and relaxation techniques.

Now you can see how stress and worry can deter you from your goals, physically cause health problems, and influence your personal and professional life. The brain's "monkey mind" can feel like it's never calm but remember that many of your worried thoughts about the future and past tend never to materialize anyway. Don't be your own worst enemy. It's essential to develop the skill of stopping yourself of imagining false scenarios about your future and hurting your own feelings and health in the process.

That's exactly what each day can feel like when you continue to worry about the future or regret the past. And in the very small chance that your worst nightmares do happen, well, it could even be a lesson you can learn from and not be afraid of. This perspective can be a mental muscle (remember neuroplasticity) that can be built and cultivated within, so be patient with yourself.

When developing this mindset and skill, be kind to yourself and cultivate self-compassion. Treat yourself as if you were your own best friend. Most of us treat our best friends better than we treat ourselves. Developing a new perspective of your worries is essential, but there are ways to combat and calm your monkey mind—or what scientists call our brain's default mode network (DMN)—to increase your happiness, focus, and fulfillment. Your brain's DMN is the constant voice that you keep hearing throughout the day that is mostly regretting the past and worrying about the future. Scientists say it's responsible for a lot of our rumination that can lead to negative thinking, worry, unhappiness, and feelings of anxiety.

Although this may be the case, research is confirming that meditation and exercising are effective ways to help calm this self-referential region of the brain. It's because of this I've devoted two entire chapters on the benefits of these two subjects to help upgrade your wellness and success in life.

Understanding your brain and body and how it operates in day-to-day allows you to increase your awareness to make better decisions in life. Whether it's dealing with negative people, negative news, your own worrisome thoughts, or even when turbulence arises in your life, you now have a life framework to build off of that you can apply daily. This knowledge puts you at an advantage because you now know that you can influence your emotions and behaviors instead of feeling like they are ruling you. Guarding your mind is all about being conscious, prepared, and equipped with the tools and knowledge to increase the likelihood of your desired goals—whether it be joy, health, or productivity.

RADICAL SELF-CARE EXERCISE:
Guard Your Mind (GYM)

Our minds are constantly bombarded with information coming in through our senses. Some of this information can be helpful toward your self-esteem, health, and achieving your goals. But, on the other hand, some of this information can be detrimental to your future self. Because of this, it's necessary to stay consciously on guard to protect your internal self.

For the next twenty-four hours, use the Guard Your Mind technique or GYM for short, by trying to stay consciously aware of new information, sensations, and emotions that you may experience. This includes conversations you may have with a coworker or friend, news you've read, something you watched on TV, or even a post you may have viewed on social media. When new information begins to elicit an emotional response, ask yourself these three questions using GYM:

1.) **Will this new information enhance my life in anyway?**
2.) **Does this information give me the insights, motivation, or knowledge I need to help me accomplish my goals?**
3.) **If I keep this information in my head and keep letting myself repetitively think upon it, will it help get me to where I want to go in life?**

If the answer to these questions is no, then use your conscious mind to kick this information out of your mind as soon as possible. You do indeed have the ability to do this quickly and abruptly with your conscious mind but most of us are not even aware of it thus we don't use it. Now if the answer is yes to each of these questions, then by all means accept the new information.

When you practice GYM for multiple days, your mind will start to recondition itself to help you recognize even more opportunities where new information may or may not be serving you. This is because this exercise mainly focuses on developing your psychological awareness. Once awareness is gained, you will become more adept in denying or accepting any new information that might inhibit or accelerate yourself toward your goals, health, or future self. Try this exercise for one full day and then two days, a week. Then try to make it daily mindset.

Use hashtags #RadicalSelfCare and #SuccessStartsWithin on social media and share with others to inspire them to join you on your path toward activating your potential.

CHAPTER THREE

UNDERSTAND MENTAL CONDITIONING

Until you make the unconscious conscious, it will
direct your life and you will call it fate.
Carl Jung

How Success and Failure Are Built

I used to be afraid of the word "conditioning." In high school, I played on the varsity basketball team, and when we heard our coach say this word, our entire team would cringe. We automatically knew it was going to be a brutal practice of running drills—which some people refer to as "suicides." I know, it's a terrible name to characterize a running drill, but these exercises prepared our bodies and minds for battle on game day.

Over the years, my definition of conditioning slowly began to change. I no longer cringed when I heard it because I understood its true purpose in life. Conscious conditioning is the process of training a person to behave in a certain way to reach their desired goal or circumstance. For example, our goal as a basketball team was to win games. For us to do so, we had to prepare our minds and bodies to keep up with our opponents on the court. We had to prepare our joints, muscles, and cardiovascular system so that we could defend against opponents. Additionally, we had to develop our own skills and confidence in order to score points ourselves. The more conditioning we did—whether it was running or strength training—the greater our likelihood of winning games. Simply put, conditioning is a process to ingrain habits to adequately prepare a person to obtain a desired goal.

We all are constantly being conditioned in life, whether we know it or not. Either we are consciously conditioning ourselves for our desired outcomes, or someone or something else is conditioning us unconsciously—in some cases, against our will.

Whether through unconscious bad habits that seem to fester over time due to external circumstances and life experiences or through good habits that we've developed consciously, our bodies and minds are continually being conditioned, for better or for worse. But sometimes, we don't even recognize that we have the opportunity to make a choice. The truth is, either you are in control of your life or someone or something else is.

Understanding the conditioning process—and the difference between conscious and unconscious conditioning—is pivotal to your radical self-care journey. If you are unaware, you could unknowingly be led down a road of thoughts, actions, and habits that do not align with who you want to become. It is important to wake up to this realization so you can become aware of how streaming media, social media, your patterns of thinking, and the people you associate with influence you. Once you are aware, then wise decisions and intelligent actions can be taken to catapult you toward the success you wish to achieve.

Unconscious Conditioning vs. Conscious Conditioning

Before we dive deeper into the conditioning process, let's get clarity on some important terms. The "unconscious" represents the processes or inputs in your life that are outside your awareness. These are things you are totally unaware of that may be influencing you; you may even be unaware of how your actions are affecting your circumstances. The "subconscious," for the purposes of this book, refers to the realm of mind or the part of consciousness where unconscious activity takes place. In other texts, both terms may be used interchangeably, but I prefer to distinguish them as such.

Dictionary.com defines "conscious" as "to be awake or awakened to an inner realization of a fact, a truth, or condition." Basically, this is a state of being where you are totally aware of what you are doing and how it influences you and your external reality. Now, "conditioning" can be defined as a behavioral process whereby a response becomes more frequent or more predictable in a given environment. The conditioning process is similar to the daily habits or routines that you've picked up over time—whether it be what time you go to sleep, how long you spend scrolling on your phone, how often you go to the gym, or what time you get to work. All of these are simple examples of how the conditioning process is either working for or against your desired outcomes in life.

Now to pull this all together, "unconscious conditioning" is the process of having no awareness of how your actions and habits influence your desired outcomes in life. For example, you may want to work out more often but instead you may find yourself unconsciously finding other tasks to do to avoid what you really desire doing.

"Conscious conditioning" is maintaining consistent awareness of how your actions influence your desired outcomes. For example, if you want to wake up earlier, you move your alarm clock outside of your bedroom, thus forcing yourself to get up and move to another room to turn it off. This increases your chances of not returning to bed and falling back asleep. This is a clear example of conscious conditioning. You are forming a habit that helps you meet your goal of waking up earlier. (I use this specific example because it's helped me ingrain a habit of creating a morning routine. More about this in Chapter Nine.)

At the center of achievement, health, and success are your habits. And you build your habits, good or bad, through consistent repetition or conditioning. Consistently doing small behaviors over an extended period of time can significantly impact who you become. This is why habits play a massive role in your radical self-care journey. Because if you are not aware of how your behaviors and habits influence your outcomes, you will rarely be in the position to change them for the better. In order for change to occur, new inputs—such as habits, patterns of thinking, and beliefs—have to be cultivated. Without this change, you will continue to garner the same results as you always have in your relationships, happiness, health, and wealth.

This is what's known as the "comfort zone." You might be comfortable, but nothing changes. This is how some people can continue to be in the same unhappy relationship or keep going to a job they hate for years. Because it's comfortable and anything different causes discomfort. Unfortunately, it does not generate the positive results you are seeking.

This is why American writer and futurist Alvin Toffler said, "The illiterate of the 21st century will not be those who cannot read and write, but those who cannot learn, unlearn, and relearn." And why Albert Einstein is quoted as saying, "No problem can be solved from the same level of consciousness that created it." All these quotations are saying the identical thing: the same thinking, behaviors, and habits you presently have will create the same future. Nothing will change unless you do first.

New behaviors may seem awkward and paradoxical at first, but, with enough consistency, results will come. Price Pritchett, PhD, author of You^2, states in his book: "If you want to accelerate your rate of achievement rapidly, you must search out and vigorously employ new behaviors." In essence, new routines and habits are a prerequisite to any change you may want to see in your life.

Furthermore, he says there is a certain irony here, which is "your historically most dependable behaviors can become the major obstacles to future success." Breaking away from your old conditioning and behaviors is necessary for new results to arrive in your life. So think about what behaviors or habits you have that are not giving your desired results? Do you feel disorganized and frazzled throughout the day because you try to take on too many tasks at once? Do you need to limit your phone screen time before bedtime, so you won't feel groggy in the morning? Current behaviors produce the same results. New behaviors produce new results. Most of us know this already; however, we are often so unconscious (the brain's autopilot mode) that we don't take a step back to look at how our present behaviors influence our well-being and success.

Developing awareness and knowledge of this process puts you at an advantage so you can consciously influence desirable outcomes in your life, as opposed to being at the mercy of old behaviors and not knowing why your results continue to stay the same.

The Process of Mental Conditioning

Take a look at Figure 2; it's one of my favorite infographics that we use in our youth mental wellness workshops we conduct as part of our nonprofit, Positively Caviar, Inc. The illustration clearly shows how conditioning can influence your outcomes in life. We use this infographic in our workshops with youth to teach them how repetitive thoughts and actions can and will influence their destiny. More importantly, we show them the progression of this process and how to consciously disrupt it to ensure they're pointed toward their goals, desires, and who they want to become.

Whether or not we are aware of this process, we are all determining the direction of our lives through our daily habits of thinking. It is how we influence who we will become and what our future will hold, and it is how we manifest the things we desire into our lives. Conversely, if we are not careful or mindful, it can also be how we bring circumstances into our lives that do not serve us or align with what we desire. Conscious conditioning is a framework that can ensure the quality of our thoughts and behaviors are not unconsciously derailing the external experiences that may ultimately influence who we become.

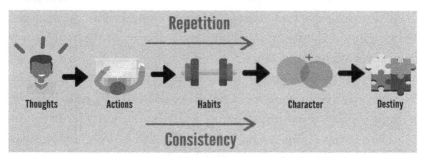

Courtesy of Positively Caviar, Inc.

Figure 2: Conditioning

Your habitual thoughts will always influence the person you become. They drive every action, desire, emotion, and habit you adopt. Proper conscious conditioning is key to ensure your mind is being fed seeds of nourishment, health, success, and happiness. You should be mindful of the digital content you view, the people you surround yourself with, and the information you read because they play huge roles in the results of your life.

Thoughts

In Figure 2, we can see that everything in our lives begins with our thoughts. This is the first step and the giant leap many of us don't tend to *think* about.

Now let's get one thing set in stone: thoughts are things. Whatever we think about is manifested into reality either unconsciously (unknowingly) or consciously (knowingly). Many of the great inventors, philosophers, scientists, and theologians have all come to this conclusion since the dawn of human existence. From the Bible, "As a man thinketh in his heart, so is he." And American philosopher Ralph Waldo Emerson said, "A man is what he thinks about all day long." When I first tell people in my mindset and wellness corporate seminars and workshops that our thoughts create our reality, some of them get nervous and begin to monitor their thoughts vigorously. As if every negative thought they think will produce unfavorable circumstances in their lives. Now monitoring your thoughts is a good practice to have but keep in mind that negative thoughts are natural to the human experience. We all have them. The most important piece to all of this is to become aware of how your thoughts are influencing your perceptions, behaviors, and outcomes in life. In Chapter Four and Eight, I will discuss how you can change your relationship with your thoughts, which can yield peace of mind and assuredness that they are leading toward your desired outcomes.

Now let's ground these famous statements and quotes in some truth and everyday life since many self-help books don't often break this down with clear practical examples.

Here's what I want you do. Take a look around. Whether you are in a coffee shop, your room, or your kitchen, look around with fresh eyes, setting your sights on every material thing you can see. Everything you see was once a thought in someone's mind, just like it is in yours now. The chair you are sitting on, the structure of the building you are in, the lightbulb that's providing you light, the cup you are you drinking out of, the pillow you rest your head on every night, and the phone you use.

Every single thing you encounter throughout your life was once an idea or a thought in someone's mind. Before Benjamin Banneker built

America's first fully functioning clock almost entirely out of wood, he saw the idea in his mind. To bring this to present day, before Elon Musk built Tesla, SpaceX, and PayPal, they were, again, ideas in his mind. And before Serena Williams, Oprah Winfrey, Lebron James, and Robert F. Smith climbed their ladders to success they had thoughts of patience, persistence, and perseverance. You can see how this internal facility plays a role in someone's external achievements and circumstances.

Now let's do another exercise with a fresh mind; turn your focus inward, toward the people in your life who you encounter day-to-day, whether on the job, in your relationships, or in your friendships. What are their primary behaviors and emotions? Are they mostly happy or sad? Are they accomplished or can't seem to find their footing? Are they givers or takers? Do they enjoy life, or do they think life is a miserable struggle?

Here's some truth: Everyone's behaviors, emotions, and actions are simply an outward display of what that person is thinking all day long. In these exercises, you can see how this might be detrimental or beneficial to someone's internal and external life.

If all this is true, then it's important to be attentive to how we habitually think about ourselves, our lives, and what we desire out of life. Repetitious and consistent internal thought will manifest itself in our external reality. The two key words here are "repetitious" and "consistent" because they are crucial to accessing the subconscious mind (I will discuss this more a bit later), which influences your beliefs and patterns of thinking and governs your reality. The repetition and consistency of the same thoughts, actions, emotions, and experiences will produce the same results—in your relationships, health, wealth, and overall fulfillment in life. This is the result of daily conditioning.

So, if you want to promote new and positive results in your life, it's important to become aware of your thoughts. To put it another way, try daily to stop and bring awareness to what you are thinking about. As I tell participants in my seminars: "I want you to think about what you are thinking about." You'd be surprised that most people are not doing this! Once you start to hear that little voice, good or bad, in your head, then you can adequately address your self-talk and discover ways to ensure these thoughts provide you with the nourishment you need for growth in your life.

William James, who's widely considered to be the father of American psychology, once said, "The greatest discovery of my generation is that human beings can alter their lives by altering their attitudes of mind." In this case, your attitude of mind is your thoughts or self-talk. When you alter your thoughts, your life changes. We will dive a bit deeper into how your self-talk governs your life in Chapter Four.

Actions

Changing your thoughts is half the battle. There are tons of people who accumulate knowledge through podcasts, attending seminars, and reading books hoping for change but nothing happens. Now don't get me wrong here, the accumulation of knowledge is necessary because it can alter your thinking. But none of it matters if you don't take any action. New thoughts are helpful. Consistent actions are even better. This is how real and lasting change is made in the subconscious mind for true results to manifest in your life.

To take this a bit deeper, say you want to accomplish a certain goal like lose weight or apply for promotion, but all your actions and behaviors are not reflecting the achievement of that goal. This may be because you have not effectively influenced your subconscious mind where a self-limiting belief (remember the elephant analogy in Chapter Two) or change in self-image may be needed for a desired change. It almost feels like you are fighting yourself and you're getting in your own way. In fact, that's exactly what's happening! Again, your subconscious mind (where your repetitive habits and beliefs are stored) is overriding the conscious mind (the goal or the desire you are seeking).

Now think about it. Nearly all your actions or nonactions are the result of your thoughts and emotions—everything from the career you've chosen, where you live, and the car you drive. Your actions are products of your thoughts and emotions, not the other way around. So, if you are interested in changing your actions, you need to begin by changing your inner dialogue. Likewise, even the actions that you haven't taken are the result of your thinking.

Many people want to change their circumstances without going to the source of the problem, which is their thoughts. Change is possible when we can gain greater levels of awareness around the types of inner dialogue that are influencing our actions, particularly those that may not be serving us. Once right thinking is in place, consistent right action begins to follow.

Habits

In short, your habits represent anything that you do repeatedly. Over time, they become automatic to the extent that you may not even notice them—like how often you go the gym, what time you go to sleep, how you shop at the supermarket, or the fact that you lock the door as soon as you come in the house. Psychologists tell us that anywhere from 40 to 95 percent of our behavior is habitual. Over time, your habits make you who you are. They essentially become your identity—for better or for worse.

In the context of Figure 2, your habits make up your repeated thinking followed by your repeated actions. The brain is constantly looking for ways to optimize itself to make space for other activity, and your habits happen to be an effective way to allow your brain to divert energy to other, nonautomatic tasks. Once you've done something over and over again, your brain essentially says, "Well, I guess this is what you want. Here you go. And don't worry, I'll make it easier for you next time." We first create our habits then our habits create us.

You can see how this pattern of thinking might be detrimental if followed by actions that are not in alignment with your desired future self. For example, say you desire to become someone who works out in the morning, but you've picked up a habit of scrolling through your phone late at night while in bed to decompress from the day. This late-night habit might be contributing to your drowsiness in the morning, thus causing you to hit the snooze button several times before finally waking up.

To change this habit, the first step is to gain self-awareness and think new thoughts that are in alignment with your desire of waking up early. Having a new pattern of thought will contribute to new actions being taken, whether it be making the conscious decision to refrain from touching your phone right before bedtime or exercising for fifteen minutes before dinner. Research published in the *European Journal of Social Psychology*, suggest on average it takes at least two months, or sixty-six days to be exact, before a new behavior becomes automatic. Of course, this is widely dependent on the person's behavior, circumstances, and current neural pathways. But don't think about the days so much, just focus on progress. Small incremental improvements every day and making a commitment to the process is what really matters.

Other bad habits could include procrastinating, paying bills at the last minute, spending more money than you make, arriving late to appointments, or gossiping about people. All your current established habits are producing the current level of results in your life. So, if you want to create greater levels of success and satisfaction in your life, you are going to have to drop the habits that are not serving you. Remember, if you keep doing things the same way, you will always get predictable results.

The best part about habits is when you consciously decide to lock in good ones, they automatically carry you toward your goals without expending much energy and effort. This is what psychologists call *automaticity*, a habit that can be performed efficiently without much awareness or cognitive effort by the individual, similar to brushing your teeth before bed. Your success basically becomes effortless and sustainable over time because you've locked in habits that are aligned with your goals. This is where you move beyond motivation and let your conscious habits drive you toward your destiny. As I am sure you know, motivation and relying on sheer willpower come and go. We aren't always going to feel like working out or meditating daily. But when you set up the right habits, you won't always have to depend on motivation to carry you toward your goals; you rely on your habits. Simply put, when motivation fails, you always fall back on your habits. This is your foundation.

Again, your habits can only be correctly influenced by making sure the quality of your thoughts and actions are in alignment with your desires. Many people try to address the results of their life without peeling the onion and examining the inputs that contribute to those results. In this case the inputs are your thoughts and actions. Fix the inputs, and the outputs will fix themselves. If you are looking for resources to get rid of bad habits and set goals, check out my free e-books here: chazzscott.com/freebooks.

Character

When your consistent thinking influences your actions and creates your habits, your character is born. Your character represents all the attributes and qualities that make you, you. All the experiences you've had since you were young have made you who you are today—whether you thrive in social settings or tend to be a bit more reserved, or if you enjoy spending time reading books rather than going out with friends.

One of my mentors, Freeman A. Hrabowski III, American educator and former president of the University of Maryland, Baltimore County (UMBC), used to tell me that our character represents everything we do when no one is looking. And that's true, especially in today's society, because we have a tendency to conform to please others instead of ourselves.

It's important to remember that your character is always being shaped and constructed by your thoughts, actions, and habits. So, while some people may believe they cannot change—"This is the way I am"— or they are stuck, this is not the case. The quality of the inputs that lead to the development of your character is what matters. When you change the type of inputs over a period of time, your character begins to change.

This entire process starts as soon as you are born and continues throughout your life. Who you believe yourself to be is outwardly displayed in who you are, which ultimately affects how your destiny takes form. And to make this crystal clear, your destiny is the results of your life. Whether it be your health, inner freedom, joy, relationships, wealth, or a certain position at work, all these results are nothing more than the physical manifestation of your previous thinking. *If you want to change your results in life, it must begin with your thinking.*

If you can understand this process and properly implement it through the exercise at the end of the chapter, change will begin to occur. Many cynics don't believe any of this but like the late self-help author Bob Proctor used to say, "Cynics don't get results either."

Social Conditioning

Whether or not we realize it, many of us are influenced by the people we surround ourselves with every day—coworkers, friends, and family. You can either be consciously controlled by yourself or unconsciously influenced by someone or something else.

Have you heard of any of the following sayings? "You are the average of the five people you spend the most time with" or "Birds of a feather flock together" or "Misery loves company." These aren't just sayings. They are facts and actually have been scientifically proven (I will discuss more on this soon). We are conditioned to think the same way and have similar beliefs and value systems to those we consistently surround ourselves with. Humans are hardwired to be a part of a tribe of people who are similar to them. It reminds us that we are safe and comfortable. And in order for us to further establish the emotions of safety and security, we unconsciously act like others in our tribes or friend groups, to make ourselves more likable. We don't just act like the people around us to feel good about ourselves; science is proving that we literally do it for survival in a field of study called mirror neurons. It's an instinct deeply embedded in humans. (I will explain more later in this chapter.)

This tendency to adapt to our environment might be detrimental if you began to unconsciously pick up a friend's or relative's self-limiting beliefs. You might begin to not believe your own ideas, passions, or dreams. If those closest to you possess poor habits, values, or health, you are likely to be influenced by them.

One of my close friends reached out to me and expressed that he'd been reading self-help books, and they were helping him change his attitude. With his new perspective on life, he began to realize that his social circle was pretty negative and that his friends were not supporting his new way of thinking or his goals.

He was learning new, positive ways of thinking in his reading, but he continued to be influenced by his immediate environment—in this case, his circle of friends. He believed this was why he was feeling like his progress was stagnant. I recommended that he use the Guard Your Mind (GYM) technique (see exercise at the end of Chapter Two) to ensure he stayed aware of how his friends made him feel so they wouldn't influence his goals. In addition, I invited him to limit his interactions with them, especially if he believed they were blocking who he was becoming in life. This is a prime example of how our social circle can sometimes negatively influence us when we begin investing in our personal growth.

Research in this area reveals that a group of specialized brain cells called *mirror neurons* cause us to feel joy when friends are happy and empathy when they are sad. Researchers have even concluded that human civilization depended upon this faculty because we learn from observing others' actions. Scientists call this *imitation learning,* and we do it every single day. We unconsciously pick up on the moods, thoughts, behaviors, and even personalities of those closest to us. Naturally, this makes the habits of those closest to us highly contagious, whether that is good or bad. This is what was happening to my friend with his social circle. As it turns out, the old "Birds of a feather flock together" adage actually had it right!

If you want to improve an aspect of your life, it's best to put yourself around people who have the attributes you wish to adopt. For example, if you wish to become a more optimistic person, it would be in your best interest to spend time with people who you know are positive and are always looking on the brighter side of life. If you wish to work out more, then it's best you find a community of people who go to the gym regularly. Social conditioning can be extremely subtle but can influence us more than we realize.

How Our Twenty-First Century Technologies Are Conditioning Us

Our twenty-first-century society has created a means of communication and convenience that has certainly made our lives easier. But our handheld devices have conditioned us in both negative and positive ways. Negative because if you are unconsciously (unknowingly) conditioned by an external force, then you are by definition controlled by it. And the things you are controlled by can have power over your time. And since time can never be replaced, how you choose to spend it is crucial to your success in life. Let me give you an example that you've probably faced recently.

I want you to think about how many times you've picked up your phone today and scrolled through your favorite social media platform or how many times you've checked your email. You may not even be aware how many times you've done this today. I know it's hard for me sometimes! Also, think back to a time when you had to complete something that required your full, undivided attention, like finishing an important work task or reading a book. Did you ever unconsciously pick up your phone or get sidetracked by a notification or a ping? And before you even realized it, you've been on your phone for ten to fifteen minutes, when you knew you were supposed to dedicate that time to an important task.

Your email and social media just robbed you of the most precious commodity known to humans: time—time that could have been spent in a conscious, productive way to help accomplish your desires. This used to happen to me a lot, and I would get so frustrated because I felt like an unconscious robot reaching for my phone every time.

These may seem like small moments, but over time those few minutes add up, and the act of scrolling can become an unconscious conditioned habit that disrupts your productivity and overall fulfillment at the end of the day. Don't believe me? Take a look at your phone's Screen Time feature, which shows you how long you've used certain apps throughout the day and week. I bet you will find these numbers are much larger than you anticipated! Start tracking this information and be mindful of where you place your time. Because what you can track, you can manage. What you can manage, you can master. It's essential to master the balance of where you place your attention and time throughout the day.

Where you place your time is where you expend your energy, which could be diverted toward things that serve your happiness, health, and desires.

In addition, because the availability of modern-day digital distractions has skyrocketed, some scientists are now saying that human attention spans are slowly declining. In fact, Microsoft conducted a study to find out how long people could focus on one thing. In 2000, it was concluded that the average person's attention span was about twelve seconds. Fast-forward to about thirteen years later, when a second study revealed that this number had dropped to around eight seconds. That's a four-second decline in just a handful of years. Researchers are now concluding that most humans have a shorter attention span than a goldfish, which is said to be around nine seconds. There is some speculation about whether or not goldfish really do have such attention spans and if this claim is scientifically backed, but one thing we know for sure is that we need to be mindful of how these technologies are influencing our focus and productivity.

What's even more startling is that a study published by Jampp, a digital mobile marketing company, concluded that our attention spans are declining 88 percent year over year. And a recent study by the Technical University of Denmark suggests that our collective global attention span is dropping because of the abundance of information (news notifications, web searches, social media alerts, email notifications, TV ads, etc.) presented to us daily. Companies, marketing conglomerates, and people demand so much of our attention that there seems to be a "rapid exhaustion of our limited attention resources," as the study puts it.

This exhaustion of our attention can foster bad habits and constantly demands that we place our attention outside of our own internal needs. If we are not careful, we could fall down a slippery slope of uncontrolled habits that may not align with who we desire to become. This can inhibit our overall success and well-being in life. We should be conscious and aware of how our current society and distracted lifestyle influence the most powerful attributes of humans: the ability to focus and remain in the driver's seat of life.

If your ability to hold focused thought deteriorates, your relationships, concentration, and even your overall fulfillment could suffer. The challenge that will need to be conquered is maintaining your ability to focus and keeping a healthy balance on your device use. Luckily, we don't have to be at the mercy of our devices anymore; new research conducted by Dr. Amishi P. Jha, a psychology professor at the University of Miami, concluded that we can practice mindfulness just twelve minutes a day and improve our attention and working memory. For more information, I encourage you to read her book, *Peak Mind: Find Your Focus, Own Your Attention, Invest 12 Minutes a Day*.

So why are these technologies so addicting? Well, some researchers claim that online distractions continue to prime our brains with the expectations of reward and release the brain's feel-good neurochemical dopamine. Robert Sapolsky, a biology and neurology professor at Stanford University, calls this process the "magic of maybe." He explains, "Dopamine is not about pleasure but the anticipation of pleasure." Furthermore, he says it's about the pursuit of happiness rather than happiness itself that we are so addicted to.

When we pick up our phones to check email or our favorite social media platform, we may find a response or notification—and sometimes we don't—but when a notification does occur, Sapolsky found that we enjoy a huge spike in dopamine. So, we really are addicted to our brain chemicals, especially when it comes to the anticipation of someone emailing us, tweeting us, or liking our pictures. This develops in us a desire to consistently pick up the phone or check our social media feed. It can become addictive if not watched carefully and can distract you from important tasks or even leave you frazzled and anxious throughout the day. It may also have a negative effect on you seeing the so-called "perfect" lives of others on social media and feeling that your life is not as good. And when not addressed, this subtle feeling can harm your self-esteem and mental health. It can short-circuit our sacred experience of life when we are constantly bombarded with thoughts that compare our life journey with someone else's highlight reel on social media.

Additionally, from a productivity perspective, a study by Sophie Leroy, an associate professor at the Bothell School of Business at the University of Washington, found that if people transition their attention away from an unfinished task, the performance of their subsequent task will suffer. Let's say you're writing an important email, and you are interrupted by a text message that needs a reply. You reply, however, by doing that you will now need time to regain your focus and shift your attention back to completing the email. It's clear that our devices can contribute to stress and lower work performance levels, which can leave us fragmented daily.

As Gaylon Ferguson says in his book *Natural Wakefulness*, "Distraction is married to dissatisfaction." Be mindful of how your notifications may be conditioning you. Put yourself back in control and pick up your phone or check your email only when you absolutely need to.

RADICAL SELF-CARE TIP:
Turn Your Focus Inward for External Growth

When you have a task you need to complete or something that needs your undivided attention or maybe you just want some time to yourself, try putting your phone on *Do Not Disturb*, even if just for a couple of minutes. You can also silence your notifications.

When we constantly pick up our phones, we slowly give them power over us. This means we give marketing conglomerates, the people we follow on social media, and news corporations the ability to influence us. It's time to bring that energy *inward* that we've grown accustomed to focusing *outward*. It's time to focus on you to get your power back. We give so much of our attention to our devices and other life demands that we very rarely have time for introspection and reflection. And introspection is the first step to growth and development of oneself.

Instead of picking up your phone when you feel the slightest sense of boredom, spend some time thinking about your hopes, goals, or a future vision that you have for yourself. What we think, we become. Do you want to become a phone or yourself? This is where personal growth, creativity, self-improvement, and productivity can truly express themselves without being interrupted by a notification ping. In fact, Earl Miller, a professor of neuroscience at the Picower Institute for Learning and Memory at MIT, says that when your brain is distracted, "Your thoughts are more superficial, and you're not getting as far down that path where new ideas emerge." He further says, "The main thing that impedes our cognition is distraction."

When you give yourself time by silencing your notifications and other distractions, you will notice greater levels of calmness, increased productivity, and focus. You will also find yourself to be more creative because when you're unstimulated by pings and notifications, your brain has a chance to explore ideas and create new neural connections for more breakthroughs, creativity, eureka effects, and aha moments!

Modern-day technology has made significant contributions to our lives—whether by allowing us to communicate with family and friends thousands of miles away or to receive all the world's information with just a simple internet search. But, like anything in life, technology can be used in negative ways that can significantly undermine our goals and desires. Our society must become conscious and intentional about where we place our attention and how we use our time. Watching TV and scrolling on social media may provide a temporary boost but may come with deeper crash later.

Remember this: *Where you place your energy is where you are placing your time.* So we should be intentional about where we place our energy and attention to ensure we are getting the most bang for our buck, to achieve and experience the life we truly desire. We should ask ourselves: *Do my current conditioned thoughts and habits support my desired goals? Does my unconscious scrolling on social media contribute to my life positively or negatively? Does my binge-watching of my favorite TV show provide me with the opportunity to truly grow and expand into who I want to become?*

Here's something you can try in the coming days. After you've picked up your phone and have been scrolling on it for a few minutes, consciously ask yourself, how do I feel about myself? Do I feel empowered, inspired, fulfilled? Or do I feel drained, anxious, sad, or fearful? If it's the latter emotions, I invite you to practice some radical self-care. Try unfollowing everyone who does not contribute to your well-being and goals. Follow pages that contribute to your life, whether those are fitness, financial, productivity, or mindset to increase your game in some of the essential areas of your life. You can even take a step further and unfollow your favorite celebrity gossip accounts. Try it for a couple of weeks, and you might be surprised how those pages unconsciously put you in a constant state of unease or even cause you to obsess over someone else's life rather than focusing on the self-care and happiness that you should be fostering in your own life. This is all about shifting your energy back into you.

And if that doesn't work for you, go ahead and delete the app for a couple of days. Don't worry, you can come back. Your friends and your favorite celebrities will still be there. Just try focusing on you and your self-development. You can come back when you feel renewed, refreshed, and ready.

Self-Awareness Is the Key to Self-Transformation

Before you can begin to take more control of your life, you must first gain awareness of your thinking so you can influence how life shows up for you. This is a process of obtaining self-awareness about your day-to-day thoughts—so, basically, *thinking about what you are thinking about,* which

I touched on earlier in the book. You might be surprised to hear that most people don't do this. We get so lost and locked into day-to-day life that our thoughts drive us toward unconscious actions that don't allow for deep introspection to manifest true change and control. Some would say, "I've been going through the motions." As self-help author Eckhart Tolle says, "Awareness is the greatest agent for change." Because whatever you can bring awareness to, you can change. How can you solve a problem if you don't know you have one? You can't!

Self-awareness is the key to progression in life. One of the most effective exercises to start this process of obtaining a sense of self-awareness is meditation, which I will discuss more, later in the book. Meditation can help you disconnect from your scattered thoughts so that you can see your life with more clarity, peace, and joy. And as you begin to obtain more self-awareness of your thoughts, actions, and emotions, you will be able to direct your attention and intentions toward your desires. If you don't foster the ability to direct your focus, then your focus and thoughts can be used and abused. In other words, you will continue to go through the "motions" of life without having the ability to make any of the conscious changes that may serve you.

As you align your thoughts and emotions to your desired goals, your brain begins to structurally change. This is called neuroplasticity, which I discussed previously. The concept of neuroplasticity suggests that our brains can rewire and adapt their neural pathways through growth and reorganization based upon our thoughts, habits, and external experiences. This means that when you begin to take control of your life, the structure of your brain changes with you. And the more that you do it, the easier it can become. It's like learning to ride a bike.

At first, it can be pretty difficult to make a change. But over time—through repetition and consistency—it becomes a lot easier. This is because when you learn something new, whether playing the violin or ingraining a new habit, the more you repeat the associated thoughts and behaviors, the more they are hardwired into the brain.

This process first begins with a conscious choice followed by repeated action. Every time the repeated action is conducted, the brain starts to deepen the associated neural pathway. Over time, the same neural pathways are reinforced, making them deeper and deeper. Slowly but surely, through repetition and consistency, this activity begins to migrate to the subconscious mind making these actions almost automatic. They are now your habits. They've become who you are. They've become you.

This process can be great if we are reinforcing positive habits, but it can be detrimental if the habits are negative or don't serve us. Every belief, thought, attitude, and decision is recorded in the neural pathways in your brain. And the more you think a particular thought or act on a particular behavior, the more it becomes you. This is why philosophers for many years have said *we become what we think about.*

The study of neuroplasticity has proven this down to the very structure of our brain. Now you can see how important it is to be mindful of your actions and beliefs because every thought reinforces the same thought you've just had. The most intriguing part about this knowledge is that you have the ability to change and modify this conditioning process. Through practice, you can take control over what you think, how you feel, and how you react to life's situations to ensure that you are conditioning your brain toward the highest ideal version of yourself.

Not only do our brains have the ability to change, but new studies in epigenetics are confirming that we have more power over our genes than we once thought. Scientists used to think that genes were just given to us by our parents and that we didn't have the capacity to influence them in any way. New research confirms that our environment—what we eat, the types of experiences we are exposed to, even the very thoughts we think—can influence our genetic destiny. Our genetics don't have to rule us. We can have mastery over them to a certain extent.

A perfect example of how life experiences can directly influence our genes is found in Deepak Chopra's book *Super Genes.* Our DNA is packaged into threadlike structures called *chromosomes.* At the end of a chromosome is what's known as a *telomere.* Telomeres help protect chromosomes from unraveling as we age. You can think of them like the plastic wrappings at the ends of shoelaces. As we get older, our telomeres become shorter as our cells continue to divide. To make this clear, as your telomeres get shorter, your life also gets shorter, too. This is part of the natural aging process of humans. When Idan Shalev, the lead author at Duke University, Department of Psychology and Neuroscience, studied how people's life experiences influence their telomeres and the aging process they noticed something very interesting. The research analyzed DNA samples first from five-year-olds and then again when the children were ten. The scientists knew some children experienced long-term stress including bullying, domestic violence, and physical mistreatment. Ultimately, the researchers concluded that the children who experienced the most stressful experiences accelerated their telomere erosion.

As we can see from this startling research, long-term chronic stress can biologically influence our genes. In short, the affected children were aging faster because of the constant stress in their day-to-day lives. This makes a strong case for why we need to be mindful of the types of people we expose ourselves to, how we manage stress, and foods we eat. Because it shows up in our genes. This study highlights the importance of regular self-care to counteract the stress we experience daily.

You may be asking yourself if we are powerless and helpless in the face of this telomere decline? Not at all! New research indicates that we can extend or elongate the length of our telomeres, which basically means we can slow down the aging process and quite possibly, even reversing it. Research has confirmed that meditation and exercise can produce an enzyme called *telomerase*, which can elongate our telomeres. For example, one study conducted by the National Health and Nutrition Examination Survey (NHANES) program under the CDC suggests that highly active adults have significantly longer telomeres and have a "biologic aging advantage" of about nine years over sedentary adults!

This is powerful because it means we now have the knowledge and actionable tools to improve our well-being and even positively impact our life expectancy just from a few simple lifestyle choices.

These new insights into neuroplasticity and epigenetics can be refreshing because they show us that we truly do have the ability to change and grow and to become who we desire to be. With the right knowledge and discipline, the body has the ability to adapt according to the will of the individual.

The Body and Brain Can Adapt

What does all this mean? We need to be especially cautious and aware of what we expose our minds and bodies to. Because what we expose ourselves to, we become. And what we do repetitiously is who we embody.

The rise of distractions in our day-to-day lives can be used as a surreptitious tool to avoid facing life circumstances. Unconsciously browsing social media feeds and mindlessly shopping online may offer short-term getaway packages, but, at the end of the day, problems or feelings of discontent will likely continue to be there. Many of these distractions, if not consciously used correctly, can influence the outcomes we expect in our life.

As my late grandfather, a sergeant major in the U.S. Army, who served in the Vietnam War and the Gulf War, and my dad, a retired U.S. Air Force lieutenant colonel B-52 radar navigator, who also served in the Gulf War, would both say, "The body is an amazing machine." They both came to understand how the body can adapt in even the toughest conditions to achieve a desired outcome. This statement has been passed down to me and has stuck with me for many years, reminding me just how powerful we really are.

The body really can be influenced through the will and heart of the individual operating it. It can be used to help advance every facet of your life or to undermine it, depending on the quality of inputs it's exposed to.

So, we should be mindful and ask ourselves: "Do I want someone or something else conditioning me, or do I want to be in control of the results in my life?" This is a question we should constantly be asking ourselves if we desire to maintain power over our lives. Consciously conditioning ourselves to focus on positive habits while developing a self-awareness of what may be influencing us are the key mindsets that should be fostered.

RADICAL SELF-CARE EXERCISE:
Conscious Mental Conditioning

The first step to conscious mental conditioning is identifying what you want or who you want to become. From this point, we will use the mental conditioning process you learned in this chapter and go backward to define a framework of thoughts, specific actions, habits, and character traits you will identify that are in alignment with your future goal. This exercise is about taking back control of your internal self, instead of letting your external reality shape you.

1.) Destiny
What is your goal or what results are you hoping to achieve? Do you want to write a book, receive that promotion at work, experience more inner wellness, become a more social person, have a more harmonious homelife, experience greater happiness, start a business, graduate with honors?

2.) Character
List the character traits you will need to adopt to achieve this dream or goal. Will you need to be ambitious, a risk-taker, independent, punctual, outgoing, compassionate?

3.) Habits
List the daily habits you will need to adopt to build the character traits you've listed above. Some examples might be waking up early, writing 100 words a day, reading twenty minutes a day in an area you want to grow in, exercising one hour a day, or sparking up one conversation a day with someone you don't know.

4.) Actions
List the actions you will take to help yourself build the habits you've identified. Perhaps you'll move your alarm clock to another room, force yourself to rise early, put a book on your bed after making it to remind yourself to read before going to sleep, or place sticky notes around the house reminding you to drink water.

5.) Thoughts
List the self-talk or thoughts you will want to adopt to motivate yourself to carry out the actions and build the habits listed above. Examples include "I am worthy of the very best," "I believe in myself," "I was born to do great things," "I am a morning person,"

"My confidence increases every day," and "Great things come when I step outside my comfort zone."*

*You can think of these as affirmations, so make them personal. (I will discuss in more detail later in the book why your self-talk and affirmations are an integral part of your success and well-being.)

Use this framework as a plan to help guide you toward your desired results in life. You can even photocopy or take a picture of this exercise and post it somewhere you'll see it every day to serve as a reminder.

Use hashtags #RadicalSelfCare and #SuccessStartsWithin on social media and share with others to inspire them to join you on your path toward activating your potential.

CHAPTER FOUR

AFFIRM YOUR SELF-TALK

Be mindful of your self-talk. It's a
conversation with the universe.
David James Lees

Do You Hear That? Yes, It's You Talking to Yourself

Now that you understand the conditioning process in modern-day society and looked at how you might be able to take advantage of it, it's time to discuss the underlining voice you hear every day that influences every aspect of your life. Have you heard this inner voice before? I bet you have, but maybe you haven't consciously recognized it throughout your day. You're using it right now to read the words on this book.

It's a silent voice that influences your every action, emotion, and experience. Your self-talk is your internal dialog with yourself. It's the voice that seems to never cease to be quiet. It's basically the thoughts you listen to every day that no one hears except yourself. It can consistently bring up your fears, beliefs, your past, and worries about your future.

One of the most critical lessons in this chapter is discovering that there are two different types of self-talk: positive and negative. Negative self-talk tells you that you are not good enough or can't do something that you know deep down inside you know you can get done or overcome. It's almost like you are fighting two different people inside your own mind to accomplish your goals, dreams, and desires. In fact, that's exactly what it can feel it if you do not know how to properly address your self-talk.

Understanding how to address your negative self-talk is an integral process in your radical self-care journey because this is the guiding force that influences every aspect of your life. In addition, as mentioned, your *thoughts* are the first step and giant leap to the mental conditioning process explained in Chapter Three to improve the results in your life. It's pivotal to understand the psychology of your mind to ensure you can effectively achieve the desires you seek. This brings you clarity and confidence. Otherwise, you are left in uncertainty and confusion about how to change the results in your life.

Throughout your life, you've likely heard two opposing voices in your head. The one that says, "I think I can, I think I can, I think I can," and the one that says, "I can't do this. I am not worthy. I don't have enough money. I don't have enough resources. I wasn't born with innate talent. I don't know how to do that. I am not smart enough." Finding awareness and differentiating between these two voices is one of the most powerful things you can do to take your mind off autopilot and turn it into a forward, conscious thinking instrument to serve you.

Getting your self-talk on your side plays an integral role in your radical self-care journey because if you can master the conversation in your own mind, you can master the circumstances in your life.

Your mind can be used to catapult you to achieve the life you desire but it first starts with knowing how to find awareness and gain control of your self-talk. As David Goggins, a retired Navy SEAL and Ultramarathoner once said, "The most important conversation that you will ever have is the one that you have with yourself." He goes on to say, "You wake up with it, you walk around with it, you go to bed with it, eventually you are going to act on it, whether good or bad."

Beyond Positive Thinking

Let me first start by saying that many self-help books don't often acknowledge the complexities of life to provide techniques that are down-to-earth and that you feel you can incorporate them into your life even when times are challenging. It is not always easy to control your thoughts, especially during stressful moments in life. It is not easy in the midst of stress to think peace or feel feelings of unhappiness and think joy. As you can probably already tell, this is not just a "be positive and your problems will be solved" type of book. Although on a surface level, movements like "positive thinking" have helped millions of people, including me, gain a better life circumstance. Still, I realize "pie in the sky" sayings like these, in some instances, don't often offer a sensible remedy to address challenging and stressful situations in life.

The principles shared and the exercises at the end of each chapter recognize that you aren't going always to feel happy and motivated all of the time. The point is to gain awareness of how you think and feel so you can adeptly use the science-based tools you are learning to ultimately change your results in life.

As you know, a healthy, positive self-talk can help you achieve a more fulfilling, healthy, and happy life. But you don't have to take my word for it. Numerous scientific studies have come to the same conclusion.

For example, one study concluded that spending just a few minutes thinking about the best qualities about yourself before a high-pressure meeting can calm your nerves, increase your confidence, and even improve your chances of a successful desired outcome. Researchers have scientifically concluded the effectiveness of affirmations to the extent that now it is an evidence-based approach to treat people with depression, low self-esteem, and other mental health conditions. This specific study concludes that affirmations have been shown to stimulate specific areas in the brain that make us more likely to affect positive changes related to our health. It's clear if used correctly—repetitiously and consistently—affirmations can have a substantial impact in virtually every area of your life.

Now let's move toward a real-world example to help you truly understand how self-talk can either be a destructive or constructive force in your life.

Imagine yourself becoming excited about an idea for a goal that you always wanted to accomplish in your life. You found some inspiration one day, and you knew this was something you wanted and could very well achieve. The idea got you so excited you couldn't wait to tell someone! As time went on, you started to research online and even read books about the topic to understand the following steps to accomplish this new goal. As you continue to investigate, you begin to hear a small voice in the back of your head get louder and louder.

It starts to tell you that you can't do this, you don't have enough experience, or you're not smart enough to learn. Over time, this voice begins to overpower your "I think I can, I think I can" voice, and pretty soon, you begin to talk yourself out of the same goal you literally just talked yourself into. Your perception begins to narrow, which causes you to unconsciously find information, associate character traits about yourself, or even meaningless situations in your life to support this negative voice in your mind that slowly keeps reaffirming that you can't accomplish this new goal. It's an extremely subtle voice, but it happens all the time whether or not you consciously realize it, whether it be accomplishing a new task on the job, ingraining new habits, studying for a test, or stepping outside of your comfort zone to start a business.

Now that I've given you an example of how negative self-talk can be destructive toward your goals, future vision of yourself, and your life, it's time to discuss what's actually going on in your body.

Your self-talk is a gateway to the life you innately yearn for. Full of abundance, joy, gratitude, fulfillment, love, and success. Now it can also be a gateway to the life you innately do not want to experience. Which is a life of lack, limited self-belief, selfishness, low energy, and even new science points to how negative self-talk could have a physical effect on your bodily functions. It's your choice and, frankly, your responsibility to choose the life you desire, and it's heavily dependent upon the little voice you hear every single day. So, it becomes necessary to master this voice to master your life.

Positive self-talk about yourself and life will carry you one way, and negative self-talk will slowly move you another. In fact, in Dr. Joe Dispenza's *You Are the Placebo*, there is research that suggests your "self-talk slips by your conscious awareness on a moment-to-moment basis and stimulates the autonomic nervous system and flow of biological processes, reinforcing the programmed feeling of who you think you are."

Your self-talk and your beliefs are powerful forces that influence virtually every area of your being, including your body's autonomous fight-or-flight responses. Self-talk and beliefs are separate but related entities that compel each other. To put it simply, your self-talk and the story you tell yourself over time, through constant repetition, eventually become what you believe to be true about yourself and your circumstances—whether it be positive or negative or true or false. In turn, your beliefs fuel your self-talk. These ingrained beliefs and self-talk we tell ourselves daily are key indicators of whether or not you are actually going to capitalize on your potential.

Ultimately, your life will move in tandem with your beliefs and your self-talk. For example, if your self-talk is "I'm never going to get the promotion at work" and your belief is "This company doesn't respect me," then it's likely your day-to-day actions will reflect this thinking pattern. And what will happen? You will probably not get a promotion because your behaviors are aligned with someone who doesn't deserve the company's respect.

It's necessary to change this script in your mind if it is not serving the goals, beliefs, and life you wish to experience. Once you begin to change the script and appropriately disrupt your inner critic, it will positively show up in how you talk, walk, project confidence, and even how your body functions. As Brain Coach Jim Kwik would say, "Your brain is like a supercomputer, and your self-talk is the program it will run." We must think and speak what we desire into existence because it will eventually materialize in our lives.

RADICAL SELF-CARE TIP:
Positive Mental Prompters (PMP)

Our thoughts are always directing and guiding us toward the emotions, experiences, and circumstances that manifest in our lives. Thus, it's increasingly important to pay attention to the type of thoughts you have. Positive thoughts direct you toward positive experiences, and negative thoughts direct you toward negative experiences. When you began to become aware of your negative thoughts arising, it's important to address them, and not let those thoughts slip by your awareness.

If you don't address them quickly and adequately, they can begin to use you. This requires a conscious shift from you toward positive thoughts to uplift you. In addition, it's helpful to know that our minds tend to wander and sometimes they wander toward thoughts that don't serve us. A study conducted by Harvard psychologists concluded that people spend about 47 percent of their waking hours thinking about something other than what they are presently doing. That's nearly half our day thinking about thoughts that may not serve us! As the psychologists concluded, "A human mind is a wandering mind, and a wandering mind is an unhappy mind."

To help address this, use the Positive Mental Prompters (PMP) technique to guide your thoughts toward the good you desire in life.

You can use PMP when you feel like you are cycling down a path of negative thoughts, stuck in a rut, feeling low energy, or when you feel like you need some inspiration. Use podcasts, self-help articles, inspiring YouTube videos, self-help books, and even positive music to help revert your thoughts toward thoughts that will support your life, not undermine it. Many times, we unconsciously allow ourselves to cycle down a long path of negative thoughts, often without addressing them early. Use the devices and technology that you engage with on a daily basis to help guide your thoughts toward positive thought patterns that can support your health, goals, and desires.

These can be especially helpful when your mind begins to unconsciously wander while driving in the car or even when you have downtime. Keep your mind nourished, uplifted, and refreshed with knowledge, motivation, and strategies so you can continue to guide your thoughts toward reaching your highest self. Here are a few resources:

- Kwik Brain Podcast
- Ten Percent Happier Podcast
- The School of Greatness Podcast
- Positively Elevate Podcast
- ThriveGlobal.com
- Impact Theory Podcast
- Spoken Word: The Strangest Secret—Earl Nightingale
- The Tony Robbins Podcast
- Tiny Leaps, Big Changes Podcast
- Oprah's SuperSoul Conversations
- Optimal Living Daily Podcast
- Success Meditation Music: Abundance – Chazz Scott (This is my song!)

Using Affirmations to Change Your Inner Dialog

Now how do you overcome negative self-talk and influence this dialog in your mind to help you maximize your potential? Affirmations is an effective way to start.

Many action-oriented and results-driven people think affirmations are useless; however, they fail to realize that underneath all that action lies a thought. A thought that can either affirm your well-being, behaviors, and results or undermine them.

It's hard for many people to believe in this technique at first, but I invite you to take a step back and understand how they can influence the brain and your behaviors. The truth is you use affirmations every single day of your life, whether or not you realize it. The ability to talk yourself into something is the same ability you use to talk yourself out of something. It's that simple. Only difference here is you are *consciously affirming* who you desire to become as opposed to *unconsciously* telling yourself who you don't want to become. Don't make this any more complicated than it needs to be. The thoughts and words you use to describe your life create your perception thus creating the reality you experience. So, it's important to use positive words to speak *life* into your life!

Naturally, negative affirmations or words can limit your self-belief and drag down your personal relationships and physical health. It's your duty to harness this power and consciously use it for your life and not against it.

I'm not smart enough.

I'm not a good public speaker.

I wish I could stick up for myself at work.

My body is never going to get better.

I just feel like I am never going to lose weight.

I'm not good with money.

I'm going to be single forever.

Does any of this sound familiar to you? This running dialog of negative self-talk can undermine your life if you leave it unchecked. Now let me be clear and say it's okay to have negative thoughts occasionally, but it is not okay to recognize them and allow these thoughts to corrupt your life.

Prolonged negative self-talk can be destructive. It can be a self-sabotaging loop that overflows into many parts of your life.

Strive to replace negative self-descriptions with positive ones. Growth in life doesn't happen when you are the one beating yourself up inside. Rather, aim to be your loudest cheerleader. Change the conversation in your head and consciously use positive affirmations to carry you toward the goals and life you wish to live.

I have the ability to learn.

I can become a better public speaker.

Sticking up for myself at work is something I'm capable of.

My body is challenged but I'm grateful for all it can do now.

Losing weight takes time and planning, but I can do it.

I can learn to be great with money.

I can find a significant other if I'm willing to put myself out there more.

Your self-talk is a self-fulfilling prophecy, and it's your job to determine if it will be good or bad. Affirmations and positive self-talk can sometimes get a bad rap from self-help gurus. Some people may think you are outright lying to yourself but that's actually not the purpose here. You are creating space for growth to allow yourself to expand to see what's possible for you. When the conversation shifts in your head from limitation to possibility, this can lead you toward the behaviors that are in alignment to your goals. If you don't shift the conversation, nothing changes. Over time, the affirmations you say to yourself, which may feel like lies at first, can often lead to changes in how you feel internally, ultimately contributing to positive behaviors.

For affirmations to work, the key is repetition, consistency, and feeling so that you truly influence your subconscious mind. Sound familiar? Yes, this is conditioning the mind at its finest, as I mentioned in Chapter Two. And sometimes, you may not even realize how destructive your self-talk could be about yourself. Many times, it's been happening for so long you've internalized these beliefs, and it becomes all that you hear. In essence, this is why it could be hard for you to speak up for yourself or step outside your comfort zone. Or why your health may not make any meaningful change. Or why diets, most of the time, never work and why losing weight never seems to stick. It's because you haven't truly changed your deep internal self-beliefs, which developed out of the story you told yourself every day.

The only thing standing in the way of what you want is the story you keep telling yourself as to why you don't have it yet.

Consciously, you may want to be better and do better in your life, but your negative self-talk subverts your subconscious mind in ways that make it nearly impossible to achieve your goals. The great part about this is that if you sabotage yourself with negative thoughts, you can most certainly heal and empower yourself with positive ones. That's because your brain is malleable and can change. As Claude Bristol clearly states in his book *The Magic of Believing*, "This subtle force of repeated suggestion overcomes our reason. . . . It's the repeated suggestion that makes you believe." In this case, suggestions happen to be your affirmations and, after time, according to Bristol, these positive and affirming words can start to reach your subconscious.

So how do you implement long-lasting positive change? Using sincere affirmations (examples of which I'll share later) happen to be an effective way to disrupt this negative unconscious dialog to train your mind toward a story that serves who you want to become. Another path to success is to begin a daily meditation practice (discussed in Chapter Eight). With meditation, you become aware of negative self-talk and distorted beliefs, and then you can learn to let them be without engaging or controlling you for the worse.

Upgrade Your Thinking to Change Your Life

Using conscious positive affirmations will combat this negative self-talk and can help you challenge and overcome the self-sabotaging voice in your mind. The end goal of this effective process is to impress positive affirmations on the subconscious to get to their deepest level, which is feeling. Because when you feel different, you act different.

At first, this process may feel like wishful thinking, but try to think about affirmations like muscles in your mind: the more you use them, the stronger they take hold. Repetition is key. Remember the conditioning process discussed in Chapter Three? Repetition and consistency of your

affirmations continue to mold you toward the person who you desire
to become.

Many of us do repetitive exercises in the gym to build our muscles
to become strong and lean. At first, it can feel tough, but then the reps
become easier overtime with the same amount of weight. Affirmations
work in the same way, only we use affirmations as exercises for our mind
to instill self-belief, a positive self-image, and a positive outlook upon life.
Over time these positive mental affirmations can reprogram your thinking
patterns, and pretty soon, you will begin to think, feel, and act differently.
And once you start to think, feel, and act differently, neuroplasticity—as
discussed previously—will begin to physically change the structure of
your brain in accordance with your self-talk, emotions, behaviors, and
actions. As I described in Chapter Two, when you begin to influence your
subconscious mind, you end up rewriting your beliefs and changing the
running script about yourself. Or, as I like to say in my seminars, "Once you
truly believe that you are somebody, that's when you become somebody."

**To make positive change in your life and move beyond the
story you've been telling yourself, you must transcend it.**

One thing to keep in mind is that your affirmation must be used
continuously; otherwise, you risk reverting back to old negative ways of
thinking. Again, back to the gym analogy. Once you get your body in
shape, you can't stop working out and still expect your muscles to remain
strong. They can quickly weaken from missing just a few days in the gym.
Same thing with your affirmations. It's important to stick with it for real
change to occur.

This is the secret as to why change is hard for people and why many
of us don't truly get what they desire. People will end up wishing for one
thing but are constantly thinking another throughout the day. People will
pray for one desire for all of one minute but end up thinking and feeling
throughout the entire day the exact opposite of what they just prayed for.
Don't get me wrong, prayer works but if you don't engage in what I like
to call *pray in action* then your one minute of prayer a day is futile and
is less effective for the results you desire. Your "praying in action," can
be anything from speaking up for yourself in a meeting even when your

voice shakes, sending a blind email, making a cold phone call, or finally being honest with yourself and realizing you may need a new way achieve progress in your health, relationships, or personal success.

As American abolitionist Frederick Douglass pointedly stated, "I prayed for twenty years but received no answer until I prayed with my legs." Your thoughts, emotions, and actions will need to be in alignment and consistent if you intend to make any real progress or change in life.

With enough consistency, your baseline thinking about yourself begins to change. And when your baseline thinking begins to change so does your perspective of your life circumstances.

Pretty soon, you'll start speaking up for yourself, taking more risks with your goals and desires, and betting on yourself more.

Here are some affirmations that can help guide you:

- If I'm struggling with a problem in my life, I trust myself to seek the resources needed to overcome it.
- I am divinely guided.
- I have all my needs coming with speed.
- I am at peace.
- I am always equal to any task set before me.
- I am abundance.
- I give myself grace when I feel like I'm not meeting my potential.
- I am tranquility.
- I am confident in my ability to meet every situation with calm and intelligent action.
- I have the ability to manifest my deepest desires.
- My memory is extraordinarily dependable.
- I am anything I set my mind to.
- I face the future with a persistent knowing that whatever is needed will appear in my presence.
- I am free from guilt.
- I am free from all fear.
- I am generous.
- There is enough money for me and everyone else.
- I can do this!

Quick tip: You can write these affirmations on a sicky note and place them around the house in your common areas like on your desk or bathroom mirror. So, when your mind begins to wander toward thoughts that don't serve you either while brushing your teeth or downtime sitting at your desk, the notes can serve to remind yourself of your power and realign your pattern of thinking. I've been placing sticky notes and notecards of quotes and affirmations all over my house for years!

It's best to use these affirmations during a time of high stress, right before bed, and right when you wake up. These are specific opportunities where you can have a substantial impact on your subconscious mind. Close your eyes and visualize the feeling of the specific statement as you say them. Visualize how it would feel to have already achieved your desired goal or outcome. Truly feel it within your mind, body, and soul. *You must see it in your mind first before you can manifest it in your reality.* Your life is a physical manifestation of the internal running dialog about yourself and life. So, if you want to change your external circumstances, changing your inner dialog is an effective step to take. It's important to be mindful, conscious, and aware of how you speak to yourself when no one is around.

You can either be your biggest cheerleader or biggest enemy, but it's your choice. It's always your choice once you become aware of this voice. Now I didn't say any of this would be easy at first. When you first begin, it may seem as though you are even lying to yourself but over time it will become easier because our brains and bodies are incredibly malleable and can change. And once you have the momentum built, the running dialog in your mind changes from self-corrupting to supportive. Slowly, your actions begin to change; you start talking different, walking different, and carrying yourself with unwavering self-belief.

Soon you won't even recognize yourself, and it will be the most amazing feeling you've ever experienced because you know in your heart you have the power to influence the results in your life.

RADICAL SELF-CARE EXERCISE:
Disrupt & Affirm (D&A)

It's estimated that humans average close to 6,000 thoughts per day. Unfortunately, many of these thoughts can be negative and cause harm to our self-esteem, careers, goals, and health. And because many of these harmful thoughts tend to happen outside of our awareness, it gives us little to no opportunity to shift toward thoughts that improve our lives.

This exercise is all about discovering self-awareness to uncover and disrupt your negative self-talk. For the entire day, I invite you to pay attention to all of your thoughts. Become aware of what you are thinking about.

To put differently, think about what you are thinking about.

You might be surprised, but many of us don't do this. We think compulsively throughout the day; therefore, we are taken by thought and don't allow ourselves to simply observe our thoughts objectively. In this new space of self-awareness, you take the reins of your mind back into your hands.

As you go through the day, you may be surprised how many negative thoughts can arise throughout the day. But this is perfectly fine as you are on the right path. As you continue to develop more awareness with this exercise, you will begin to notice more negative thoughts so you can make the conscious shift toward more positive ones.

Here's what I want you to do as soon as a negative thought arises:

Disrupt It and Affirm (D&A)
This will look like this:
1.) Become aware of the negative thought.
2.) Disrupt it!
3.) Affirm yourself of who you desire to be.

Here's a quick breakdown of how to use this:

Step 1: You become aware of the negative thought. It's important to take a step back here from whatever you are currently doing and give yourself space for inquiry and self-compassion.

Step 2: Once you are aware, it's vital to disrupt it. To adequately disrupt your negative thoughts, you could say to yourself out loud, "Stop," or "I am in control." Another option is wearing a rubber band on your wrist to give yourself a good snap if a negative thought arises to disrupt it!

It's essential to actively do something to disrupt the negative thought to ensure your subconscious mind (which remembers everything) picks up on it. You can even ask yourself a reframing question like "Is this thought even true?" or "Is there any valid evidence to support how I am feeling right now?" or "How would my highest self respond to this?" The simple act of questioning your thoughts can offer a new perspective of your challenge that might turn your anxiousness into excitement, which can often lead to living with more compassion and new possibilities.

Step 3: Affirm yourself. This is when your affirmations come into play. Say them with feeling and it might be helpful to remember that practices like these can rewire neural pathways in your brain to reinforce this habit. Feel free to use the affirmations in this chapter and the example that follows.

Here are some examples:

Negative Thought: My boss is making me lead on this new project, and I don't think I have enough experience yet.
Affirm Yourself: This may be a challenge, but I know I can get this project done if I seek the proper resources and ask for guidance along the way.

Negative Thought: I don't think I have what it takes to achieve this goal.
Affirm Yourself: I trust myself to succeed! If I don't have the right information or resources now, I trust myself that I can go find it when I need it.

Negative Thought: I'm not a natural writer or public speaker.
Affirm Yourself: Through practice every day and with help from mentors, I know I can improve my writing skills and become an effective public speaker.

Over time, through practice, you will create space for yourself to adequately disrupt your negative thoughts so you can consciously choose a pattern of thought that serves you. As you use D&A throughout your life, you will become more capable of questioning and examining your thoughts before they influence your mood, actions, performance at work, and health. This exercise is powerful because it takes you off autopilot and puts you in the space to have more freedom of your emotions and thoughts.

Make D&A a part of your DNA to activate your potential.

Use hashtags #RadicalSelfCare and #SuccessStartsWithin on social media and share with others to inspire them to join you on your path toward activating your potential.

CHAPTER FIVE

DISCOVER YOUR WHY

He who has a why to live can bear almost any how.
Friedrich Nietzsche

The Foundation to Life

As a speaker, I was once invited to speak at the Central Virginia Community College located in Lynchburg, Virginia, in celebration of Black History Month. The session was packed with faculty, students, and university officials. I was surprised to see a decent turn out even on a cold rainy day in the middle of February. During the session, my friend and I shared the stage, and we discussed our past failures, successes, and our experiences being Black engineers in our fields of Systems Engineering and Cyber Security.

We discussed how we were able to secure our unique internships at some of the most prestigious laboratories and agencies, including NASA, National Institute of Standards and Technology (NIST), and National Nuclear Security Administration's Lawrence Livermore National Laboratory (LLNL). We shared our tips and strategies for finding internships and securing jobs. It's always a pleasure for me to speak on these topics to students because I see it as our duty to help guide the next generation of leaders.

I've always challenged myself as a speaker to ensure the audience could leave with a practical takeaway that they can immediately put into action after the event. As anyone who's ever spoken before it always seems as if time flies when you are giving a presentation or a speech, so you have to be clear, concise, and intentional with every word that comes from your mouth.

During the Question and Answer (Q&A) portion of the event, we received a number of really good questions ranging from how we found internships to the importance of mentors. But one of the last few questions during the Q&A surprisingly rocked me to the core. It wasn't the first time I've heard the question either, but something came over me that allowed me to answer the question a little bit differently then I normally would. A student stood up in the back of the audience and asked us, "How do we stay motivated despite failures and setbacks?" I could have answered this question like how I normally do with a creative psychological technique taught by hundreds of self-help authors—which can be very helpful—but instead the cold hard truth came out.

Without conscious thought something came over me and I started to speak with so much clarity and focus that I almost didn't feel it was me who was actually talking. I told him that it really comes down to your why. I remember saying, "If your why is strong enough you can overcome anything and achieve anything you set your mind to." I continued and turned to everyone in the audience and said, "It's essential to have a sturdy *why* for why you wake up in the morning, a why for attending school, and a why for heading to work. If you have a strong enough why, you will never quit on yourself or life. It will supply you with strength and resilience to keep going even when you can't push yourself any harder or farther."

At that moment, I felt a rush of energy fill the room that I can't even put into words. It really had nothing to do with me or what I said. I was just being used as a medium to articulate what is deeply intertwined into our existence as humans. It's an underlying persistent yearning that all of us search for whether we realize it or not. It's the innate desire to have a sense of purpose and meaning in our lives. And in order to truly satisfy this deep longing for purpose and meaning, a why should be discovered to truly live a meaningful, resilient, and fulfilled life.

After the speaking engagement was over, I spoke with several audience members, and I kept hearing the same common thread of questions and comments related to this ineffable truth that we all continue to search for. We are all looking for our personal power to propel us over the hardships, daily struggles, and adversities that we may face in order to have a satisfying life. The underpin of this is found in one clearly knowing their why for living.

At the foundation of every successful human is a strong why for who they are. From what they do, where they are going, and what they want to accomplish to the type of clothes they wear, morals they abide by, values that guide them, the choice of words they use, and who they spend their time with. Your why is your guiding light for all the decisions you make in life. For if you do not know your why, almost every decision or problem that is presented to you will be faced with mental turmoil, indecisiveness, and lack of direction. This is because you haven't ingrained a mechanism or light within to help lead you toward your higher purpose.

Knowing your why is like your GPS that continues to give you correct and most effective directions to get you to your desired location or goal.

Your why can also give you the strength and ambition to remain steadfast in your journey despite roadblocks, adversity, or any negative circumstance you may face. As most of us know already, life isn't always positive or happy-go-lucky all the time. As a matter of fact, it can be difficult and confusing if you do not have a guiding light that leads you along the way. Think of your why as your shepherd. It's your North Star for every area of your life. Knowing your why will keep you uplifted, resilient, discernible, and can give unwavering security and peace.

You can think of your why as the solid foundation of your house. If the foundation is not built on solid ground so that it is strong and sturdy, then when it is challenged, it will be compromised. So when you are challenged in life, your why will naturally become the foundation to keep you driven toward your goals and who you want to become.

In addition, your why will help you define your goals in life to keep you from burning out. Many of us are working hard and striving for things in life we really don't care about or value—those things society tells us we need or should want. Working hard without true alignment with your soul's purpose promotes burnout. Do you ever notice when you work on things you enjoy or value doing, you seem more energized and feel more alive? But when you are working on things you don't value, your energy feels depleted and worn out at the end of the day.

Personally, when I used to leave my job that I didn't enjoy or value, my mind, body, and soul felt so depleted at the end of the day. The job was "paying the bills" but it didn't excite me. And after work I felt like I didn't have enough energy or time to do things I valued personally in my life. But when I took baby steps toward what I like to call my "aligned self" I started doing things I enjoyed doing, like public speaking, writing, mentoring youth, and teaching corporate seminars, I realized how energized I was throughout the day. As crazy as it sounds, I got more done, and I felt I had more time in my day to work on things I truly valued and enjoyed.

What does stepping into your aligned self look like for you? What do you truly value? What energizes you? Is it an instrument or hobby you used to enjoy as a child you never found time for? Or maybe you really value helping others and want to donate more of your time to a local nonprofit. Try stepping into your aligned self and watch your energy, well-being, and happiness all increase! As Mark Twain said, "The key to success is to make your vocation your vacation."

So many of us are working hard but are not in alignment with our values and purpose. You don't want to get to the end of your life and realize you've been working hard but climbing the wrong mountain. *Success without fulfillment is failure.* And fulfillment only ensues as a byproduct of doing what you love or working on something you value. Your why helps you to align with yourself so you can fast-track the desires and well-being you are aiming for. This is why you must ensure you have a clear and strong why for your life for your radical self-care journey.

Meaning and purpose are so necessary for the human psyche that neurologist and psychiatrist, Viktor Frankl, developed a scientific concept for it. It's called *logotherapy.* Logotherapy is a form of psychotherapy that was founded on the belief that "human nature is motivated by the search of a life purpose." Frankl believed that one can discover their meaning in life in three different ways: "(1) creating a work or doing a deed; (2) by experiencing something or encountering someone; and (3) by the attitude we take toward unavoidable suffering."

For Frankl he found meaning while fighting for his life in a Nazi concentration camp. In his memoir *Man's Search For Meaning*, he describes how many prisoners in the camp responded to their suffering with despair and simply lost their will to live. While others in the camp found some way to continue to fight and suffer through despite the extraordinary physical and psychological torture. He slowly began to realize it was because these individuals found meaning and purpose to continue to persist.

They found a reason to live.

As Frankl states poignantly: "What man actually needs is not a tensionless state but rather the striving and struggling for a worthwhile goal, a freely chosen task." Finding meaning and purpose in your life is literally the fuel you need to continue to ignite the flame in your soul so that you can continue to persevere and activate your potential. This is what the human spirit desperately craves.

Being Prepared with Your Why

Whether it's lack of self-belief in attaining a particular goal, being stuck in a rut, overcoming a loss, failing a class, battling an illness, recovering from a failed relationship—life can be challenging. Whether we unconsciously cause the harm to ourselves or an external circumstance does it to us—having a strategy or framework to overcome life's adversities will put you in a much more manageable position. Not in the sense of expecting difficult situations to come but always being prepared when they do.

You can think of this like the safety precautions built into a car such as a seatbelt and airbag. Every time we get into a car and drive to our destination, we do not expect an accident to occur, but we prepare ourselves in the event one does happen. Same thing for life. Imagine driving around in the car today without airbags, a seatbelt, headlights, antilock brakes, or traction control? You wouldn't feel comfortable getting into a car without these safety precautions, right? So why would you unconsciously walk through life without your own safety precautions to put yourself in a better position to bounce back despite life's most difficult moments?

This is what a strong and clear why can do for you. It can set you back on track to bounce back so that you can continue to ascend toward who you were meant to become. There are so many people walking around through life with no primary aim, no mission statement, or why for their lives. So when life challenges them, and they have no foundation or why, many suffer defeat and give up without a fight. Unbeknown to them, this affects their self-worth, self-image, motivation, and joyfulness throughout day-to-day life. Your why keeps you steadfast toward your desires and life you innately desire full of opportunities and personal freedom.

Unfortunately, it's becoming even worse as most of our society is forced to continue to focus their energy on things outside of themselves. For example, most of us know more about our favorite celebrity than we do our goals, desires, and "why" for living. And spending countless hours on social media and mindless web browsing has made this much easier to distract us from what our soul truly yearns for. It's so easy for us to set time aside for our favorite Netflix show but most of us have not taken time in our lives to sit down and consciously think of what our values are, who we want to become, our morals, or our deepest desires. Our minds are filled with other people's thoughts, desires, and goals—not our own. As result, our souls feel depleted, and our potential isn't activated.

This makes it that much harder to know who we really are or who we want to become because we've lost touch with our inner souls that yearn for expansion, clarity, and personal growth. Setting time aside and thinking about who you are and your why in life is by far one of the most important life activities that you can do. This is quite simply the foundation for your life.

RADICAL SELF-CARE TIP:
More Life Moments (MLM)

Gratefulness is an excellent way to boost your mood, enhance a healthy perspective about your life, and widen your perception to find solutions in your life. Robert Emmons, a professor of psychology at the University of California, Davis, and the world's leading scientific expert on gratitude concluded in his research that those who practice gratitude consistently report having stronger immune systems, more stress resistant, increased levels of joy, more compassion, and even lower blood pressure.

It's essential to spend time celebrating the present moment and focus on things you do have as opposed to things you feel like are lacking. Research has confirmed that human beings cannot experience emotions of gratefulness and unhappiness at the same time. Once you begin to consciously think of things that you are grateful for, the more grateful you will become. It sends you toward an upward spiral of emotions that can be used as a catalyst to improve any aspect of your life.

Before the start of every team meeting at our nonprofit, Positively Caviar, Inc., we share what we call *More Life Moments or MLM* for short. These moments are experiences in life that are positive or joyful that has recently made an impact on you. It could have been a spontaneous conversation, a breakthrough, a sense of clarity, a feeling of inspiration, or even a simple change in perspective for the better. These types of experiences happen more than we realize but because we are locked in a busy, always-on lifestyle, we tend to forget the simple moments that are really the most precious to our life journey. It's imperative that we relish the good happening in our lives and hold on to these moments to invigorate our souls to remind ourselves that life is a gift, and we should treat it as such.

Once a day, preferably in the morning, take some time to think about your *More Life Moment* that happened the day before. It could have been anything from catching up with a close friend, learning something about yourself, or something that made you smile. This is a great way to foster self-awareness so you can pull yourself out of your fast-paced lifestyle and focus on the good happening in your life. Many times, our gut reaction is to focus on the bad (this is what scientists refer to as negativity bias) when really there are so many good precious moments happening every single day. But they easily fade into the back of our minds, outside of our awareness, thus easily forgotten.

Cultivating gratefulness for what you have, where you've been, and where you are going is necessary so you expand toward your highest self. Not only that, but you also become more receptive and open to allowing the goodness of life to continue to pour into you and through you. Because once you train your mind to focus on the good, the more *good* you begin to notice. You start to see and experience *more of life* right before your eyes.

And as a result, it continues to compound giving you more ammunition to realize that your life is a joyous journey and is always moving you toward more love, peace, happiness, and abundance.

Living Life on Purpose

Our strongest desires as human beings are to have purpose and meaning. Life doesn't automatically hand out purposes to us or show us the meaning of life. To find purpose and meaning in our lives, we need to cultivate and foster our desires, talents, and experiences.

My grandfather knew all too well about the importance of purpose and meaning in life. While attending North Carolina A&T State University, Ackneil "Neil" Muldrow II, was one of the very first to participate in the civil rights lunchroom protests against segregation at the Woolworth department store lunch counter in Greensboro, NC. The official policy at the time was to refuse service to anyone who was not white. In addition, the notorious Jim Crow laws that segregated Blacks from whites in almost every aspect of daily life continued to permeate across the South. This left Blacks with poorer quality facilities and services than whites. With this in mind, students from A&T, including my grandfather, planned a staged sit-in that eventually sparked a movement that spread across the United States to over fifty-five cities and thirteen states, according to *History.com*. This pioneering act, resulted in the Governor of North Carolina, threatening expulsion of him and other participants. The action was eventually averted, with the support of the NC A&T administrators and faculty. Because of the extraordinary success of the sit-in movement, many restaurants across the South began to modify policies for integration.

For my grandfather, he found purpose and meaning in his life during the 1960s when racial discrimination and the civil rights movement begin to reach a critical tipping point. He fought for equality among Black Americans for a better future. From that moment on, his entire life was centered upon this goal. Every action, conversation, and choice he made reflected upon his purpose of civic duty.

From creating access to working capital of nearly forty million dollars for Black businesses and entrepreneurs in the commercial lending space to serving as a board member for Bon Secours Baltimore Health System, University of Maryland's Chancellor's Advisory Board, the University of Maryland Medical System, Stevenson University, Coppin State University, and the College of Notre Dame of Maryland. He knew that access to capital and developing minority entrepreneurship played a pivotal role in creating equitable opportunities and to effectively combat what is now known as the racial wealth gap.

Former Baltimore Mayor Kurt L. Schmoke claims that "A lot of people owe their successful careers to him," and "You could say he was a financial godfather in the minority business community. His style was low-profile, but he was well known in his field." My late grandfather found purpose and meaning through serving others to ultimately live a purposeful, goal-oriented, and meaningful life. He lived a full life because he was fueled by a strong and clear why.

There is an innate longing for purpose and meaning intertwined within our human souls that without it we naturally feel lost, isolated, and perceive that life is happening *to* us rather than *for* us. It makes us feel like we are in the back seat of life rather than the driver's seat.

Having a clear and strong enough why is one of the most powerful ways to give yourself strength and clarity to bounce back that can make life much more manageable and meaningful. It can give you the energy and persistence to keep going when life gets tough. Our why for life is our highest goal and mission because this is what our human nature continues to long for. And if you don't feed your innate human desires adequately, you may feel lost in life and naturally lose your desire to keep going when faced with difficult decisions or tumultuous circumstances. This is because you've lost sight of your highest target—your why for living.

Your why will ground you for life.

> *Character cannot be developed in ease and quiet. Only through experience of trial and suffering can the soul be strengthened, ambition inspired, and success achieved.*
>
> Helen Keller

Finding Your Will in Suffering

As I continued to study the mind and experience ways to further my own journey in finding meaning in life, I started to pick up long distance running as a hobby. This was a tough challenge for me because I was not a natural runner growing up. But I continued to challenge myself because I was obsessed with the numerous long-distance runners I had researched who had experienced states of enlightenment, bliss, and the feeling as if they could transcend and conquered anything. I wanted that feeling. And I wanted to challenge myself mentally and physically to see if I had what it took.

In fact, there have been stories of monks living in Mount Hiei, located in the mountains of Japan, who have put themselves through excruciating endurance challenges of running 1,000 marathons in 1,000 days in their quest to achieve spiritual enlightenment. And get this, apparently, they run in straw sandals! In a *Guardian* article, it states that in the last 130 years only forty-six men have achieved this feat. The idea behind this excruciating task is to tire out the mind and exhaust the body until nothing is left in order to achieve a state of "oneness with the universe."

So, what does all this have to do with your why? Well, one of the main reasons why monks in the mountains of Japan actually run for this long is to answer the simple question that most of us ask ourselves in some part of our lives, which is "Why am I alive?" or "What's my purpose in life?" To the monks in Japan these types of endurance challenges happen to be a unique meditation to answer those deep questions that innately exist within all of us.

When I started to run as a hobby, my goal was no way near 1,000 marathons. My first goal was to finish one marathon. I trained for about three months, which by the way was way too short! Running in the early mornings before work, at lunch time, and sometimes after work. Whatever I needed to do to modify my schedule to train, I did. I challenged my little brother, Austin, to sign up for the Baltimore Running Festival in Baltimore, MD, and we were both extremely excited for the challenge. After training for months and researching everything that we could from the race route to proper nutrition, and even receiving advice from past runners, we were ready (at least we thought we we're). We woke up early Saturday morning in October for race day. It was still pitch-black outside by the time we got to the starting line. The race was about to begin and just like that we were off!

My brother and I ran with each other for a good portion of the race. Both of us felt amazing and comfortable; we were on cloud nine to say the least. The race day energy was in full effect, and we thought this was going to be a piece of cake. About mid-way through my brother had some issues with his shoes so he had to stop but I kept chugging along doing the best that I could.

After about nineteen miles of running, I began to feel excruciating pain in my legs and lower back. I quickly realized this was going to be a challenging experience. I had reached the inevitable "wall." I had prepared for this moment through tons of online research and training but *knowing* something means nothing until you actually *experience* it. Hitting what's known as the runner's "wall" is a point where the human body depletes a lot of its stored glycogen and the feelings of exhaustion, mental fatigue, and negative thoughts begin to arise. Glycogen is a carbohydrate stored in our muscles and liver to give our bodies energy. And when the body is low on glycogen the "brain wants to shut down activity as a preservation method, which may lead to negative thinking," naturally causing this well-known "wall." I quickly realized this marathon, which is considered to be a physical test on the body, is really more of a mental test. A test of mental fortitude and pure will. My physical training was really about preparing my mind for states of total mental exhaustion.

As I continued to run while trying to break through this mental "wall," I could feel every step and it was painful. My toenails were sore, my knees and lower back were in agonizing pain, and I still had about five more miles to go. Because I had mentally prepared for this moment, I remained keenly and consciously aware of the dialog in my head. It was appalling.

It's similar to the voice you have in your head when you're cycling down a negative thought loop that spirals you out of control, and before you know it, you've become consumed by it. This was that moment times ten. This moment stripped me down to my deepest fears, self-doubt, and insecurities. With each step, my brain continued to ask a series of questions over and over again. And each of those questions, ironically started with the word "why."

Can you see where I'm headed with this? All I could hear in my head was *Why are you continuing to put one step after the other? Why are you putting yourself through this mental and physical suffering to finish this race? Nobody is making you do this. Why are you still continuing? Why did you even train for something like this? You are not a runner.* My negative self-talk was a little bit nastier than that, but I think you get the point.

During life's challenges, adversities, and even striving for a goal we are put into situations just like what I experienced at mile nineteen of my first marathon. When our external circumstances challenge our mental fortitude, we are faced with a subtle question: Why? I realized during my marathon that our minds are constantly looking for the path of least resistance. We are always looking for a way out of being uncomfortable, adversity, or an obstacle. This is an innate desire as our brains are designed to protect us. They are designed to keep us away from anything that might make us uncomfortable to ensure our survival.

So, if we force ourselves to strive for a particular goal or face an uncomfortable situation, our brains naturally have the tendency to choose the easy route to keep us comfortable thus increasing our percentage of *survival.* Unfortunately, if you fall into this trap and mindset day-to-day, life will not yield you the results you desire in accordance with your professional and personal goals. When you are forced into a stressful situation, it's important to be prepared to answer this simple question: "Why?"

Because if you cannot clearly and consciously answer this question you will likely not stay committed to your pursuits. You will likely give up on your goal, on your relationships, on your dreams, and on the life you desire. It's in moments like this that answering this question can give you the clarity and power to effectively reason with that little voice in your head that tells you to stop or that you can't overcome or accomplish something.

When I hit the wall during the marathon, I was fortunate to be able to answer this very important question, which provided me with the incentive and drive to continue the race.

Throughout your day you constantly hear a similar voice in your head that I heard when I was running my race. It's that voice that nearly all of us have heard before while trying to attain a goal, during life's challenges, managing a dysfunctional relationship, working out in the gym, preparing for a presentation, studying for a test, or even the monotony of washing a sink full of dishes.

It's necessary for humans to have a why to overpower and combat this voice in your head that tells you can't do something or to quit. The better you become at recognizing and shutting off this voice, the more manageable it will become for your brain to overcome obstacles that you may face in your life. And again, this is neuroplasticity working in your favor. Through repetition and consistency in gaining awareness of this voice and consciously choosing to reason with it, the easier it can become. Thus, your willpower continues to grow!

As previously discussed, your brain is like a muscle and over time you can improve your mental threshold for tolerating negative emotions, uncomfortable situations, discomfort, and even pain. Despite current societal trends toward comfortability and convenience, being uncomfortable in life is where true growth derives from. And all growth depends upon your ability to consciously choose the path of most resistance so that you can continue to develop, grow, and stretch yourself. If you remain comfortable throughout life it can lead to discontent, boredom, and dissatisfaction. You will continue to just "survive," since that's what the brain is designed to do, but it won't feel like you are truly living. We are about truly thriving here!

So, in essence there are two choices in life, you can either be comfortable, which promotes stagnation or stretch yourself to grow to reach the fullest expression of you. This is mental fortitude and resilience, and it should be cultivated within so that you can continue to tackle your goals to achieve the life you envision for yourself.

During the marathon, I learned one thing about life—that mental and physical discomfort can be overcome with a strong and clear why. And that much of this discomfort we face in life can be managed a lot more effectively with the right mindset. That's why it's important to cultivate a strong enough why to use as leverage and courage to endure any obstacle or persist in achieving any goal. This is the determining factor in giving up or succeeding in life. As Friedrich Nietzsche clearly stated, "He who has a *why* to live for can bear almost any how."

What's Your Why

Do you have a clear and deep why for your aspirations, dreams, and life? If you don't think that you do, that's okay, it's time you consciously ask yourself this sometimes-elusive question and begin to structure your life around these answers. As discussed previously, your why is your guiding light. It will yield psychological strength, emotional stability, and confidence within yourself to know who you are and where you headed, despite the difficulties and uncertainties that may arise.

And as bad as you may want to go online to look up this question, your why is one of the few things that can't be answered by a search engine or by anyone else. This is a question only you can ask yourself because no one knows you better than you know yourself. You may be able to receive guidance from a mentor or loved one but ultimately this answer will come from you.

A strong why can give you the necessary motivation and passion for executing your dreams and goals. You can have all the knowledge in the world, but your human psyche requires reason and purpose to put newfound knowledge and strategies into action. I've always been astonished to see and meet really smart people who weren't happy, successful, or healthy. They can recite facts verbatim and know strategies like the back of their hand, but they don't put them into action for positive results to manifest in their lives. This is where your why comes in, to ensure you always have a reason and the necessary passion for following through and executing on your dreams and goals.

As discussed, your why can also be used as a preparedness tool, just like a seatbelt, in moments of lack of self-belief, striving for a goal, when you want to give up, or when life throws you a curveball. These types of situations will inevitably come so it's best to be prepared. As mentioned, you would never get into a car without a seatbelt so don't unconsciously walk through life without a clear and concrete why for your relationships, health, aspirations, and life. Your why is the foundation for your life.

Thomas Carlyle said it best: "The man without a purpose is like a ship without a rudder." Purpose and meaning are wrapped into our genes and souls to help guide us. Having a clear why is closely linked to your purpose and helps define meaning in your life. It will help you overcome daily adversities, invoke motivation and passion, prevent burnout, make decisions that align with your purpose, and yield discernment when faced with tough choices. This is an innate desire and a necessary component in your radical self-care journey.

RADICAL SELF-CARE EXERCISE:
Discovering Your Why

Let's take some time to discover or rediscover your why so you can become a better you and achieve your highest self. Grab a pen and notebook or a piece of paper and begin thinking about who you are, what you stand for, or who want to become. This may seem hard at first but after a while the thoughts will naturally flow. As I mentioned before, we all have a natural human desire to expand and grow. You just have to take the first step.

Your why should get you excited about life, and it should be something that means a lot to you. If it doesn't mean a great deal to you then it won't be helpful for you throughout life nor will it provide you with a solid and meaningful foundation for life's tough moments or decisions. It should help guide you toward the type of relationships, friendships, contributions you want to make, and life that you want to enjoy. This will help you narrow your focus to allow yourself to spend time and energy on activities that matter the most to you.

To help, here are some questions you can contemplate on that will help guide your thoughts toward your chief aim.

- What will be my legacy?
- How do I want my kids or grandkids to remember me?
- How do I want my community to remember me?
- What do I want my closest friends to say about me?
- What gets me excited about life?
- What are my core values?
- What are some of my most rewarding accomplishments?
- What types of emotions do I want to feel every day?
- What gives me peace of mind?
- How do I want to be remembered?
- What keeps me aligned?
- What keeps me driven?
- What do I really care about?
- What social issue makes me upset that I want to help solve?

Once you have discovered your why, which could take some time, make sure you write it down as clearly and succinctly as you can. It could be a sentence or two sentences or even a paragraph. To provide with you an example, here's mine currently: "To help others build resilience, to equip minds with knowledge, and to emit authentic positive energy to uplift others." Other examples could include: "To have fun in my journey in life and learn from my mistakes." "My why is to help people be more connected in their life, career, and business." "To leave the world better than I found it and to be remembered by the people whose lives I touched."

Remember, this is *your* why and no one else's. And of course, it's perfectly okay to change it throughout your life. It's important to write down whatever centers you so that you are reminded of who you are and where you are going. Place your why somewhere where you can see it every day. I would recommend your bathroom mirror or somewhere in your bedroom so every morning when you begin each day you are reminded of your chief aim in life.

Use hashtags #RadicalSelfCare and #SuccessStartsWithin on social media and share with others to inspire them to join you on your path toward activating your potential.

CHAPTER SIX

WORK TOWARD ASCENSION

In the absence of clearly defined goals, we become
strangely loyal to performing daily trivia until
ultimately we become enslaved by it.
Robert A. Heinlein

Develop Childlike Faith

When I was young my family and I moved around a lot. My father served in the U.S. Air Force flying the B-52 Stratofortress as a Radar Navigator. This long-range strategic bomber was originally built in the 1950s to carry nuclear weapons for Cold War-era deterrence missions. At the time of writing this, the Air Force continues flying them today. In fact, the B-52 has been widely accepted as the "backbone of the strategic bomber force" for the United States for more than sixty years. Needless to say, I was my dad's number one fan growing up. Although I was too young to realize it, his discipline, sacrifice, and strength displayed while I was growing up are attributes that have continued to guide my life.

My father served on the 96th Bomb Squadron unit located on Barksdale Air Force Base in Shreveport, Louisiana. During his time stationed on Barksdale, I came into the picture born right there in the hospital on the Air Force base. From Shreveport, we then moved to Colorado Springs, Colorado, where my father taught at the United States Air Force Academy for a few years. After spending some time in the beautiful Colorado Rockies, we settled in Arlington, Virginia, until I was about six years old.

While we lived in Arlington, my grandparents on my father's side came to visit periodically from South Carolina. During one visit, I vaguely remember playing outside with a new toy that I very much enjoyed. Unfortunately, after a couple of moments of having the toy outside on the front lawn, I accidently dropped it. It was in the middle of fall so there were a lot of leaves that had fallen in the area that made the toy nearly impossible to find. I was terribly upset at first as I remember having a deep yearning to find this toy by any means necessary.

As I walked around the front yard, I kindly ask my grandfather if he would help me look for it. Even though I barely remember this—my mom continues to tell me this story over the years—apparently, as we continued our search, I quietly whispered to myself, "Lord, lay my eyes on it."

As you might imagine I did not truly understand what I had said to myself from a spiritual or religious context. My parents were regular churchgoers, so I unconsciously developed a strong sense of faith so undoubtedly many of these spiritual principles were instilled in me growing up. But I really had no idea what I was saying. And apparently when I said this statement, it was spoken at just the right volume in which my grandfather could hear it loud and clear.

Sure enough, after a few moments of saying that statement, the toy was able to show itself through the leaves in our front yard. Although I vaguely remember this experience as a child, I do remember the incredible state of euphoria I felt when I saw the toy peek out from beyond the fallen leaves. As I went down to pick it up, I was full of joy and satisfaction. I may not have realized it at the time, but that little moment has continued to shape my life to this day.

All children are filled with tons of creativity, imagination, unshakable hope and, even if they don't realize it yet, an incredible amount of faith in something much greater than themselves. Some people may call this "childlike faith." These are innate traits that are embedded within every person's soul when we are first born into this world that inevitably make us *human*.

Unfortunately, as we continue to grow and experience societal structures, life hardships, and external influences these qualities can easily deteriorate overtime. Life circumstances can force us to become skeptical and overly analytical in some cases. Analytical decision-making may be good for some parts in our lives but in others, overthinking and being overly critical can backfire.

To depict this better, picture the following scene in your mind: Imagine you're a child nervous about jumping into the deep end of the pool while your friends are already in. You've taken swimming lessons before but your're still scared. The more you overthink about it, the more afraid you become. But once you stop overanalyzing and just jump in, you realize you never had anything to worry about at all. Now you're enjoying the pleasures of triumph, success, and fellowship with your friends.

We find ourselves in many situations in life that require us to "trust our gut" and develop our intuition. A healthy balance between planning and acting on instincts is necessary. Taking risks and narrowing your focus on what you desire in life takes "childlike faith" that cannot necessarily be analytically thought out. This is where setting proper goals come into play to unleash the proper direction of expansion for your radical self-care journey. Many people overthink what they want in life because they are unsure how to accomplish it. Thus, they never decide to go after it. This requires "childlike faith" so you can choose what you want first and then take baby steps toward your goal. As self-help author Jack Canfield once said, "Life is like driving in the dark. Your headlights show you the 200 feet in front of you, and as you move forward, the next 200 feet are shown to you. You don't need to see the entire path to reach your destination." Once you start to take action toward your selected goal, the next steps will be revealed to you. The first step is knowing what you want.

Focus on the *what* first, then the *how* will be revealed to you.

Know What You Want

Having direction in life comes from what you desire out of life. In my story as a six-year-old child, I faced what I thought, at the time, a very large difficulty in that moment in my life. But let's be honest anyone who's ever raised a child can understand that to a child, everything can feel like the end of the world. So, I was clearly faced with a challenge and although I didn't know how or if I was going to be able to locate the toy—something in me *knew* I was going to be able to find it. It was a gut feeling. In that moment of quiet desperation, I set my intentions, clearly defined my goal, mustered up faith, surrendered to the unknown, and took action.

And because I knew exactly what I was looking for, maintained expectation in my desired outcome, the opportunity arose in front of my eyes. I simply took advantage and found the exact thing I was searching for. I didn't fuss, shout, or give up. I just believed in my objective without questioning or overanalyzing how I was going to be able to get it done.

This story can relate to many areas of our lives when we are trying to accomplish our goals and attain the highest vision of ourselves. Especially when sometimes we can't consciously see or believe the end result can come into fruition. But in order for you to expand yourself and accomplish anything, you must first know what you desire. (See Radical Self-Care Exercise: Conscious Goal Setting at the end of this chapter.) You have to know what you want before you can *find it*.

Imagine rushing up the stairs heading toward your bedroom closet. You remembered that you left something but when you finally got to your closet, you abruptly forgot why you went up there in the first place. Distressed and rushed, you walk out of your closet but then after a couple seconds you quickly realize what it was that you left. It was your hat but unbeknown to you, your eyes quickly glanced over the hat when you first walked into your closet. It was sitting right in front of your eyes, but you didn't *see* it because you didn't know what you were looking for.

When you don't know what you are looking for, you won't have the opportunity to find *it*. It could be directly in front of your eyes, but until you set the inner intention, all you see are external miscellaneous circumstances. Inner clarity and intention are your shortcuts to your desired results in life.

Many of us walk aimlessly through life pointing out the things we don't want as opposed to focusing on the things we do want. As a result, the things we say we do not want call into action *unseen energy* that bring the exact thing we did not intend to have or experience into our consciousness. And thus, into our lives.

This is because when we focus on the things we don't want, we unconsciously give our energy to it, which correspondingly draws those things into your life. Energy always flows where attention is directed.

You've experienced this yourself but may not have been consciously aware of it. For example, not wanting to drive in traffic might be something you've thought a lot about. You hate congestion and every time you set foot in your car you think about traffic and how it prevents you from getting somewhere on time. Just thinking about traffic makes you *see* it—even when the number of cars on a road is relatively light. By getting angry at cars, you're inviting negativity. You begin to tense up. You behave as if traffic is everywhere and start cursing. Pretty soon, your perception narrows, and traffic and congestion are all you see. You focus on traffic so much that you unconsciously congest your own body and mind with negativity.

Whatever we consistently think about, we experience more of. Whatever we talk more about, we see more of. If you continue to talk about issues and obstacles that may be blocking you, then that's all you're going to see. Your train of thought will match your reality. This is because if you consciously believe you can't have, do, or be something your subconscious mind will create and find the same circumstances to prove yourself that you are "right," regardless of if it's true or not.

Your subconscious mind is always working. So be sure to feed it with what you want, not what you don't want. Here are some examples:

Starve Your Mind: What *Not* to Say	Feed Your Mind: What to Say Instead
I don't want to be broke.	I desire to live abundantly.
I don't want to have an unhappy relationship.	I desire to experience a joyful loving relationship.
I don't want to fail.	I desire to succeed.
I don't like my body.	I desire to change my body for the better.

Even when you say statements like "I'm not complaining" (which I used to say all the time when someone would ask me how my day was going) signals to your subconscious mind that at a deep level you might be complaining about some area in your life. And we all know complaining never gives us the results we desire in our lives. Your subconscious mind can't process negatives. It interprets everything you think or say as a command. This is why we must state our goals in the positive so our subconscious can go to work for us rather than against us.

When I realized I had been saying statements like these unconsciously every day, I realized I was setting myself back. Since then, I promised myself never to say canned statements like these ever again. Instead, when someone asks me how my day is going, I say, "I'm learning and growing." Or "I'm having a great day." And even when I'm not having the best day, I still try to keep my responses optimistic because we know our mind will search for information in its external environment to reaffirm what we think and believe. It may sound cheesy but simple habits like these play a huge role in how our brain interprets information so we can consciously improve the results in our lives. This doesn't mean we don't acknowledge the bad or ignore the problems we may be facing. Quite the opposite. With our newfound mindset, we can adequately address our problems constructively and see them clearly for what they are, not what our minds exaggerate them to be. It's a delicate balance so we can reach our goals faster.

When you can focus your attention on things you want to bring into your life, your subconscious mind will begin to create, filter, focus, and align yourself to circumstances that meet the desires you are searching for. It's been stated that Mother Teresa would never participate in an anti-war demonstration but said, "As soon as you have a pro-peace rally, I'll be there." In other words, anti-war marches have positive intentions but contain the same energy that creates more war. We must focus on what we do want, not what we don't want. Energy always flows where attention goes. What's your attention on?

Demystifying Goal Setting and How It Shows Up in Daily Life

Goal setting can be somewhat daunting but in reality, you unconsciously do it every day. For example, before you go to the grocery store, you likely make a mental or physical list of items you need so that you don't forget anything for the week ahead. You have just set a goal (to go to the store) and developed a plan to follow through on the goal (a shopping list). If you are anything like me, without this goal and plan you might walk around the store with no intention, confused and anxious, and probably spend a lot longer time in the store than planned—and, invariably, more money than you intended.

Being lost in the supermarket is exactly how life can be when you do not have check list or goals laid out for yourself. You may end up walking around in life mindlessly with no intention, spending a lot more time focusing on what you don't want rather than what you do want. With clear goals, however, you can increase clarity, alleviate uncertainty, and *develop* a success map to get you to your desired goals faster.

Let's look at another example. Imagine you are about to hop in the car for a long drive cross country from Washington D.C. to San Francisco but didn't know how to get there. You don't have GPS, a map, not even an address. You may start driving thinking you can just wing it, but after a few hundred miles you'll start to realize the importance of knowing your desired destination and having a tool to guide you there. This is exactly how life is. Goals help define your desired destination, but they are also your guiding light or your GPS to let you know if you are off track or if you need to make adjustments along the way. You would never wing a drive from D.C. to San Francisco so why would you wing your life and expect to receive all of your wishes, goals, and dreams without knowing where you are going?

Well, that's exactly what you are doing when you do not set goals for yourself. You are leaving your life to chance. You may end up somewhere, but it's almost a guarantee it won't be where you truly want to be. One of my favorite *quot*ations that I have framed in my office as reminder to myself is "If you don't know where you are going, you'll end up someplace else."

To help put things in perspective, imagine you are playing darts, but you **are** blindfolded and ha*ve* no idea where the red bullseye is. If you don't know where the red bullseye is located, then you have no idea what *success looks like*. The bullseye represents success or your ideal location of where you would like to throw the dart. Unfortunately, so many of us live our lives on autopilot, blindfolded not recognizing where we are going and have not determined where we want to go. If you don't have clarity of your bullseye in life, then you have no idea what "success" looks like for you in your life. And only you can define what success looks like in your life.

Your significant other, boss, parents, or teachers cannot tell you. They may be able to guide you, but they can't decide for you. Every human has their own unique desires and only you have the power to truly peek inside to understand what you truly want out of life. As the late American rapper and entrepreneur Nipsey Hussle once said, "Don't be surprised if you don't get what you never wanted." The premise of searching for something is knowing what you are searching for. In essence, you will never find what you are looking for until you clearly define it. You could be staring right at it and not even know it. For example, someone in your network could have successfully overcome a personal or professional problem you're interested in tackling, or you may have recently met someone with connections that can significantly advance your business or career goals. It's only until you know what you want that those people and resources around you can help you actually attain them. It starts internally first. Remember the closet hat example!

You have to define what success looks like in your life and the most effective way to do this is to look deep within and define goals that truly matter to you. So, what's your bullseye in life?

Your Soul Yearns for Expansion and Growth

You may be asking why goals are important as it relates to radical self-care. Well, let's break this down.

Humans are goal-oriented beings. There is simply no way around this. It's deeply embedded into our psyche. As mentioned previously, self-care encompasses a lot more than just taking care of your physical and mental health needs. It also ensures that you're achieving your desires, obtaining fulfillment, and expanding toward the highest version of yourself. This is the core of who you are. And part of that is ensuring that you know what you want out of life to allow your soul to expand.

Here's the truth: **Your soul cannot expand appropriately if you are not able to see a future vision for yourself.**

Whether it be for your relationships, the amount of income you desire, or what you want to offer to the world—these are desires that help us expand our potential.

Many of the highest states in life come from the satisfaction of accomplishing our goals as a reminder that we have creative control over our destinies and livelihoods. And if we don't set goals for ourselves and don't believe we have some control over our lives—this robs us of our most basic innate desire—free will to do and become who we want. When we are not achieving these states or progressing toward our goals, we can feel stagnant, stuck, and feel like we have nothing to offer to ourselves or to the world. Unconsciously, this causes us to feel like we have nothing to offer to others and as a result our relationships, careers, and health can suffer. Goal achievement is necessary for the advancement of your soul and well-being.

As humans, we have tons of innate unconscious goals that continue to influence our lives. For instance, eating, reproduction, and self-preservation are great examples of unconscious goals. Meaning we yearn for these desired states or actions without the need for conscious thought. Now here's where it gets interesting. Not only do we have "unconscious goals" as the ones I just mentioned, but we also all have conscious goals. The brain's prefrontal cortex, which sits just behind your forehead, is associated with behavioral flexibility, working memory, and even planning functions that are extremely vital for setting and achieving the goals we have in our lives. Some of these conscious goals could be improving your health by going to the gym more often, finding a loving and supportive significant other, searching for more fulfilment out of life, or even looking for ways to increase your income.

Humans have an innate desire to grow and develop and *goals happen to be an effective way to do just that.* Paul Stoltz, author of the *Adversity Quotient*, says, "We are born with the core human drive to *Ascend.*" If we are not ascending or going somewhere toward a meaningful goal or future vision, then our souls feel stuck.

On the other hand, in the Bible, Proverbs 29:18, it is written that "Where there is no vision, the people perish." This is indelibly true as well. When there are no goals or higher vision for companies, militaries, government agencies, schools, countries, or even a family household—there is no guiding light to direct individuals toward desired behaviors to produce desired outcomes. This is why mission statements, vision statements, and quarterly goals are so vital for companies and even for our personal lives. They set our sights on something. They keep us motivated. They give us purpose and meaning. And they remind us of who we are, what we are achieving, and where we are going.

Since we have the innate desire to grow, it's necessary that we set goals for ourselves to give us the opportunity to *ascend*. In essence, if you don't set clear goals for yourself, then you're not ascending. And if you feel like you are, you may not be going in the direction you *intended*.

It's necessary to take charge of your life and clearly define your goals just like any great leader should be doing for any successful company, father or mother in a household, or president for a country (see "Radical Self-Care Exercise: Conscious Goal Setting" at the end of this chapter). Without it, you leave your life open to uncertainty, doubt, and lack of direction.

Just like corporations have a bottom line to meet the desires of their shareholders, you too should be reaching your bottom line or your desired outcomes. As Earl Nightingale famously said in *Lead the Field*: "Think of yourself as a corporation." He says to think of yourself as the CEO or president of the corporation, and just like any organization, you are responsible for its success or failure. Imagine that your family members are the shareholders of your company, and it's your duty to ensure the stock rises over the long term. Your family has faith in your abilities, but ultimately, it's your responsibility to demonstrate that their faith is justified. It's your job to set and achieve goals for your life to ensure your stockholders, which could be your family or friends, are pleased with the bottom line. The people in your life are always a byproduct of your successes or failures.

Using goals is a great way to set you on the course toward achievement of the future vision you have for yourself, otherwise, as written in the Bible, your life and the people around you could "perish."

What most people don't understand is that success (discussed in Chapter One) is actually the process and journey of growing and expanding to become your best self. Let's break this down further.

Humans are constantly growing and developing. It's called evolution. We are evolving every single day. Whether or not we realize it, the world is growing, expanding, and learning from itself and it's imperative we do the same. If you're not growing mentally, physically, or spiritually then you are by definition going backward. You are either going backward or forward. There is no in-between. Think about it, I am sure there have been moments in your life when you've felt stagnant, stuck, or in a rut. You're not sure what's blocking you, but you feel as though you're not progressing—whether it be physically, mentally, or spiritually. Maybe you've been stuck in a rut for so long that you don't even realize it. Trust me, I've been there. One of the ways I was able to pull myself out of many ruts in my life was setting my sights on a future vision for myself.

According to self-help author Bob Proctor: "A person is successful if they know where they are, they know where they are going, and they're progressively moving in that direction." But here's where it gets interesting. Most people don't have clear goals.

In fact, it's estimated that close to 80 percent of people never set goals for themselves. So, what does this tell you? If it's in our basic nature to grow and develop and success is moving *toward* a particular goal, then it's clear most of us are not taking the first step in achieving our potential. That's why many of us can feel lost in life because we don't know where we are going. It is even increasingly harder now because most of our downtime has been replaced with unconsciously scrolling on social media or watching countless hours of TV.

We are longing to express our deepest desires, talents, and abilities. The best solution to counter this is to spend to time with yourself and start mapping out who want to become. This can be accomplished through goals!

**Goals and having a future vision for yourself provide
a life map for the expansion of the human soul.**

It's no wonder why people can feel lost and stuck in life. It's because they have not set time aside to truly figure out where they want to go. And if you don't know where you are going in life it can lead to stagnation, ruts, and even depression, which can correspondingly begin to spill over into your friendships, the love you express to your significant other, your performance at work, and even your health. Because if you are not growing inside then neither are your relationships, career, your well-being, or your overall satisfaction with life.

Goal setting is one of the highest forms of radical self-care.

Using Goals to Counter Living Life on Autopilot

Our minds love to wander unconsciously. As a result, it can feel like we are just merely existing instead of truly living. Have you ever been asked, "How was your day," and not been able to remember any specific parts of it? Hello autopilot! That's because your mind was stuck in autopilot to make room for other cognitive tasks. This happens in most of our waking hours throughout the day.

It's estimated that the common adult makes close to 35,000 decisions per day. Because of this mental cognitive overload of decision-making, our brains constantly kick into automatic decision-making to free up energy placed on our conscious minds. Imagine if every single day we had to decide whether to put on clothes each morning, which route to take to work, or how to operate a computer. Many of these tasks and others have become automatic as a life necessity.

As a result, it becomes easy for us and very efficient for the brain to slip into autopilot mode. The problem arises when we are in autopilot mode too often for things we need to give our full attention to and we make unconscious decisions that are not aligned with how we want to live.

Have you ever sat down with a bag of potato chips to watch a movie and halfway through the movie the chips are all gone? That's eating on autopilot, and it might not be the best move for you if you value a slim waistline.

Goals can help you to refocus your attention on your definition of what success looks like for you in your life instead being unconsciously pulled left and right.

There are two ways to live life. One stuck in autopilot leaving life to chance and uncertainty, hoping someday your desires will fall into your lap and another driven by clear intent and direction.

One of my favorite Zen parables clearly depicts this by saying:

Imagine a man riding a horse, galloping quickly. It seems as if he is going somewhere very important. Another man standing along the roadside shouts, "Where are you going?" The rider replies, "I don't know. Ask the horse!

This is the story of most people, especially in today's society. They're riding the horse of their unconscious conditioning and habits with no idea where they're headed. To reach and sustain the highest version of yourself, you must take control of the reins of life and move it in the direction of what truly matters to you.

It's important to use your goals as guideposts. Otherwise, your mind may slip into autopilot mode, and you may end up with a poor decision that's not in alignment with your desires or what you value in your life.

Goal Setting in the Brain

What many people don't know is our brains are set up in such a way to support clear goal setting. In fact, there are functions in our brains that help guide us toward our goals and desires. Science points to how clear goal setting actually changes the structure of your brain allowing you to accomplish your desires more effectively. The *Behavioral and Cognitive Neuroscience Reviews* journal explains that when clear goals are identified in the brain, matched with emotional significance, both the prefrontal cortex and the amygdala light up almost simultaneously.

Let's break this down a bit more so it's clearer.

The amygdala is a region of the brain where emotions are given meaning. The prefrontal cortex is responsible for planning, decision-making, and most importantly, for the context of this chapter, helping to define your goals.

So, when you set a clear goal by using your prefrontal cortex, your amygdala begins to evaluate the degree to which the goal or the desire is important to you. Both the prefrontal cortex and the amygdala work together to keep you focused on this particular goal—unconsciously moving you toward specific behaviors, situations, and opportunities to fulfill your desired outcome.

This is what I like to call the brain's sweet spot! The two most essential pieces to take away from this are:

1.) Set clear goals to optimize your prefrontal cortex.

2.) Ensure you have a strong desire (or emotion) for the goals you want in order to stimulate your amygdala. Usually, these are goals you deeply care about.

Quick note here: this is the real reason as to why all those self-help books and gurus talk about the importance of feeling strong emotions as if your goal has already been accomplished. It activates your amygdala. According to William E. Towne: "A thought is powerful only when it is backed by feeling. Feeling gives thought its reactiveness. To merely make an affirmation of what you desire, without faith or feeling, will accomplish little." As discussed in Chapter Three about the conditioning process, here's how manifestation really works: your thought begins the process, your emotions amplify it, and your action increases the momentum of bringing what you want into fruition.

Again, you can see this is another perfect example of neuroplasticity or should I say *self-directed* neuroplasticity because you are in charge. When done correctly your brain begins to recondition itself to look for opportunities and you can begin to develop the behaviors that are conducive to your goal. And of course, you may even start to encounter synchronicities or coincidences arising in your life that continue to guide you toward your goal. At the end of this chapter, you will be guided through a goal setting exercise so you can put this new knowledge into action.

RADICAL SELF-CARE TIP:
Guide Your Thoughts, One Task at a Time

It can seem as if our days are consumed with never ending projects and tasks. On top of that when you have no clarity on what you need to accomplish during the day you can easily get sidetracked on things that don't serve your goals for the day. This can lead to stagnation and feeling unfulfilled at the end of the day.

Here's a technique that many refer to as the Ivy Lee Method. Named after Ivy Lee, a highly respected productivity consultant in the 1900s. It became popularized when Charles M. Schwab, who was at the time one of the richest men in the world, desired to create more efficiency amongst his top executives at Bethlehem Steel Corporation. The story goes that Mr. Lee was brought into the company to work with the executives and only spent fifteen minutes with them. When Mr. Schwab asked Mr. Lee: "How much do I owe you?" Mr. Lee replied, "Nothing. Unless it works. After three months, you can send me a check for whatever you feel it's worth to you."

After Lee spent fifteen minutes with Mr. Schwab's executives, in a matter of months, productivity skyrocketed across the company! Mr. Schwab was so impressed with the progress and gave Mr. Lee a check for $25,000. In today's dollars that would be more than $400,000.

Although this method was originally introduced in the early 1900s, it's still very effective in present day to help combat endless demands and distractions. That's because our brains virtually remain the same, but our external environment has changed.

The night before your day starts, plan your day. Write down a list of six tasks you know you have to get done. This is your mental dump of all the thoughts and ideas that are in your head. Get them on paper or in the notes section of your phone. It will provide you clarity. (Remember, your prefrontal cortex loves clear goals.)

After that, number your tasks from lowest priority to highest priority. This will help guide you to focus your efforts on tasks you know you need to complete either by a certain deadline or you just need to get off your plate quickly.

Once you have your list of tasks numbered in priority, take action and use it! It's very important you actually use and refer back to your list. Remember our brains have upward of 6,000 thoughts per day so you can easily get yourself sidetracked or *forget* what needs to be accomplished. It's also important that you focus on one task at a time. Keep this in mind, do not, I repeat, do not, move on to another task before the previous one is finished.

Put all of your concentrated effort into one task—not all of them at once! You will learn that your brain is much more efficient when you give it one task at a time or what some call "monotasking." This tip may seem too simple and even paradoxical, but it's one of the most remarkable productivity strategies to alleviate stress and accelerate your productivity. As an article in the *Los Angeles Times* mentions, "Research has shown that attempting to multitask can create cognitive stress each time you switch tasks, which can accumulate and lead to fatigue, overload and burnout."

To be frank multitasking is a myth, especially if you desire to do your best work on a given task. Your brain works a lot better when you give it one task—one by one. Steven Kotler writes in *The Rise of Superman*, "By trying to improve performance by being everywhere and everywhen, we end up nowhere and never." Stick to one task at a time and watch your brain work and your productivity skyrocket!

Not only will you do your best work because all your energy is focused on one task, but you will also be able to do it much faster with much less mental energy because it's not focused on so many things at once. And once you knock one task off your list, you start to build momentum that will carry you through your day. This tip also helps optimize your mental energy to shorten the time it takes to figure out what task you need to start next after one is completed.

Bonus Tip: **You can even take it a step further and add each of your tasks to your calendar on your phone or computer with time blocks!** This provides a when and where to increase the clarity for your brain, making it more likely that you will actually execute on the task.

This is a great way to use your brain effectively to increase your productivity, create less stress, and improve overall satisfaction when the day is finally over. Do this for at least a month and watch your entire life change. Don't wait for the day to happen, make the day happen for you.

Now let's get back to this amazing goal-setting brain of yours.

Another function in the brain that helps you with goal setting is the Reticular Activating System (RAS). All your future goals are a direct reflection of your subconscious thinking but are mediated by what's known as the RAS. The RAS is a section in the brain that is located in the core of your brain stem. The RAS serves a filter between your conscious and subconscious mind. You may not even realize it, but you use the brain's RAS every day.

A great example I am sure you've encountered before is when you are thinking about purchasing a particular car, and after a while you begin to notice the same car on the road similar to the one you are interested in purchasing. This is your RAS in full gear! It's working to benefit your desired goals and intentions. The object of your desire has most likely always existed around you, but your mind and eyes were not *able* to recognize it. Your awareness expands with new knowledge, and it shrinks when it's left in the dark.

Again though, the key here is knowing what you desire so you are consciously equipped to recognize opportunities in your life that support, guide, and match your desired outcomes. If you don't know what you want, how will you recognize it when you see it? Remember the closet hat example I described earlier? You can only see what you have *in mind* first. If your goal is to cultivate meaningful relationships or a larger income, your RAS will work for you to find information, opportunities, and circumstances that meet this desire.

Are you wondering what your RAS is currently tuned to? My friend and CEO of ShineHard Network, Johnny Bailey, introduced me to a simple but marvelous exercise by heading over to your favorite social media site and scrolling to view your suggested content. For Instagram, it could be viewing the content on the Explore page or scrolling on your Twitter, Facebook, or YouTube feed to view suggested tweets, posts, or video content of people you don't follow. Whether you like it or not, this gives you a pretty good picture of what's going on in your mind and what your RAS is currently tuned to. This is because of social media platforms' incredible recommendation algorithms that automatically select similar content they think you may like based on your past activity of likes, tweets, comments, and searches.

Suppose the suggested content is full of celebrity gossip, negativity, or nothing that has anything to do with your future self. In that case, it's entirely possible you may be experiencing the same thoughts and circumstances related to them. For example, my Explore page on Instagram is currently full of book recommendations, fitness videos, and real estate. This makes sense because I'm looking for a new leg workout to incorporate into my routine. I'm always searching for new books to read, and my wife and I have been thinking about buying a home in the next couple of years. This is what my RAS is tuned in on currently! Suppose you notice your suggested content on social media is not anything positive or related to your goals. If that's the case, you can change it instantly by setting new intentions, thus retuning your RAS.

We are bombarded with billions of bits of information daily so it's necessary that you begin to use your RAS to your benefit to fine-tune your desired outcomes. Remember when I said in Chapter Two that we are only consciously aware of about fifty bits of information per second, while our subconscious mind can sense up to eleven million bits of information from our environment? It's because your RAS is mediating and refining the amount of data coming into your conscious mind. Otherwise, it would be overloaded! This is why writing goals down and setting intentions is so important so you can set a target for your outcomes, and your brain will start to notice information that's in alignment with your intentions. Ironically, when you know what you want, your brain's RAS makes you notice more of what you want. Your RAS tells your brain what to pay attention to so it can help you!

When you write your goals down, you trigger your RAS to help you find opportunities, circumstances, and people to achieve your goals. And it does this subconsciously, without you even realizing it. This is a prime example as to why people create vision or dream boards. Vision boards are a collage of images, pictures, words, and/or affirmations pasted on a poster board as a source of inspiration and motivation. They are essentially a visual representation of your goals or future vision of yourself. Do they work? Absolutely! There's powerful science behind them. After all, how can you move toward a vision of your future self if you don't have any inkling what that may look like?

This is what some people call the law of attraction, law of vibration, *The Secret*, or the power of the subconscious mind. At this point, I don't care what you call it as long as you are aware this power is available to you at any time to help you achieve the life you desire and benefit others around you. Understanding many of these studies requires another book but I would highly encourage you to research them and begin experiencing with it in your own life. I also write about how to use these principles on my blog, chazzscott.com/blog.

> *Rare is the man and wise who perceives that all possibilities are right where he is. He need only change his perception to see them. He doesn't create them by changing his perception. He only becomes aware that they are there; they existed all the time.*
>
> U.S. Andersen

Become a Conscious Creator

If you begin to study many successful people in life—it doesn't just have to be monetarily—you will see they've often set lofty goals for themselves. As my mentor, Eddie C. Brown, one of the most successful American Asset managers, told me one day: "You must have 'big ideas' for yourself and be a 'risk taker.'" That's exactly what he did after being hired as the first African American portfolio manager at T. Rowe Price, and then decided to leave and start his own investment company, Brown Capital Management.

Some of his friends thought he was "absolutely nuts." They said you're the Vice President of T. Rowe Price, you've been here for ten years, and you're doing exceptionally well; why would you want to leave? But, in an interview, Eddie said, "It's always been my vision to have my own business, and I've always been a risk-taker."

He saved up some cash before leaving T. Rowe Price and gave himself five years to accomplish his goal of stepping out on his own and starting his own investment company. Unfortunately, shortly after starting the company, his wife was diagnosed with breast cancer. As you might imagine leaving a steady-paying job under these circumstances was extremely challenging. Fortunately, they eventually found the medical care they needed.

With persistence, a great deal of resourcefulness, and some help along the way, Brown Capital Management, a Baltimore-based firm, went from zero assets under management and zero income to amassing more than $17.5 billion under management and climbing since it opened for business in 1983.

Today it employs thirty-eight people and is the second oldest African American owned investment management firm in the world. In Eddie's 2011 memoir, *Beating the Odds*, he describes his life in a small, segregated town in the Jim Crow South of Apopka, Florida. As the son of a thirteen-year-old unwed mother, he grew up without electricity or indoor plumbing in the home. Yet, Eddie overcame extraordinary odds through dedication, perseverance, an awful lot of networking, and as he says in his memoir, "some luck" along the way.

Now Eddie and his wife, Sylvia, have continued to pay it forward and have donated tens of millions of dollars over the years to support the arts and education. The couple recently donated five million to their alma mater, Howard University, the largest donation the university has ever received. What strikes me the most is Eddie's remarkable humbleness and sound character. If you were to meet him, you would have no idea about his amazing feats and significant accomplishments. He's a true trailblazer and inspiration to those who yearn to reach their potential in every area of their life!

If you think back to Chapter Three regarding the mental conditioning process and how ideas held in mind and aligned actions ultimately manifest to determine our destiny, Eddie's success is an excellent example of this entire process being displayed. He held ideas of success, dedication, diligence, patience, and in the case of his profession, stock profitability in mind to *create* the life he currently lives, which enhanced his family's life and his contributions to the world. Through the process, he **guarded his mind** against naysayers when leaving T. Rowe Price, set a **clear goal** of five years to accomplish his dream business, and **took consistent action** through tons of networking and studying his craft.

Successful people know what they want, maintain an unwavering faith, remain persistent, and hold a consistent positive intention until their ideas are realized, even in the midst of difficulties that may arise. I should add that there are many successful people who may not even be aware of the power of their subconscious mind, the right self-talk, goal-setting strategies, or the law of attraction. If you asked how they became successful, they might say "hard work," and not mention any of the strategies in this book. In life, there are things at play that influence our outcomes that are sometimes beyond our awareness.

This is what some call *unconscious competence*. Meaning, they were unconsciously using these methods and laws but might not have necessarily attributed it to specific strategy, word, or process. Nor did they even consciously know they were using it. Once you begin to know the knowledge, repetitiously apply them, and start to see results that's when you'll know it's working. At this point in time, you will start to become a *conscious creator* of your life. And once you become a conscious creator, it's necessary that you stay conscious and pay attention to the insights and signs that show up throughout your life experience that help guide you toward your goals and desires.

Some people may call this your intuition or a "hunch" that you might have when faced with a particular decision. In reality, you are becoming more aware of your external experiences displayed in your life to use them to reach your desired outcomes. At this point you become an active participant of your life experience, instead of feeling like life is happening to you. One of my favorite quotations that ties all of this together is from Esther and Jerry Hicks *Ask and It Is Given*, which states:

> *Without making the correlation between your thoughts and feelings and the manifestations that are occurring, you have no conscious control of what happens in your experience.*

To a certain degree, you may already be using these frameworks or strategies either when attracting negative experiences in your life or positive ones. You just may not have been consciously aware that you are using them all the time. Before I studied them, I was using them myself and my life circumstances reflected what I was thinking but I totally was unconscious, which means I didn't have any control in my outcomes. The objective here is to become a conscious creator of your life so you can influence the results you desire.

Let Go and Let God

Changing perceptions and expectations can shape your reality. It can turn problems into solutions. It can shift blockages into opportunities.

Anyone who lives in the Washington D.C. area knows how atrocious parking can be around the city. When I first moved to Arlington, VA, located just a few miles south of D.C., I even became petrified of driving into the city to meet up with friends. I would always resort to taking the metro because I was afraid I'd never finding a parking spot. After doing this for a while, I started to realize how much effort it took to walk to the metro station, hop on the metro, get off at my stop, and then finally walk to my destination. And then doing it all over again going back home. Because of this hectic cycle, I started driving my car into D.C. just to try it out.

As I started driving, I intentionally changed my perspective on being nervous of not finding parking spots near my destination. Something in me told me to let go of fear and set my intentions on locating the perfect parking spot. It was an effortless conscious intention. One where you know what you desire but you let it go and have faith that it will be shown to you.

Sure enough, I began finding parking spots either right in front or very close to the restaurant, bar, or building I was going to. My friends would joke and say, "I don't understand how you always find great parking spots every time we come into the city." In reality, at first, I didn't know why either. I chucked it up to *luck* but after researching and experimenting I quickly realized exactly what I was doing. I knew it derived from changing my perspective of my problem, releasing fear, and acting in faith.

My friends would usually say, "Well how do you know if it's the result of your *parking spot intention* strategy. I usually tell them: "I can't necessarily prove it, but one thing is for sure the results have continued to be consistent every time I do it." And at the end of the day, the outcomes or results are all that matter. Never question the results. Just believe, act, and truly feel the feelings of the result already manifested, and your intended outcome will come into your experience. This is where your "childlike faith" comes into play nicely. Sometimes it can be hard to see the end results of what we want, but once you take the first step, you can be sure that you will be guided along the way. Just focus on your first step and be courageous enough to be patient. Remember the driving in the dark analogy!

Another great example of this that I am sure you've experienced in your own life is when you've lost something of value, and you can't find it. Whether it be a wedding ring, the remote to your TV, your wallet, or keys. You vigorously search the house for it, in the crooks and crannies of your living room sofa, and even ask the people closest to you if they've seen it. When you ask them, they usually reply with: "Well, when is the last time you've seen it or used it?" Like most people you reply, "I don't even remember. That's why I am asking you."

Over a period of time of not locating the item you finally stop rushing around and just "let it go" and *hope* the item shows up again. Sure enough, that's exactly what happens, it just shows up right before your eyes in the place where you probably already looked. These situations in our lives represent a microcosm of life itself as it relates to our goal, dreams, and desires.

When we frantically run around with fear (activating our sympathetic nervous system) in our body hoping to find and achieve the things that we desire out of life—our perceptions narrow and they run from us. Which leads to us not even seeing opportunities that may be directly in front of our eyes—similar to an item you've lost. The very things we yearn for but have a fear of not achieving them seemingly continue to evade us. It's only until you know what you desire, change your perspective of the situation, let go, have faith, and persistently act can your desires or goals be truly manifested. When we've done our part, we must learn *to let go and let God*, the Universe, the Creator, or Nature work through us in our lives.

The Power Within You

I'm sure you've heard the saying, "Whatever the mind can conceive, it can achieve." At this point you should be able to see that this isn't just some fancy saying that isn't grounded in any truth. Our minds, based upon how we think, can skew our perceptions, both negatively and positively, which ultimately affect the results in our lives.

Both the parking spot and lost items examples are microcosms of life and how our minds can directly influence what we want to achieve. So, if you can use the same principles described in finding a parking spot or items that you've lost, imagine what you can do for your health, career, relationships, and wealth you desire to attain. They say that "luck is when preparation meets opportunity," which is often true. Having good habits and a consistent drive are essential to prepare your mind to take advantage of life's opportunities. And taking action ultimately drives your luck. But you cannot be so anxious or impatient that you fear not having or not attaining your goals because this can draw the exact thing you desire away from you.

In the parking spot example, I changed my perspective of the problem, set a clear intention of my desire (locate my ideal parking spot), let it go, took action, maintained faith, and sure enough I took advantage of the opportunity when it arose. In essence, I simply created my own "luck" by just taking advantage of it. I just had to take the first step. As written in the Bible, "Ask, and you shall receive; seek, and you shall find; knock, and the door shall be opened to you." We must do our part first by asking, seeking, and knocking before we can achieve the results we want in life.

Speaker and author, Michael Beckwith—recognized by Oprah's SuperSoul 100 list of visionaries and influential leaders—is quoted by saying that *luck* stands for "living under cosmic knowledge." I believe luck is a term we use to explain away things that we don't quite yet understand about how the universe works. Consistent intention, belief, action, and faith can guide you toward your desired results and this is when *your luck* helps create the life you desire. When these ideas are held in mind, this is when all those amazing synchronicities and coincidences begin to happen in your life that you can't explain. It almost feels like life is guiding and giving you hits along the way toward your desires. And, of course, consistent action is required as well. You can't just wish and think it will come to you. Thought, feeling, word, and action all need to be aligned to not only achieve the desires you seek but also keep them. Like the Bible clearly states, "Faith by itself, if it is not accompanied by action, is dead."

Once you become aware of your power and trust your intuition to guide you, you will often begin to see results derive from your thoughts. This is conscious manifestation at its finest and not unconscious manifestations cycling you down a path you don't want to end up on. According to Dr. Joe Dispenza, "If the results you seek happens once, it can be considered an incident. If the outcome happens a second time, then it's a coincidence. But if the outcome happens a third, fourth, and fifth time then you are looking at a trend or pattern." Anything that is repeatable is a science. If used correctly, the goal-setting techniques presented in this book and the exercise at the end of this chapter are literally a science or strategy that you can apply to effectively achieve the results you desire out of life.

Think of it like this: say you want to bake a fantastic pound cake for an upcoming holiday party. You start by researching online and find an article titled "James's World-Renowned Best Tasting Pound Cake Ever," along with the exact recipe. If you followed the recipe precisely and maybe with some practice, do you think you could bake his world-renowned pound cake? Sure you could! If you knew the exact ingredients, the quantity of each, and the correct order in steps, you would receive the same results as James could.

A recipe is nothing more than a strategy to guide your thoughts and actions toward a desired result. And it can be replicated and repeated, thus consistently producing the exact same results if followed correctly.

Life is the same way. Successful people have strategies for sustaining happiness, managing stress, accumulating wealth, and building meaningful relationships (many of them are in this book). Any strategy they use, you can replicate in your life, thus producing the same results they have.

Initially, it seemed difficult, but eventually, it got much easier through practice, thus requiring much less effort as time progressed. In this case, goal setting is a strategy or skill that can be repeated to guide you toward the results you are seeking. Just as a recipe for James's world-renowned pound cake, you need the recipe or steps for goal setting, which in this case would be understanding how your mind works, setting an intention, and writing down your goals. I will discuss this more in the chapter exercises at the end.

If our thoughts influence our lives, then our goals help guide our thoughts toward the outcomes, experiences, feelings, and circumstances we truly desire.

When you begin to clearly define what you desire you give your brain the ability to search for opportunities, people, and possibilities that support your goals. Not only that, but you will begin to notice flashes of inspiration and ideas arise from your subconscious mind that will help you achieve your goals. Goal setting is an innate function in your brain and if you can begin to use it effectively, your goals and dreams will begin to manifest right before your eyes. Effectiveness is the key. At the end of the chapter, I will show you how to set goals now so that you understand the underpinnings of goal setting in the brain.

Keep Pressing On

Once you work with this knowledge, you may start to feel what some people call "lucky." You will observe your life experiences as being in the "right time and right place." You will begin to feel that life or the universe is working for you, rather than against you. In reality, you are just consciously taking advantage of the power within you to set goals to ultimately guide your thoughts toward the circumstances that support you.

As the world continues to evolve everything is growing, even humans. As a result, it's in our basic nature to grow and develop along with it. And if we do not, we are moving backward, as I said before. One of the most effective ways to grow, evolve, and keep life an exciting adventure is to constantly set goals for yourself. Setting goals for your life is like telling the universe that "I am here" and sets into motion various circumstances, synchronicities, and what some people call "luck" to meet your desired outcome. Being clear of what you want, maintaining positive attitude about your goals, reviewing them frequently, matched with deliberate action will set you apart.

Remember your soul innately yearns for higher experiences of itself. So, it's important that you feed your soul with a future vision of yourself to continue to grow and expand your own consciousness. And the only way to do that is if you use your mind effectively and set goals for yourself that truly matter to you. Once you accomplish one goal, make sure you write down another. Don't stop progressing toward reaching your highest self. This is radical self-care at its highest level.

RADICAL SELF-CARE EXERCISE:
Conscious Goal Setting

Setting goals raises the bar to make room for growth in your life. If you don't set conscious goals for yourself, then you may not be growing toward where you want to go or feel like you're drifting through life aimlessly. It helps to focus your intentions, so you don't leave your life completely to chance. Otherwise, your intentions remain unfocused thus not producing the desires you want. Remember: *unfocused thought leads to unfocused results.*

Here's an exercise you can do. I want you to take some time to put everything away. Put your phone on Do Not Disturb, turn off the TV, and go to a quiet place. Get a pen, a piece of paper or notebook, and start thinking of a vision for your future self: What do I really want? What do I desire? What makes me happy? If I wanted to live my fullest potential, what would need to happen?

Once you begin to visualize a vision for yourself, start writing down some goals that align to this vision. This future vision could be anything from improving your friendships, making more money, obtaining a new job, writing a book, finding time for more things that you enjoy, or living a healthier lifestyle. Nothing is off limits! Don't focus on the how right now. Just focus on what you desire. Although writing your goals down might seem like an obvious first step, it is one of the most important steps that many people ignore! And if it helps, research at the Dominican University of

California confirms that you are 42 percent more likely to achieve your goals just by writing them down.

This may be challenging at first but if you stick with it the thoughts will flow. It's also necessary that you be specific on what you want. *Clarity is power.* If it's more income that you desire, then write down a specific number that you want to accumulate monthly or yearly. The more specific you are, the better it will be for your mind to visualize your *future desire in its entirety.*

Remember your prefrontal cortex is searching for clarity. *It's simply not enough to think it or even say it, it's essential to* write it down to kickstart the many powerful forces that help guide you toward your desired outcome. Here are a few examples:

- Marry a passionate partner who is committed to a long-term marriage.
- Start a side hustle business doing what I love and earn $1,000 monthly.
- Make at least $100,000 a year doing what I love.
- Lose fifteen pounds and get in the best shape of my life.

Once you've determined a couple of goals for yourself that align with this future vision, now it's time to integrate them into your life. There are a few steps I recommend you follow once you've written down some of your goals.

1.) Review your list of goals right when you wake up and before you fall asleep.

As previously discussed, psychologists have confirmed the subconscious mind is more suggestible during certain periods of the day. As you start to fall asleep your brain waves cycle down from beta, alpha, theta, and delta. Most people don't realize that a child's brain between the ages of birth to six years is primarily operating in theta waves. This is why kids pick up ideas, information, and words so fast! Their brains are like sponges. (Meditation and prayer are also another way to influence the subconscious mind that I will discuss in a later chapter). Reviewing your goals during these two time periods will effectively impress your goals from your conscious mind into your subconscious mind so you can actually start to *truly believe and know* you can accomplish the desires you wish to obtain. This also helps to install the behaviors that correspond to the desires you are seeking. Pretty soon you start to walk, talk, and act like your goals because you've become exactly what you desire. You won't be chasing them. You've become them. You've developed an *inner knowing*. It may also be helpful to play a recording of yourself reading your goals as you fall asleep as well. Remember: *you don't get what you want; you get what you believe.*

2.) Visualize and feel the feelings of already achieving the goal.

If it's a new car you want, visualize yourself in that new Porsche driving down the highway. Feel the breeze rushing past your cheek as you press on the gas. If it's more money you desire, mentally rehearse yourself receiving a check for the amount money that you've written down. Feel the feelings of already achieving your goal is the key. Remember, your brain cannot tell the difference between an actual physical experience, and one produced by thought alone. So, if you really feel the emotions of attainting the goal you've written down, your body and brain will believe as if you've already achieved it. It essentially becomes neurologically real to you thus yielding you the behaviors that are in alignment to your desires. If you stick with this practice every day, synchronicities will begin to arise, you will begin to meet the "right people," and be at the *right time at the right place.*

3.) Trust the process, but also take action!

Belief, faith, and gratitude are key ingredients to this process. Have faithful persistence. One of the most important parts to this is to take action! When a moment of opportunity arises (and it will), it's necessary to act with persistence with the inner belief you are cultivating within yourself. Taking action may be uncomfortable initially, but your nervousness will become excitement once you take the first step. Remember: *Faith without action is dead.* Therefore, it's essential not to forget the last step in this process to fully receive your desires. You will start to notice opportunities that arise in your life that will require action by you. Don't miss them. As Wallace Wattles would say, "By thought, the thing you want is brought to you; by action, you receive it."

Use hashtags #RadicalSelfCare and #SuccessStartsWithin on social media and share with others to inspire them to join you on your path toward activating your potential.

CHAPTER SEVEN

SCHEDULE REGULAR EXERCISE

If you don't make time for your wellness, you will be forced to make time for your illness.
Unknown

The Pill Everyone Is Searching For

Suppose I told you there was a pill you could take that could combat your illnesses, guard against stress, give you states of euphoria, increase productivity, improve your relationships, enhance your mood, and boost your psychological resilience to combat adversity? What if it could reduce your risk of cancer by 40 percent or slash your risk of diabetes by 50 percent? Suppose I told you this pill was free and available to you whenever you wanted it? Would you take it? I know I would! I am not a fan of stress or not feeling well about myself. In reality, this pill is available to you and can be used at your disposal. And it's not even a pill. It's actually physical fitness. A big component of catapulting your success within your radical self-care journey involves consistent exercise. Daily exercise ensures sustainability over the long-term so you can continue to enjoy and enhance the life you're building.

Many of us attribute exercising to physical health and that's true; it's responsible for a large part of that. But one of the greatest benefits exercising offers is the significant influence it has on the brain—from better emotional stability, improved focus and attention, increased self-confidence, and helping to increase your resilience to bounce back from tough times. As an avid runner, I started to realize just how much how much physical fitness fostered better habits in nearly every other area of my life. Including significantly increasing my focus at work and even improving the satisfaction in my relationships as a by-product. In fact, I attribute my success with writing this book to my consistent exercising habits in the morning. Without my early morning runs, I believe maintaining my increased levels of focus and sustained concentration would have been very tough for me.

Our current society reinforces long periods of time of not moving our bodies as much as we should. Nowadays we move not more than a finger to swipe on a smartphone, click the remote, and type on a keyboard. The only exercise we may get is getting up from the bed and walking to the kitchen. On top of that many of us are spending time in the house not focusing on things that can allow us to become better version of ourselves. This can contribute to physical health problems, bad habits, a decline in self-esteem, and even overflow into our relationships.

Remember; *wherever your attention goes, your energy flows.* The more attention you give to one particular area, the larger it grows, while the others begin to shrink. It's essential to refocus your attention on yourself to ensure you are growing physically and mentally so you can become the best version of yourself. An excellent way to refocus your attention toward your brain and body's needs is through physical fitness.

If you take some time to think about it there is nearly a gym in most office buildings, apartment complexes, and many community neighborhoods. Most by now understand the importance of regular exercise, but it wasn't always like this. There was a time in our history when gyms on the corner of every other street or office building didn't exist. After thousands of scientific studies, we've reached a moment in our history where physical fitness isn't just fad, it's a requirement if you want to maintain a healthy brain and body.

If you truly want to cultivate self-care within yourself then you would make sure your body and brain are in tip top shape so that you can be prepared and equipped to take on the world, tackle your goals, and be a self-sufficient contributing member of society.

It can be difficult to start and maintain a good exercise regimen, especially in our busy lifestyles. Demands, distractions, and sustaining the necessary motivation can make it feel like an uphill battle. However, with clear meaning and purpose with our behaviors, I've found we can make time for things in our lives if we know their potential value. You'll practice how to do this in the exercise at the end of the chapter. It's a perfect exercise if you want to further enrich your current physical fitness routine or if you need some purpose-driven motivation to get started. And if you think you don't have enough time throughout your day to receive the benefits of an exercise routine, did you know that simply walking twenty to thirty minutes a day could cut the chance of dying prematurely from heart disease in half? Finding time to improve the quality of your life so you can execute your dreams and enjoy the life you're building has never been easier.

As most of us know by now physical fitness can significantly influence our psychological and emotional health in day-to-day life. When you move your body your brain releases tons of "feel good" chemicals called *endorphins*. When you don't move your body, you don't have an opportunity to release these chemicals. So basically, bad physiology reinforces negative feelings. Great physiology reinforces positive feelings. It's as simple as that.

Have you ever walked away from a great exercise feeling empowered, happy, or recharged? This is exactly what I am talking about. Who wouldn't want to feel these emotions every day? Consistent exercising makes you a better you. If want to build self-confidence—exercise. If you want to overcome negative thought patterns—exercise. Are you stressed? Exercise. Want to increase your focus or productivity—exercise. If you want to feel better about your life then I would urge you to again give exercise a try.

As Tony Robbins would say, "Motion creates emotion." Changing your physiology means you are changing your mental state and how you feel about yourself. Exercising and moving your body is one of the most effective ways to getting unstuck in life and to help you achieve a better you.

Research has confirmed that regular exercise can reduce stress, combat feelings of anxiety and feelings of depression, boost self-esteem, improve resilience, and improve sleep. The *New York Times* published an article titled, "Fight Depression, on Your Treadmill" that reported how aerobic exercise, such as walking on a treadmill, "could begin reducing symptoms of depression faster than many drugs could." In addition, research at the University of Toronto conducted a longitudinal study that concluded that not only does consistent exercise play a role in maintaining good mental health, but it also helps in "preventing the onset of depression later in life." The researcher of the study further explains that "it's definitely worth taking note that if you're currently active, you should sustain it."

If you're not physically active, don't worry with some purpose-driven motivation, I'll get you there. This research shows promising evidence that the impact of being active goes far beyond the physical. With the steady rise in depression rates, physical exercise seems to be an effective way to help combat this mood disorder.

Many of us spend our day-to-day lives sitting in a car commuting to work, at the office sitting at a desk, back in the car commuting home, and then again sitting at home on the couch. We are not moving our bodies. Innately, this is not what our bodies need to increase our potential and to live a full and healthy life. Experts are now saying "sitting is the new smoking" because of the increased risk of diabetes, heart attacks, and strokes.

Our modern-day society has created unparalleled levels of convenience in our lives but simultaneously it's contributing to feelings of depression, unhealthy eating habits, and promoting lack of self-confidence. It is because of this that many of us are unhappy and why depression rates are continuing to rise, especially as we are consistently connected to our digital devices more than ever. It's because we don't move our bodies. Move your body to feel good. And once you implement a regular routine, you will begin to feel like you have more control over your body, and thus your life. If you're feeling emotionally and mentally stuck, move. Exercising is literally a *life hack* to feeling better and fostering positive emotions for an overall better life.

Work Smarter, Not Harder

Not only does exercising help you reduce stress and make you feel good about yourself, but it can also make you "smarter" and improve your rate of learning. Carl Cotman, a neurologist and neuroscientist at the University of California Irvine School of Medicine, ran a groundbreaking study with lab rats determining that physical activity "induces gene expression changes in the brain." Cotman proved that animals, in the form of voluntary running, show an increase of brain-derived neurotrophic factor (BDNF). BDNF is a protein molecule that increase neural survival connections, enhances learning, and protects from cognitive decline.

His research supports the argument that physical fitness can literally upgrade your mental capacities. In addition, German researchers conducted a study of humans and found that people learn vocabulary words 20 percent faster after "intense physical exercise" rather than before. Researchers say this is, again, due to the sustained levels of BDNF in the brain directly after physical exercise. As John J. Ratey, an associate clinical professor of psychiatry at Harvard Medical School, says BDNF is like "Miracle-Gro for the brain" to help you achieve more, focus better, and streamline your mental processing.

So, if you have to achieve a task and want to give it your best shot, I recommend placing that task directly after your workout. It could be the difference between a promotion, more revenue for your business, or a breakthrough idea that could improve the life for your family. And when you make exercising a priority in your life every day it tends to compound on itself upgrading other aspects of your life.

Growing up I remember always being taught how important physical fitness was for our physical health. As I mentioned in Chapter Three,

I played on our varsity basketball in high school and lifted weights often. My only purpose for going to the gym and running back then was to stay physically fit. It never occurred to me that physical workouts could actually improve my mental functions and enhance my emotional stability. In fact, I never fully recognized it's benefits until I finally graduated from college and got out there in the "real world." That's when it really hit me. Physical fitness became a perfect tool to enhance my day-to-day life.

My body was already used to lifting weights, so I continued going to gym mostly after work, which become really tough because, at the time, I had a long commute to and from work in the Washington D.C. area. A full day of work would absolutely drain me to the point that a workout around 5:00 p.m. almost felt impossible. At that point, I started working out in the morning before work and running more as well. It was a tough schedule change at first until I realized how I felt after my morning workouts when I finally made it to my desk at work.

This was the life changing moment for me. I felt like I took a limitless pill. I would sit down at my desk and every work task felt much more manageable. I had mental clarity and pristine focus that I didn't even know was possible. Writing long emails became a breeze, concentrating on one work task was much easier, and not to mention I experienced a rush of energy and feel-good emotions in-between. I felt like I could take on challenges more often, not only in work, but even in other areas of my life. I even began to speak up in meetings a lot more when before I may had been timid or nervous.

Working out in the morning boosted my self-confidence, improved my work productivity, and actually improved the quality of my entire life. My mornings didn't feel like a chore, and I began to feel like I was in control of my life instead of feeling like life was controlling me. This is why it's critical to maintain a consistent exercise regimen that empowers you! As you can see, when we feel good physically, it significantly affects the way you perceive the world and the results in them. The same relationships, work, business, and personal challenges don't seem as tough anymore because the vehicle you rely on to make it through life is taken care of and feels strong and coherent.

Once I started to see the benefits of working out manifesting in my life, I became obsessed. It was like a drug. In reality, that's exactly what it is. When you exercise, dopamine is released in the brain, which triggers the reward system to automatically put you into a state of euphoria. Dopamine is the same chemical that is released when an individual has taken drugs such as Adderall, ecstasy, or meth.

New research also confirms that exercise, specifically aerobic, releases a chemical called *endocannabinoids*, which are self-produced chemicals that are similar to those found in marijuana. This is where the famous term the "runners high" derives from after a run. Ironically, this is a feeling and state we can create at will without taking any drugs. Furthermore, physical exercise increases alpha brain waves in the brain, which can help in maintaining attention and focus to help retain information faster.

And remember the brain's Default Mode Network (DMN) I introduced in Chapter Two? The brain's chattery voice or self-talk that tends to be negative throughout your day. Many scientists suggest it can be responsible for most of our unhappiness in life. New studies show the brain's chattery voice or DMN tends to quiet down after aerobic exercise. No wonder people feel a state of elation after a good workout—our brain is quieter. Thus, yielding you the ability and bandwidth to stop ruminating over negative thoughts and past regrets, so you can maintain pristine focus on your tasks, goals, and who you are becoming rather than what you feel like you're lacking.

This is exactly what I felt when I started to work out in the mornings. I began to realize that you can literally hack your brain to improve your mental capacities. This is when I ingrained the philosophy of *working smarter, not harder* into my life. Our society continues to glamorize working hard and over-extending ourselves when ironically our brains actually excel doing the complete opposite. If we invest in ourselves properly through regular exercise and intentional rest, we can take care of our body's needs while simultaneously improving our performance and quality of life.

In fact, one of the most compelling scientific studies by the California Department of Education (CDE) backs up these claims, which concluded that students with higher fitness scores also perform better academically. Delaine Eastin, who was the State Superintendent of Public Instruction at the time of the study, said in a press release that "We now have the proof we've been looking for: students achieve best when they are physically fit. Thousands of years ago, the Greeks understood the importance of improving spirit, mind, and body. The research presented here validates their philosophic approach with scientific validation."

RADICAL SELF-CARE TIP:
Self-Induced Flow to Gain Focus

Here's a radical self-care tip that can yield you laser focus, increase your performance, improve effectiveness in daily tasks, and increase happiness. Positive Psychology has termed a state of consciousness called "flow" that I am sure you've experienced at some point in your life.

Flow is when you are in complete immersion in the task at hand. It's when you are "in the zone," as athletes like to call it. It's when you're so involved in a task that you lose sense of time, lose sense of self, your focus is out of this world and eventually you look up at the clock and an hour or more has passed. The task challenges you but is not terribly hard where you feel like you can't complete it. Your skill level is just right where the task is enjoyable but not completely boring. You are essentially in a state of relaxed high performance. It's the sweet spot.

Mihaly Csikszentmihalyi, the leading positive psychologist who is credited for the concept of flow, said in *Flow: The Psychology of Optimal Experience* that "control of consciousness determines the quality of life." He believes that by using flow, we can gain a sense of control over our lives by directing our own optimal experiences thus increasing productivity, happiness, and fulfillment.

So, how does this help you? Well, you don't have to get into flow just when the task is enjoyable. You can help yourself get into "flow-like states" *on purpose*, either for a tedious work assignment, doing your finances or budget, writing a book, or a series of tasks that requires all your mental capacities. Basically, anything that requires your undivided attention or focus. I like to call this "Self-Induced Flow."

Try scheduling an aerobic exercise right before starting any of your work tasks or workday. Have you ever experienced the famous "runner's high" after a run? You may feel at ease and maybe even blissful. Try taking this "high" you experience and applying it to a task that needs your undivided attention and watch your brain work! You may feel a sense of increased concentration, focus, creativity, and overall mental clarity. Not to mention you actually *feel* good while doing it. In a time where attention spans are slowly dropping because of large amounts of information, pings, and interruptions, this could be a very effective technique to stay ahead of the curve. In fact, exercise is becoming so effective that scientists are now discovering that it can act as a supplemental treatment for ADHD patients.

Concentration, attention, and focus are primary assets for anyone looking to accomplish their goals and improve the quality of their life. When I have to write an article, complete a difficult work task, or even as I wrote this book, I always intentionally scheduled my hardest tasks of the day right after my exercise routine. Physicians recommend at least thirty minutes of some type of aerobic exercise in the morning to catapult your mind. This radical self-care tip can elevate many areas of your life and will help you achieve your potential if you can get into a good rhythm. Remember, it's all about *working smarter, not harder.*

There are many other ways to obtain states of flow. Just do a quick internet search.

What's Stopping Us

Acquiring knowledge is great but if you don't actually put it to use to yield results in your life then it's almost pointless. One of the things I realized is that most of us already have a general understanding on how to achieve a happy and healthy life. It's been taught to us our entire lives. If this is the case, then why don't most people actually do the things they know will improve their lives? Just because "we know better, doesn't mean we do better." We know that it's important to eat healthy to improve our waistline but instead many of us resort to a bag of chips or heading to a local fast-food joint. We know we are supposed to exercise regularly to not only maintain a healthy body but also contribute to greater levels of productivity, happiness, and fulfillment. Instead, we sit on the couch all day and unconsciously get lost in our phones, TV shows, and surf the web hoping to find external things outside ourselves to drown out our innermost desires, goals, and dreams.

Our souls are meant to be expressed in their entirety and maintaining a healthy body and mind is one of the surest ways to allow our full selves to express through. So why is it so hard to do the easy stuff that will significantly improve so many areas of our lives? Some of it has to do with the conditioning I discussed in Chapter Three and others happen to be people not having a clear purpose or "why" for exercising. We have to get past the superficial external motivators like looking nice in an outfit or losing weight and dig a little deeper to focus on things that are really meaningful to us. And sometimes we can't clearly see the end result we are looking for. As Stephen Covey says, "We must begin with the end in mind."

Exercising can seem like one of the hardest habits to build and stick to but once you get clear on its purpose in your life, take one day a time, build momentum, and consciously see the results manifest in various areas of your life, it can be one of life's most rewarding experiences. It puts you in control of your body and health which, in turn, puts you in the driver seat of the vitality and longevity of your life.

For any goal you set for yourself, including exercising, it's necessary to consciously attach a strong enough why to your desired goal. This is necessary because many of us say to ourselves we want to get healthy and active but don't make a conscious and personal connection to our end goal. When you can clearly and consciously define your why, the *how* becomes much more manageable and easier to grasp in day-to-day life. Again, clarity is your superpower here.

For example, when I began going to the gym, I started to see how my consistent exercise routine started to affect my self-esteem, which then naturally overflowed into my relationships with friends and family in a positive manner. I felt more secure, able to share my inner joy easier, and even bring my full self into my relationships. Once I made the conscious connection of attaching exercising to the end result of developing more meaningful and deeper relationships in my life, that's when everything began to change.

I wasn't motivated by having a perfect body or a certain run time. I was motivated by ensuring I could bring my very best self to every relationship in my life. My family and friends deserved the best of me. After consciously recognizing the feedback loop derived from the act of my exercise routine, it became much more manageable during times I wasn't motivated or did not feel like working out. This was my why and it meant a lot to me. When I thought about my why, it would push me when I couldn't push myself. It would give me the drive and motivation to wake up in the morning when I knew I did not want to leave my warm bed. My why for exercising each day wasn't about me anymore; it was about the people in my life and how I could contribute to the world more efficiently, abundantly, and not to mention feel good while doing it.

Now think to yourself for a moment, what's your why for exercising? How can it enhance some of your personal qualities in life? If you need some guidance, I've created a powerful exercise at the end of this chapter to help guide you.

Your why could be to become a better you, to develop more meaningful relationships, or to instill more self-belief to overcome daily challenges you are facing. It could be anything, but keep it very personal, clear, and specific to who are or who you want to become. Your why should motivate you and remind you why you do what you do every day.

If you are able to pinpoint your why for exercising, it's important to reflect on it when you don't feel like getting out of the bed in the morning to work out or when you are feeling frustrated with learning a new exercise. Once you begin to consciously and repetitiously do this, again, neuroplasticity begins to work in your favor. You begin to build new neural pathways in your brain that can reinforce the new behaviors you are adopting, making it less challenging over time.

As you maintain these new behaviors, they eventually become habits that are integrated into your life. And when you start to see your life change, you begin to make an emotional connection or bond between exercising and the by-products that are manifesting in your life.

This is when you move from exercising feeling like a chore to becoming an exciting challenge because you began to consciously realize you have the ability to improve the quality of your life. What an amazing feeling to know!

Eventually you find yourself saying, "I'm going to make time in my day to exercise" instead of "I don't have enough time in the day for exercising."

You began to realize the more discipline you have over your mind, the more freedom you have over your life. And once you get here, you become relentless and excited in becoming a better you every single day. Don't get me wrong though, some days will be tough, but like I said, it will become a lot more manageable knowing your why and clearly knowing the results you wish to achieve.

On the other hand, if exercising does not come natural to you or you feel like it's a burden, consider this: studies have confirmed that "people who find the act of exercise inherently unpleasant have a positive mood swing the minute the workout is over. If you know what's on the other side, it's easier to push through the difficulty," says John Ratey, author of *Spark: The Revolutionary New Science of Exercise and the Brain.*

Developing a strong why and remembering the emotional and psychological benefits once the exercise is over can be a great tool to counter that voice in your head that rationalizes every excuse to not workout. In addition, once you start exercising it can become a self-reinforcing tool in itself that ingrains the urge to continue to work out more. In other words, the act of exercising gives you the motivation to continue to do so. As you continue, the more you harden the neural pathways that reinforce the act of exercising and, at the same time, the old pathways that do not support your new lifestyle habits begin to atrophy. Essentially, your brain is helping you along the way!

Exercising can feel like a chore sometimes, but it doesn't have to be. Here are some great ways to integrate and receive the benefits of exercising without feeling so burdensome in your daily life:

- Sign up for a spin cycle class. (Check out Spiked Spin & Wellness Co. if you're ever in the NYC area!)
- Go for a hike.
- Take a Yoga class on YouTube.
- Take a dance class.
- Get involved with team sports.
- Learn how to play golf.
- Clean your house.
- Go roller-skating.
- Go ice-skating.

Satisfy Your Desire for Expansion

We all have the innate desire to strive to become better than we are. It's so enveloped into our psyche that we can never seem to escape the little voice in the back of our head that constantly says, "I could be doing more." We hear this voice as a parent, leader, employee, entrepreneur, and spouse. In nearly every role we play in our lives. It's an impulse that exists in all of us, and physical fitness is an effective way to satisfy this urge that is a basic human desire. It's the perfect tool to become a better you and evolve and grow in every aspect of your life. Exercising is a form of radical self-care that can catapult your health, peace of mind, productivity, relationships, and overall fulfillment in life.

RADICAL SELF-CARE EXERCISE:
Move with the End in Mind

How often have you been told that you *should* do something (knowing the benefits it may provide) but don't always *do* it? Like sticking to a balanced diet, getting enough sleep, budgeting, and of course, exercising. Don't worry; I'll raise my hand with you! Change and consistency can be challenging.

Just because we know better doesn't mean we do better. You can learn all the scientific benefits in the world, but that doesn't mean change will occur. Change and motivation occur from within and must strike a chord with your core intrinsic self. So let's get past all the superficial reasons for wanting to start a workout routine and dig a little deeper to find an internal motivator that's meaningful to you.

This chapter exercise is about *starting with the end in mind* and getting to the core of your why (addressed in Chapter Five as a core human need) for improving yourself through the instrument of physical fitness. Gaining clarity of your internal motivators and knowing the positive results of how physical fitness can ultimately manifest in your life can be powerful motivators and sustainers.

So even if the thought of physical fitness and all its scientific benefits doesn't motivate you enough now, maybe enhancing a personal quality about yourself will. The idea here is that physical fitness can be a tool to improve other aspects of your life that you truly value.

Whether you are looking for motivation to begin a workout routine or already have one but want to amplify its purpose in your life, this exercise is perfect for you. Always remember: *you don't have to be sick to get better.*

1.) List at least two personal qualities in your life that you might want to improve. Think back to all the fantastic benefits regular physical fitness can provide.
Examples: *self-confidence, willpower, more openness, more optimistic, better memory, improve mood, more energy, regulate emotions better.*

2.) If you could improve these personal qualities, how might they show up and enhance your day-to-day life? Remember to keep it positive and say what you want, not what you don't want.

You can use this sentence syntax to make it easy: If I can [personal quality you want to improve], then [how it will enhance your life].

Examples: If I can *improve my mood throughout the day*, then *I can treat myself and my loved ones and coworkers better*. If I can *increase my energy throughout the day*, then *I can spend more quality time with my friends, kids, or partner after work*. If I can *improve my memory*, then *I can remember names better to demonstrate my care for others and excel in my professional career*. If I can *enhance my creativity in my business or professional life*, then *I can create better solutions to amplify my impact to help more people*. If I can *regulate my emotions better*, then *I can demonstrate more patience and compassion with myself, my partner, or my friends*.

3.) Now, let's think back to the chapter. Think about all the fantastic benefits physical fitness can provide. Let's combine Steps 1 and 2 to develop a clear, compelling why for how exercising can improve this personal quality in your life. You can think of this as your affirmation! (And we know how powerful those are for your brain.)

You can use this sentence syntax to make it easy: I exercise because I want to [personal quality you want to improve] so that I can [how it will enhance your life].

Examples: I exercise because I want to *improve my mood throughout the day* so that I can *treat myself and my loved ones and coworkers better.* I exercise because I want to *live my life with more energy and vitality* so that I can *spend more quality time with my friends, kids, or partner after work.* I exercise because I want to *improve my memory to remember names better at work* so that I can *demonstrate my care for others and excel in my professional career.* I exercise because I want to *enhance my creativity in my business or professional life* so that I can *create better solutions to amplify my impact to help more people.* I exercise because I want to *regulate my emotions better* so that I can *demonstrate more patience and compassion with myself, partner, or my friends.*

Once you've written a clear, compelling why for exercising, write it down on a post-it note or index card, and place it in common areas around the house, such as your desk, kitchen, or bathroom mirror.

Connecting or realigning to your why for exercising keeps *the end in your mind,* so you remember why you started in the first place. It reminds you of the bigger picture and can solidify your motivation from within. So be sure to *move your body with the end in mind.*

Use hashtags #RadicalSelfCare and #SuccessStartsWithin on social media and share with others to inspire them to join you on your path toward activating your potential.

CHAPTER EIGHT

MAINTAIN A MEDITATION PRACTICE

You should sit in meditation for twenty minutes a day
unless you're too busy then you should sit for an hour.
Zen Proverb

Make Amends with Your Thoughts

Maintaining your physical fitness, consciously knowing your why, and getting clarity of a future vision of yourself are all essential practices of radical self-care. Now to bring everything together, it's essential to take care of your mental wellness and focus. And yes, I said focus. It's one of the most important because it governs your entire life. As the famous saying goes, "The mind is all." It controls every thought you think, influences every feeling you have, how you perceive life, and even affects how life shows up for you.

It's necessary that we become self-aware to create space between us and our thoughts thus yielding us the ability to *choose* how we want to experience life, instead of life becoming a series of mundane reactions.

Since I discussed in the earlier chapters that our thoughts influence nearly aspect of your life, it's necessary that you properly take care of this mental faculty—your mind. Again, it's estimated that the average human has about 6,000 thoughts per day, and many of these thoughts can be quite harmful. Not to mention most of these thoughts can be unconscious and slip by us undetected. As discussed in Chapter Four, scientific research has concluded that mind-wandering, which is our brains' automatic unhealthy habit of unconscious thoughts that can be mostly negative, occupies 47 percent of awake time. Of course, I don't need to tell you, but that's nearly half our entire lives awake that has the potential to be filled with thoughts that can negatively influence our health, relationships, and goals.

To disrupt this process and create a space of acceptance and peace with your thoughts, aim to stop letting them control you. One of the most effective ways to do this is through the practice of meditation. Many people think the goal of meditation is to control your thoughts. This is not necessarily the case. The purpose of meditation is to stop letting your thoughts control you. When you make amends with your thoughts and realize that not every thought you have is *actually real* or true, then you begin to create more self-awareness throughout your life and can began to consciously choose thoughts that are in alignment with who you want to become.

Now I know what you are thinking. In Chapter Three, I said, "thoughts are things," and everything we think is influencing our reality, but now I'm saying all thoughts aren't actually true or real. While these statements seem to contradict each other, they don't. Remember our brains are constantly on autopilot, and the "monkey mind" chatter discussed in Chapter Two is continuously trying to warn us of potential threats with the hopes of keeping us safe. But here's the key to all of this, a lot of this chatter can either be fabricated, false assumptions, or down right lies.

In essence, meditation can help develop your ability to focus and guide your 6,000 thoughts toward the behaviors, desires, and results you hope to achieve in your health, relationships, wealth, and overall satisfaction in life.

The integration of meditation daily can catapult your well-being thereby affecting your performance and achievement.

Many people have a hard time understanding how meditation or mindfulness helps us deal with day-to-day life experiences. To effectively communicate this, let me tell you the story about the hungry fox and the turtle.

Mr. Fox thought, *I am going to have some good food today.* The turtle said to himself, "Oh, my goodness. My enemy is out there. Shall I run? I'm not fast enough." And since we all know a turtle cannot outrun a fox, Mr. Turtle swiftly went inside its shell and stayed put. Mr. Fox walked around the turtle and continued to pace while trying to find a way to get to the turtle. Eventually, Mr. Fox got tired of waiting for the turtle, so he ended up leaving Mr. Turtle alone and running away.

Now how does this story relate to life and meditation? Well, think of the fox as your daily stressors—whether it be anxiety, low energy, failure, nervousness, sadness, depression, or disappointment. When they arise in your life, you should be like Mr. Turtle. Now to be clear, that doesn't mean running away or hiding from your problems. It merely means finding awareness within yourself to observe your reaction to those problems or stressors instead of engaging with them. Over time, through practice, you can learn to appreciate these thoughts and feelings as just passing products of your own mind.

The best part about this is you can control your relationship with these stressors or negative thoughts by obtaining awareness. You can bring about awareness through the practice of meditation. You don't need to fight or surrender to your problem. Through meditation, you can *make friends* with all of your thoughts. And over time, as you meditate daily—just as you go to the gym—you can become stronger and better at recognizing stressors or negative thoughts that arise so that you can transcend them. Once you get to this point, your work, relationships, and accomplishing personal goals become much more manageable to work through and attain.

So rather than meditation becoming a practice that separates you from life, it enhances it and your results.

Use Meditation to Excel Goal Achievement

Most people associate meditation with relaxation. This is true but the principle point of meditation is to help train your brain to focus. When you are meditating you are training your brain to focus on relaxing, which gives way to a surprising number of health benefits that include a stronger immune system, reduction of age-related memory loss, and lower blood pressure. Because our brains get so caught up in the day-to-day hustle (that pesky autopilot mode), it can be quite difficult to focus our brains on the thoughts that serve us.

The same can be said for accomplishing our goals and desires. In order to reach your goals, it's essential that you make time to focus on them. This gives your brain the bandwidth to recognize information and circumstances that support your intentions. In other words, in John Assarf's book, *The Answer*, he says, "Our brain's hectic activity often drowns out finer signals and precludes any hope of picking up on the information that is most crucial to helping us achieve our goals."

Remember when I discussed your brain's Reticular Activating System (RAS)? It's constantly searching for inputs from your senses to help guide you toward your intentions or goals. Well, to encourage this particular system to serve you, meditation is an effective tool to condition your brain to help you focus on what it is that you wish to bring into your experience. When meditation is consistently practiced, your brain will continue to condition itself through neuroplasticity, making it easier for you to gain awareness of your thoughts to "re-focus" your attention on thoughts that are in alignment to the goals you wish to achieve. Furthermore, Dr. Andrew Newberg of University of Pennsylvania, says that "the longer you focus (i.e., meditate) on your goal, the more real it begins to feel, and if you stay focused long enough, you'll alter the neural circuitry in your brain."

This is why meditation practitioners and personal growth gurus encourage people to visualize or think about your goals and who you want to become in a calm and relaxed state (i.e. meditation). Research is consistently confirming that these ancient practices are an effective shortcut to change the circuitry of your brain, making it more likely you will adopt the corresponding behaviors that help you accomplish the future vision or goal you have for yourself. In other words, there is less friction between thought and execution. As I like to say, you reclaim your inner child, eager to learn and excited to grow. This hints at the old adage that the secret of a genius is the adult who can carry the spirit of a child into old age. To bring this closer to home, here's a client story that may help.

During one of my coaching sessions, a client came to me for guidance on how to strengthen his mindset and achieve better results on his job. He worked in sales at a company that sells business products and cleaning supplies to other businesses. His goal was to become Top Ten in sales in his region. This would put him the prestigious President's Club in his company and would result in the company awarding him an all-expense paid vacation! Throughout our coaching sessions we discussed the power of the subconscious mind, self-talk, and how the mind works as it relates to adopting goal-seeking behaviors.

I invited him to meditate every morning along with visualizing his goals and behaviors he would need to adopt that were in alignment with his future self. In this case, his behaviors would be picking up the phone and making sales phone calls, having a cheerful personality, and maintaining a persistent positive attitude even when a potential customer wasn't interested.

Over the course of just a couple months, he went from fifty-five in the region all the way up to sixth in the region. Last I talked to him he mentioned he was on track to make the President's Club!

The daily morning meditation allowed him to heighten his awareness of his self-talk, cultivate a sense of gratefulness, get centered before the day started, and clearly see how his behaviors were not fostering the results he said he wanted. Shortly after he started the daily meditation practice, he noticed he was happier, work seemed easier, and he was noticeably more productive, which contributed to his positive results at work. Still to this day he notices a huge difference on the days when he does not meditate. He feels less grateful and more agitated, which certainly do not support his professional goals.

I'm not suggesting all you have to do is sit there and meditate to achieve your goals, but the practice can be transformational with how you perceive your day and navigate stress, thereby improving the quality of your day-to-day life experience. And as I've discussed repeatably throughout this book, your inner well-being directly influences your outer success and results you wish to achieve. So, if you're looking to accelerate the accomplishment of a particular goal, regular meditation might be an effective practice to integrate into your daily routine.

There's a saying, "When we can quiet the mind, we can let the soul speak." By doing this, we let it guide us toward the well-being and desires we innately seek.

Meditation on the Rise

Meditation is quickly becoming one of the fastest-growing health trends. A recent report by the US Centers for Disease Control (CDC) states that meditation has increased by more than threefold in the US over the past five years. This is no surprise as we've seen a stark rise in the importance of meditation and mindfulness in almost every major company from Google to Nike to Apple. Many of these Fortune 500 companies have built meditation rooms throughout their company facilities. They are even offering opportunities to take free meditation courses during the workday.

In fact, when Salesforce opened their San Francisco Office, they strategically put a meditation room—what they call "mindfulness zone[s]"—into just about every floor of their 1,070-foot office skyscraper building headquarters, which happens to be the tallest building in San Francisco. The CEO of Salesforce is quoted by saying these rooms "are really important to cultivating innovation." Suggesting that the benefits of meditation extend far beyond health and wellness.

Even our smartphones and devices are seeing a rise in meditation app downloads. In fact, Sensor Tower, an app intelligence firm, reported that the top ten meditation apps alone ended up generating $128 million in revenue. The year after, this number grew to $195 million. And even Harvard neuroscientists have found that meditation conclusively alters and positively changes our brains' structure to reduce stress. *Harvard Business Review* states that spending just ten minutes a day on mindfulness can change how we treat ourselves, others around us, and our work. In recent years, we've seen a shift from doctors prescribing pills to treat illnesses to physicians prescribing mindfulness activities to treat everything from pain, loneliness, anxiety, and burnout. Research has even concluded that meditation and mindfulness are effective treatments for PTSD and depression.

So, what's happening here? Why are meditation and mindfulness practices creating such a buzz? It seems Fortune 500 companies realize its importance from a work performance and economic bottom-line perspective. Also, it appears that most of our society is craving for its benefits. Whether if it's increased performance, a better attention span, improved memory, or as an avenue to treat depression, anxiety, or combat stress, meditation almost seems as if this is the true "limitless pill" we've been trying to find.

Meditation has been around for thousands of years, specifically practiced by many Eastern religions such as Hinduism and Buddhism. It's described as a "mental regimen or discipline to promote concentration and the capacity for what is called 'one-pointedness' (*ekāgratā*) of mind."

Ekāgratā means the intentional pursuit of one object, close and undisturbed attention. It's only until very recently where Western science has finally caught up to Eastern spiritual practices that have been known to transform human lives for centuries. Using brain-sensing technology, we now have the unique opportunity to uncover just what is going on in the brain when we meditate. And scientists are seeing measurable effects on the mental and physical health of a meditator. Neuroscientists have found that daily meditators can achieve states of focus, attention, and concentration and even seem to affect their nervous, immune, and endocrine systems positively.

New research conducted by Dr. Sara Lazar, a Harvard neuroscientist, suggests that a fifty-year-old with a daily meditation practice can have a brain of a twenty-five-year-old! Whether this is a stretch or not, one thing is for sure, our stress levels have a lot to do with how quickly our body ages. So, I'll ask you the same question as Mr. Hudson famously sung in Jay-Z's "Young Forever" song, "Do you really want to live forever young?" Meditation may be the key to help you do just that!

What You Resist Will Persist

Have you ever felt like you wanted to run away from your own thoughts? Or have you ever felt like your thoughts have gotten the best of you?

Whether it's regretting the past, worrying about the future, or constantly reimaging negative scenarios play out in your mind, many of us have experienced fear of our own thoughts. When this happens, we try to push back against our thoughts, try to avoid them by constantly keeping ourselves busy, or pretend they don't exist. An everyday practical example is being afraid of what the doctor might say to us because we don't want to think about the ramifications of being sick, so we avoid thinking about going to the doctor. We all know how that turns out.

But beyond the negative impact of avoidance, I'll let you in on some science: If you're afraid of your thoughts, you're giving them power over you.

Let me tell you why that is. A famous saying coined initially by Swiss psychiatrist Carl Jung in which he says, "What you resist, persists." Have you ever had a negative thought about your past or future that continues to arise, and for some reason, no matter how hard you try, you can't avoid it?

You desperately try not to think about that particular thought, yet it still manages to stay in your head. You try to keep yourself busy by watching TV, listening to music, going to happy hours, or even spending time with friends, but those negative thoughts continue to bubble up to the surface. This was me when I felt lost back in 2017. It almost feels like you're running away from yourself with no end in sight. It's not a healthy place to live, and unfortunately, this can throw you into a cycle of fighting your thoughts, leading to discouragement, guilt, and anxiety. This, in turn, can manifest and overflow into your relationships, your career, and overall health.

Despite best efforts to distract yourself from these thoughts either through external influences or by trying to not think about them—they continue to persist. This is because the fundamental nature of this approach naturally gives power to your negative thoughts.

Let's relate this to a real-life example that my dad continues to ingrain into my brothers and me. When you're driving down the street, and your engine light comes on or hear a strange noise coming from your car, the right thing to do is pull over and address the situation. On the other hand, some people continue to drive their car "just one more day" before taking the car to the shop and getting it properly addressed.

Unfortunately, if you continue to drive the car knowing that the engine light is on, you might likely damage the car even more. The problem continues to persist and can get worse over time if not addressed. We try everything to avoid looking at the engine light or come up with another excuse by saying, "I don't have enough time to go to the shop" or "I don't have enough money right now." The problem is you could end up spending more money and time if you don't address the issue as soon as you were made aware of it. This analogy is precisely how negative thoughts can work in your mind.

If you continue to run away from your thoughts, they will use you. If you try to block them out, they will control you. If you don't address them properly and timely, they can overflow and possibly cause more damage to other areas of your life. It's crucial to properly address your negative thoughts as soon as your *emotional light* comes on—just as if your car engine light comes on. A great way to address them and see them for what they are is by facing them. Meditation is a great exercise to do just that and help you make amends with your thoughts and find peace in your mind.

I want to explain how meditation can help you. Many people believe that meditation is about deliberately stopping the natural movement of your thoughts and emotions. This is not the case. Quite the opposite. When you meditate and begin to watch your thoughts rise and dissipate, you can truly see them for that they are—just thoughts. The brain's "monkey mind" will continue to chatter, and you will begin to make amends with your so-called negative thoughts. Eventually, during meditation, your thoughts start to settle down, and the brain's executive functions decline in activity. Once this happens, you begin to disconnect or disassociate from your thoughts. Nothing crazy or elusive about this—your mind is just settling and relaxed just as if you've woken up from an amazing nap.

You will begin to watch your thoughts arise and then leave. Once detachment happens, you start to retransform the relationship you have with your unpleasant thoughts. This helps to dissolve the constant stress and anxiety of running away from your thoughts. When the relationship begins to change between you and your thoughts, you gain more familiarity with your own mind as you continue to examine it in meditation. You start to detach from the thoughts or feelings of attachment, stress, fear, or uncertainty and recognize they are just simply a fabrication of your own mind. And the most amazing revelation you will soon discover when detachment happens is that you are not your thoughts. Instead, you are the observer of your thoughts. Because if you can be *aware* of your thoughts floating by, then YOU can't be your thoughts. I hope I didn't lose you, but if I did, let's break this down, so it's clearer.

We plan. We predict the future. We regret the past. We wonder. We react. It's so easy for us to get wrapped up in our thoughts that we mistakenly believe it's who we are. When you practice meditation regularly, you realize you can listen to your thoughts without attaching yourself to them, which yields your detachment from them. Again, nothing crazy or mystical about this. You simply realize that all those crazy, stressful, and worrisome thoughts are not you because you can literally watch them float on by. This puts you back in the driver's seat of life, allowing you more mental bandwidth to regulate your emotional state better, make conscious decisions aligned with your goals, and enjoy the fullness of life.

In the *Joy of Living* by Yongey Mingyur Rinpoche, he describes meditation as "simply a process of resting the mind in its natural state, which is open to and naturally aware of thoughts, emotions, and sensations as they occur." He compares the mind to a river that naturally flows and how pointless it is to try to stop the river's flow. And goes on to say, "When you don't understand the nature and origin of your thoughts, your thoughts use you." Meditation can ultimately be a practice to show you how to use your thoughts instead of being used by them.

When your own thoughts use you, they can easily control you to react to life as opposed to consciously responding, as previously discussed. And since many psychologists believe we have an innate desire for self-preservation, we constantly fear and worry to ensure our survival in day-to-day life. Unfortunately, as mentioned in Chapter Two, these types of stressful thoughts and emotions for long periods do not serve us well or those closest to us. It can wreak havoc on our health, force us into a scarcity mindset, decline our performance, and keep us in competition with each other. When you meditate, you become more aware of these types of thoughts and emotions, and you create a better chance for yourself to *choose* who you desire to be. Ultimately, this practice will help you foster more self-compassion and empathy toward yourself and others around you.

How Can Meditation Improve Your Life?

Here are a few examples of how the daily practice of meditation can improve the quality your life.

- Do you ever notice how your attention begins to drift when you're writing an email or reading a book? You may get halfway down the page of a book, and you forget what you even read, and you have to force yourself to reread the same paragraph several times. Meditation can help increase self-awareness to allow you to refocus and concentrate for more extended time periods.

- Have you ever felt like it was hard to focus your attention during a conversation with a friend, significant other, or business associate while they are talking? Your mind can't stop telling you what you may have forgotten to do yesterday or you unconsciously pick up your phone. All the while, your spouse or coworker talking to you may be telling you something very important. Correspondingly, your nonverbal communication—lack of eye contact and body posture—is perceived by the other person talking as if you don't care what they are saying. Meditation can improve your concentration so that you can deliberately listen to the people closest to you which can, in turn, create richer relationships.

- Are you interested in cultivating silence and unshakeable peace within yourself to get a break from your busy, frantic schedule?

- Are you looking to uncover unconscious self-limiting beliefs that may be preventing you from accomplishing your goals, taking action on your ideas, or reaching your fullest potential?

- Are interested in decreasing stress throughout your day to enhance your physical and emotional well-being?

- Are you interested in boosting your immune system's ability to fight illnesses?
- Are you looking to consciously respond more empathetically to those close to you instead of reacting with negative emotions that don't serve you or the other person?
- Do you want to build more self-compassion and grace so you can stop being so hard on yourself?
- Are you feeling lethargic or low on energy due to lack of sleep or rest? Research shows a regular meditation practice can be up to two to five times deeper than sleep! It's essential to remember meditation doesn't replace sleep but can supplement it.
- Do you constantly forget the names of people you just met?
- Are you interested in growing spiritually to become more connected and aligned to your purpose?
- Are you looking to cultivate more empathy or compassion for yourself or others around you?
- Do you desire to be emotionally present with your significant other?
- Do you want to combat your negative thought patterns and increase positive thoughts to improve your confidence and self-assurance?
- Are you looking to improve your mental focus and productivity at work?

Well do I have news for you; daily meditation can help address all of these examples. Meditation creates awareness of your thoughts so you can be equipped to address situations or problems in almost any aspect of your life. Without awareness, it is challenging to be conscious of your thoughts, actions, and emotions to make positive changes in your life.

Meditation can improve concentration, self-esteem, and memory; it can help you foster more kindness, improve emotional health, lengthen your attention span, and increase the density of gray matter in brain regions linked to learning, memory, regulation, and empathy. I share these benefits because it can be tough at first to start and maintain a meditation practice, but what really helped me to keep up with my practice was reflecting on the science-backed benefits it can contribute to my life. In short, *when we believe that a behavior will benefit us, we are more likely to do it!*

With meditation, you're not always able to see the immediate progress like you can from lifting weights at the gym. When you lift, you can see your muscles getting bigger and stronger. Unfortunately, you can't see your brain get bigger or stronger with each mediation session, but over time, you will slowly feel the results come naturally, sometimes unexpectedly, in your everyday life. As you continue with your meditation practice, you may not even have the urge to honk or get mad in traffic when someone cuts you off on the road. And even if you do have the desire, you will become more skillful in being aware of your thoughts and gut reactions in the moment, so they don't take control of you. You will slowly start to learn to consciously choose thoughts that support you despite stressful external circumstances that may arise in your life. This is seriously a superpower that is overlooked.

External events will not phase you as much because you've cultivated enough awareness to know how to respond to life and choose thoughts that support you and not undermine you or the people closest to you. In today's busy world, meditation can literally be your life vest to keep you afloat to not only survive but *thrive*!

> *One of the most courageous things you can do is go inward and begin your journey toward self-discovery. Once this happens, you'll realize the everlasting peace, serenity, happiness, abundance, and strength that you've been searching for have always been within.*

RADICAL SELF-CARE TIP:
Mindfulness in Daily Living

We are constantly bombarded with notifications throughout the day. Whether it be emails, social media, calls, or text messages. It seems like it's never-ending. And because we feel compelled to pick up the device every time it rings or pings, our brains are slowly becoming controlled by them. Experts say this contributes to the decline of our attention spans and effectiveness in getting tasks done throughout the day.

So, here's a simple, yet challenging, tip: The next time your phone buzzes, chimes, or rings, don't touch it! Look at it, mentally acknowledge the notification, and let it ring or vibrate. (If someone important is calling, you can decide whether or not to pick it up.) You can even put this exercise into good use while you are standing in line at the supermarket or in the waiting room at the doctor's office. Resist the urge to pick up your phone when you're bored or waiting for something. Calvin Newport, an associate professor of computer science at Georgetown University and author of the book *Deep Work*, says, "The brain has to get comfortable not getting some shiny new stimuli from a device every few seconds."

This simple act of not touching your phone slowly builds self-discipline, so you don't always feel compelled to pick up your device every time it demands your attention. Over time, through repetition and consistency, you can build new neural pathways in the brain, making it easier not to feel obliged to pick up your device every time it demands your attention. Again, this is self-directed neuroplasticity working in your favor.

This simple tip helps you develop complete awareness of how devices, distractions, or even unexpected demands may be pulling you away from a vital task or an important personal or business conversation that may need your undivided attention. Over time you may even notice your focus, self-awareness, and productivity increase from the simple exercise. As actor Denzel Washington once said in an interview: "Are you using your phone, or is your phone using you?"

Spiritual Practices Can Improve Mental Capacities

Very recently, scientific research is confirming what many of us already intuitively feel while meditating. Most regular meditators feel a deep connection to a much higher source of power when meditating. Some of us feel spiritually aligned, connected, or even empowered. Some people have even said they feel a sense of "oneness with the universe," and this feeling is sometimes difficult to put into words. This "oneness" or wholeness has allowed them to foster a tremendous amount of personal freedom and peace in their day-to-day life.

This is where neurotheology comes into play, which is the study of the brain's neural connections as it relates to spiritual beliefs, experiences, and practices. Dr. Andrew Newberg, a neuroscientist at the University of Pennsylvania, bridged the gap between science and spirituality that led him to find some unique revelations about the human brain. By using neuroimaging technologies such as an fMRI and SPECT, Dr. Newberg can peek inside the brain to understand how meditation, thinking about God, and prayer influences our realities and brain structure.

In Dr. Newberg's book, *How God Changes Your Brain*, he studied a group of nuns who had been practicing prayer for a minimum of fifteen years and compared their brain scans to a group of Buddhist practitioners who were long-time meditators. The nuns and the Buddhist practitioners clearly held very different beliefs, but the brain scan results were nearly the same. Dr. Newberg says this research confirms the hypothesis that the benefits obtained from regular prayer or meditation have less to with a specific theology or religion that people may practice but rather the practices of relaxation, focused breathing, and concentrating your mind on ideas that elicit feelings of compassion, peace, and joy. He also points out that our response may be stronger "the more you believe in what you are meditating or praying about."

I am sharing this research because no matter what your religion or spiritual foundation may be, many of these ancient practices passed down from generation to generation, from a scientific perspective, have the propensity to enhance the quality of your life. We get so caught up in what religion we practice, thus separating us, when in reality, each of our goals is the same: to improve the quality of our lives and live the highest expression of ourselves with compassion, hope, empathy, and love.

Further research of meditators with over ten years of practice reveals something particularly interesting in the brain's thalamus, which is responsible for every sight, sound, taste and touch we perceive. The thalamus is referred as the "Grand Central Station" of sensory information coming to our brains. Dr. Newberg's research concludes that the more you meditate on something, whether it be joy, love, success, God, or financial abundance, the more your thalamus becomes active until it "reaches a point of stimulation where it perceives thoughts in the same way that other sensations are perceived." And since your thalamus makes no distinction between inner and outer reality, your belief becomes neurologically real to you. Based on this research, meditating on a specific desire or goal could further enrich your belief in whatever it is you are focusing on. Thus, making it more likely for you to adopt the corresponding behaviors of your intended desires!

These revelations are astounding because we now can understand how sacred spiritual practices such as meditation and prayer can positively influence the physical structure of our brains thus yielding us a more satisfying and healthy life. Dr. Newberg took a leap of faith, literally, to turn 300 years of scientific research on its head to further humanity's understanding of some of our most revered spiritual practices.

Neurologically Moving from Fear to Faith

Remember when I said that in today's society, our brains' primitive functions are consistently being forced into a constant state of fear for survival? Well, Newberg's neurotheology research concludes that these types of regular practices (meditation and/or prayer) can increase our empathy toward others, enhance social awareness and compassion, and improve our ability to combat the innate biological responses that can keep us in a constant state of fear or worry. They can significantly reduce anxiety and stress and even suggest that you can slow down the aging process by meditating just twelve minutes per day. I mentioned this in Chapter Three as it relates to meditation lengthening our telomeres, thus prolonging our life expectancy!

There is also research to suggest that meditation can significantly influence our perception of reality and goals. In an email exchange between Dr. Newberg and me, he discussed how the "data seems to suggest that the more we focus our mind on anything, the more it becomes our reality. So, if people are focusing on the positive or on resilience, then the neural connections that support these ideas help to lead that person's brain to thinking about reality in the same way." This essentially means your brain can restructure itself and develop specific neural pathways that literally map in accordance with your goals and desires, particularly during slower states of consciousness like meditation or prayer. In essence, your thoughts about your goals and desires have the ability to become neurologically real to you. Newberg believes we still have a long way to go to understand our brains and our perception of reality.

Nevertheless, these groundbreaking scientific studies can completely transform and improve our lives. Whatever we focus on truly does grow in our brains, and our realities correspondingly take form. We really can define our own "truths" to a certain extent, whether they be "positive" or "negative."

Break Free to Ascend!

For so long, spirituality and science have been kept separate, and yet they keep making their way back to each other. Now we are seeing them collide to further humanity's health and well-being. This is a topic my mother and I discuss quite often as we further our research in our respective passions. My mother, known as Dr. Denise Scott to most, is a Geneticist and Associate Professor of the Department of Pediatrics and Human Genetics at Howard University. She mainly focuses on gene-environment interactions in psychiatric disorders and the ethical, legal, social implications in genomic healthcare. At the time of writing this, her job also consists of translating evidence-based genetic research to train healthcare professionals in genetic counseling. Her work aims to provide patient-centered prevention and intervention education to healthcare professionals to develop a patient plan of action, particularly in African Americans, to combat substance use.

Side bar: My mother is the first person in our family, from both my mother's and fathers's side, to receive a doctoral degree. She literally broke through a generational ceiling, especially since Black Americans just a few decades ago did not even have the opportunity to pursue formal education or let alone be permitted to read during the years of slavery. As a thought leader in the field of genetics and addiction medicine, my mother has significantly advanced genetic research as it relates to substance use in underserved communities.

As my mother continues her research in genetics, we continue to discuss new sciences emerging from epigenetics to neuroplasticity. Sciences that can give many of us, particularly in the Black community, a sense of hope, self-determination, and the ability to break free from the emotional and psychological trauma that stem from racial injustices we continue to face. This type of breakthrough research tells us that our bodies can adapt, we can grow, and more importantly, we can influence our genetic destiny no matter what our past may be. So just as Dr. Francis Collins suggested, the former Director of the National Institutes of Health (NIH), "genetics loads the gun, and environment pulls the trigger."

One primary example of this is a study conducted by researchers at the Medical College of Georgia that found that African American adolescents trained on meditation practices began to show a significant decline in school infractions, suspension rates, and absenteeism. Because of these striking studies and others, it's been our mission at Positively Caviar, Inc. to disrupt mental health stigmas by bringing these effective relaxation techniques to youth who may not be exposed to these practices.

The more we bridge the gap between spirituality and science, the more we will understand how to effectively treat many diseases, decrease depression, create a more empathic culture, expand our consciousness, and develop a more equitable and sustainable society.

If we desire to change the world, change from within must happen first.

Whether you consider yourself spiritual or not, meditation can be a secular practice to positively influence your life—from your health, relationships, and even your professional pursuits. I believe meditation is the key to unlocking the many hidden treasures found deep within us that can give rise to necessary global solutions that can further enrich and create more equitable societies.

Meditation will continue to take off in popularity and integrate itself more in our daily lives in wearable technologies, phone apps, and will continue to ingrain itself into company cultures. Just like when our sciences began to prove that physical fitness significantly improved our wellness and achievement in life, meditation will follow suit, and it will radically transform our lives as we know it. Meditation will become an essential form of your radical self-care journey for your mental, physical, and even spiritual health to truly move you toward your fullest potential.

RADICAL SELF-CARE:
Exercise: Daily Meditation

Many people tell me that they don't have time to meditate. Or they don't know how to. Not knowing how to do something new is something I completely understand but not having time to meditate at least ten or fifteen minutes a day is not a valid excuse.

You may be hustling toward your goals or have a ton of family responsibilities, but I'm willing to bet that you have ten to fifteen minutes every day that you can utilize to improve your well-being, accelerating you toward your highest self. Investing just 2 percent of your day to meditation to improve the other 98 percent seems like an amazing choice to me!

At the risk of sounding like a broken record, your well-being must be prioritized above everything else.

Here's a quick meditation exercise you can practice daily either in the morning or evenings (ten to fifteen minutes) to help upgrade your mental facilities and well-being:

1. Find somewhere comfortable to sit that is quiet and peaceful. It could be on a chair, pillow, somewhere outdoors, on a bedroom floor, or even in your closet (Yes, I am a closet meditator!) Note: To effectively implement a meditation practice, it's best to pick a location and stick with it. Over time your body and subconscious mind will begin to recognize or associate a particular place with "this is where I meditate." Similar with your bed. Your body knows that when you lay down on your bed, it says to itself, "It's time to go to sleep."

2. Now that you're comfortable, set a timer and close your eyes, if you wish. You can even meditate with your eyes open by focusing on a particular object.

3. Once you feel settled with your eyes closed or open, focus on your breath. You can bring your awareness to the tip of your nostrils as air comes in and out. If you've never focused on your breath before, it may feel uncomfortable at first, but you will become accustomed to breathing naturally as you practice. Don't force your breathing into a certain rhythm.

4. Now, as you focus on your breath, what you will notice is a whole heap of distractions, thoughts, emotions, or even that darn email you forgot to respond to. As thoughts arise, gently bring your focus back to your breath, going in and out your nose. Every time you recognize your thoughts straying away from your breath and bring it back, you are building a muscle of focus, awareness, resilience, and willpower. Don't get discouraged if it feels challenging at first. Just as you go to the gym to build your muscles, refocusing your awareness back to your breath is the same. The more you do it, the stronger you become.

5. Continue to follow your breath for the period you've set on your timer or phone. When you are done, sit for a moment after your practice. Refrain from jumping up and getting active immediately. Gently ease your way back into your day.

Some things to remember:
- At some point in your meditation practice, you may start to feel a sense of peace, calm, and inner fulfillment that you can't describe in words. And there will be other times when your thoughts and emotions will pull at you, and you may get frustrated. Just remember, this is all a part of the process. The fact that you are aware of all these nagging thoughts while meditating is a win in itself! As Deepak Chopra says when people ask him if you are meditating correctly, he says the litmus test is simple, "If you're doing it, you're doing it right."
- As you continue to practice your daily meditation, you will begin to notice subtle and even substantial changes in your mood, increased patience with yourself and others, ability to make good decisions, sufficient energy for long workdays, more focus, strong coping skills in stressful situations, better attention when in conversations, emotional resilience, and a stream of new ideas and solutions. More benefits come as you continue your practice!
- If it helps, again, even Oprah meditates daily. (Yes, I just used Oprah as a motivator for you!)

I've also pulled together a list of some of the best wearable meditation and wellness apps that you can use to help guide your meditation practices:

Shine App (https://www.theshineapp.com/)
FitMind (https://www.fitmind.co/)
Alkeme Health (https://alkemehealth.com/)
Headspace (https://www.headspace.com/)
Core (https://www.hellocore.com/)
Muse (https://choosemuse.com/)
Calm (https://www.calm.com/)
InsightfulTimer (https://insighttimer.com/)

Remember, this is your life and well-being we are talking about, and we don't get another one! Find time; I recommend in the morning when it's quiet and no one is up so you can focus and invest in yourself. This is the perfect time to ground yourself to center upon the inner peace and joy that you should cultivate before you go out into the world. If you genuinely desire to improve your sense of self, relationships, professional career, and health, give meditation a try.

Use hashtags #RadicalSelfCare and #SuccessStartsWithin on social media and share with others to inspire them to join you on your path toward activating your potential.

CHAPTER NINE

JUMPSTART LIFE WITH A MORNING ROUTINE

Early to bed and early to rise, makes a man healthy, wealthy, and wise.
Benjamin Franklin

Wake Up on the Right Side of the Bed

Now it's time to bring all of this together to integrate within your day-to-day life. How you wake up in the morning can affect your mental clarity, health, productivity, and overall fulfillment in life. Before you start your day, it's crucial to prepare your mind to tackle your goals, possible obstacles, or speedbumps that may arise. The best way to do that is to develop a morning routine to give yourself momentum, energy, and sense of control heading into your day. This puts you in the right frame of mind to tackle your day in accordance with your intentions. This sets you up for success, so you feel a sense of control over your day, and thus your life. *If you win the morning, you win the day.* Many high-performing CEOs, athletes, and entrepreneurs attribute their success and overall sense of fulfillment in day-to-day life to waking up early to accomplish their morning routines. Even I was a skeptic at first until I began to implement one and it completely changed my life.

Have you ever heard of the saying that he or she "woke up on the wrong side of the bed"? It's a common proverb that dates back thousands of years ago that many people sometimes say today when their day just is not going right. People attribute their unhappiness and bad moods to this famous phrase. Unfortunately, this phrase is becoming more of a norm in our current society. If we are not careful, it can self-perpetuate the negative feelings we don't want to feel. Overtime, simple sayings like these force us to believe that we don't have control over our internal thoughts, feelings, and attitudes.

On top of that, it continues to solidify a false belief in our minds that we can't change how we feel or how we show up for the day. In fact, we can, thereby enhancing the quality of our lives.

This was me—when I felt like life wasn't on my side, and I knew I needed to change. I was continually "waking up on the wrong side of the bed" and feeling as though I was at the mercy of circumstances in my life. I knew I needed a morning routine to kick my day off with the right mindset, but nothing changed, unless I did.

One morning I arose, and just like I always do, my phone alarm rang in the other room (this is a technique I use to increase my chances of waking up earlier), and I woke up quietly trying not to wake my fiancée at the time, now my wife, Kiara, to tippy toe to the other room to turn off the alarm. After I turned it off, I crept back into our bedroom, and Kiara said, "Back in the bed again, huh?"

That's when it hit me. I was pathetic. All I could see in my head was a pathetic future husband and father who couldn't show up for himself to be a caretaker and provider. Okay, as you can see, my mind definitely exaggerated a bit! But this is how I felt standing there in the cold dark room trying to ease myself back into bed at 5:00 a.m.

I had heard and researched the benefits of waking up early and implementing a morning routine but for some reason that was not enough. It was a complete struggle for weeks. I kept thinking something was going to change, but nothing was. I knew I had to make a change if I truly wanted to see new results in my life. It's like that saying, "The definition of insanity is doing the same thing over and over and expecting different results."

Well, this was me, and according to this quote, I was insane to think my life would change if I didn't change myself first. I didn't change, so the same results continued to manifest. Who was I kidding?

Shortly after Kiara said that to me, I immediately put on my clothes and went straight to the gym. Something clicked, and my willpower went right into action.

After completing my workout and morning routine, I happened to be working from home at the time (due to the pandemic) and experienced an enormous sense of satisfaction around 9:00 a.m. that day. The satisfaction stemmed from knowing that I can muster up willpower even when it's tough and, of course, the famous dopamine rush you get after from a good workout.

After waking up around 5:00 a.m. for a week after that day, I felt like I was getting some pep in my step. I started to gain the feeling that I wasn't at the mercy of circumstances in my life. I felt like I was in control of my life. Not only that, but I also felt like life was working for me, rather than against me. It was a sense of ease, and it flowed throughout my day, which I fell in love with. This control over my day yielded me the ability to bounce back from adversities quicker, regulate my emotions more effectively, and greatly enhanced my productivity. Ever since that cold dark morning, I've started my day off with a morning routine. I share this personal story for two reasons. One to share how a morning routine changed my life and so many others and the importance of taking 100 percent responsibility of how you show up and prepare for life.

It's vital to not place blame on external things influencing our internal moods. This responsibility belongs to us to ensure we can address it adequately. Otherwise, we will continue to foster a false belief that external things like "waking up on the wrong side of the bed" are not our fault. We have more control over our moods, decisions, and mindsets than we think we do and how we show up for life.

Don't fall into this trap. There is another side. A side that can drastically improve your life. I will teach you how to wake up on the *right side of the bed* to maximize your potential to be equipped with increased energy, mental focus, and personal power to rise to any occasion that you may face.

A proper morning routine can help you fulfill your potential daily.

There are two types of people in life: people who prepare for life versus people who don't. Notice the difference? One is reactive toward life while the other is proactive. In today's society, being proactive in life is almost a necessity because as soon as we wake up in the morning, the game begins.

Emails are flying in, social media notifications are pinging, and hundreds of news publishers are trying desperately to get you to view their latest content or article. Everything externally is trying to seize your attention before you even have a chance to grab your own. What you read, view on social media, and what you do right after you wake up can negatively or positively influence the rest of your day—and you may not even consciously be aware of it.

To adopt a proactive approach to life, it's vital to prepare your mind and body. In essence, you have to prepare your mind for your day before someone or something else controls it for you. This is an essential habit to adopt; otherwise, external circumstances will drive and control your internal emotions, behaviors, and destiny. You have to set up yourself for success mentally, psychologically, and spiritually. If not, the rest of the day can feel like an uphill battle of never-ending distractions and miscellaneous tasks leaving you constantly frazzled and unproductive. You may be busy "doing" but you feel like you're not making any progress.

Who's in Control?

Ask yourself this question: Do I want someone else, social media, or some news conglomerate to determine how I feel about myself and my life, or do I want to be able to make this decision for myself?

This is the question you are bypassing each day you wake up, and the first thing you do is unconsciously reach for your phone and start scrolling. Since our external circumstances influence how we feel internally, we have to be mindful of how we spend our most precious hours of the day—our mornings. It can either catapult you toward your desires, goals and positive feelings or undermine them.

A study from International Data Corporation (IDC) sponsored by Facebook found that at least 80 percent of smartphone owners reach for their smartphone device within the first fifteen minutes of waking up before doing anything else. The report states that "these statistics alone drive home the utility of and reliance on smartphones." And as the percentages continue to grow, so do individuals' chances of being negatively influenced by their device as soon as they wake up in the morning.

Now let me be clear and say that our devices are considered tools to provide convenience for our lives. And just like every other tool we use, it can be used positively or negatively depending on the operator. It can either undermine your progression or empower you. It's your choice depending upon who you follow, what you view, and how you use your device. Smartphone devices can be a great servant to you, but they can become a terrible master if you are not mindful. "Immediately turning to your phone when you wake up can start your day off in a way that is more likely to increase stress and leave you feeling overwhelmed," according to Dr. Nikole Benders-Hadi, a psychiatrist at Doctor On Demand.

So, let me give you a real-world example that you might have probably faced before.

You wake up in the morning, and the first thing you do is reach for your phone. After checking the time, you might even unconsciously open your email inbox, head over to your favorite social media platform, or check your text messages. All this happens in the matter of a few seconds.

Unconsciously you may have read a negative news article or viewed a social media post that sends you down a cycle of negative emotions or brings to the surface a self-limiting belief. Interaction with your device may even bubble up feelings of stress and anxiety because of the excessive number of external stimuli that your brain is forced to keep up with.

As you rise from bed, brush your teeth, take a shower, and get ready for the day, your self-talk begins to attach itself to the things you viewed on your phone, or anything related to it—whether it be worrying about the future or regretting the past. As you make your way out the door, in the car, and to the office, the same unconscious thoughts continue to unsettle you. You try to avoid these negative thoughts and replace them with conversations with others or scroll on social media (again), but nothing seems to provide any comfort.

On top of that, your performance at work seems to be lousy and you feel like "something is off." All of this begins to compound on itself until you say to yourself or someone else, I am just having "one of those days" today where nothing seems to be going right. And just like that you "woke up on wrong side of the bed." Unbeknown to you, your day started with a beautiful clear, blank canvas until you reached for your phone that morning and began to scroll unconsciously. This is how our brains tend to work throughout the day, and this is how you can get locked into a repetitive cycle of negativity if you are not aware of how your external environment can influence your thoughts and emotions throughout the day.

Let me be a little bit clearer and say: Your thoughts, focus, ideas, and beliefs about your life can be immediately hijacked by text messages, notifications, and social media posts as soon as you wake up. Instead of taking proactive actions toward your goals based upon your internal thoughts, you are being forced to react by someone else's thoughts. The smartphone example is just one example that can ultimately force you to become reactive in your day instead of proactive. I specifically chose this example because it's something that so many of us face every morning in our current society, and most of us don't even realize it. And as our lives become more integrated and connected to our devices, it can create more opportunities to hijack our attention, emotions, and undermine our beliefs about ourselves.

This is just one example of why a consistent morning routine can be a saving grace for your overall productivity, health, and fulfillment in life. You need to set up a morning routine to enable you to flourish in your career, relationships, and well-being. And once you set up a good morning routine and stick to it, you start to build momentum, and it *compounds*, just like money sitting in a good stock portfolio. This compounding effect slowly begins to make you unstoppable because your morning is the centerpiece of all of your habits. Once you change your mornings, virtually every other area of your life will follow suit.

Benefits of Building Success Rituals

Humans have performed rituals for thousands of years. Even though this word is sometimes associated with religious practices, it can be considered much broader than that. Many of us do them on a day-to-day basis and don't even realize it. Rituals have been known to provide us with purpose, consistency, clarity, and a sense of grounding to help us achieve our highest self. They can be our anchors during a time of uncertainty and constant distractedness. A ritual is defined as any pattern or practice of behavior regularly performed in a set manner. Rituals make us who we are. They make us human. Because no matter what happened yesterday or what you may encounter today, you're constantly reminded of who you are and who you want to become. A consistent morning routine is no different.

Many highly successful people in life consider their rituals to be a large part of their success. Steve Jobs, Tony Robbins, Oprah, former President Barack Obama, and President of Ariel Investments, Mellody Hobson, attribute their productivity, success, and emotional well-being to their daily morning rituals. Tim Cook, the current Chief Executive Officer at Apple, has even said he goes to the gym every morning to keep his "stress at bay." Oprah starts her morning with twenty minutes of meditation, which she says in an article she wrote on Oprah.com, fills her with "hope, a sense of contentment and deep joy." After she meditates, she takes about an hour to workout. When former President Barack Obama was in office it was said that he started his day around 5:00 a.m., at least two hours before his first scheduled event. This allowed him to prioritize his day, and as Business Insider reports, alternate between strength and cardio training. Even Tony Robbins, who has spent the last three decades as the world's foremost performance coach for Bill Clinton, Usher, Oprah, Serena Williams, and billionaire investor Paul Tudor Jones, has a morning ritual that he calls "priming." Which is a type of mindfulness meditation exercise to help cultivate positive emotions and "set a productive and powerful tone for your day."

Are you noticing a pattern here? The successful people I've discussed all have a powerful morning ritual that keeps them centered, focused, emotionally grounded, and productive. If you don't realize it by now, *success always leaves clues.* Successful people don't become successful because they are "lucky." They don't have great friendships by chance. They don't have strong marriages because they are just "winging it." And they are surely not genuinely fulfilled and radiate an aura of joy just because "they were born that way." They know something. And they are doing it purposefully and consistently to achieve the life they desire. It's not by accident.

They have become "successful" because of their consistent habits, thoughts, and day-to-day actions. And morning rituals can bring it all together to catapult your day and overall life satisfaction. Rituals help you ingrain healthy habits and discipline needed to succeed in any area of your life. The best part about all of this is any habit or ritual they use, you can learn and implement it in your life with a little effort to produce massive results in your life!

RADICAL SELF-CARE TIP:
Wake-Up Morning Strategies

A lot of people tell me it's hard for them to wake up in the morning. I get it, trust me. It's a tough battle because you know deep in your heart no one is telling you need to. This process takes time to create new neural pathways in the brain to replace old habits with new ones. The great thing about this is, it gets easier, but I always find people need somewhere to start. Here are a couple of tips to help you wake up earlier to make time for your morning routine:

- Let me clear the air and say you don't have to wake up at 5:00 a.m. to receive the benefits of a morning routine! I recommend waking up at least one hour before your busy day begins, so you have enough time to complete your routine. We will discuss what you should include in your morning routine in the exercise at the end of the chapter.
- Charge your phone in another room. This forces you to rise from bed and physically walk to your phone to turn off your morning alarm to get your day started. This automatically increases your percentage of not getting back into the bed because you are already physically up.

- Layout your gym clothes by your phone to ensure they are the first thing you see when you turn off your alarm. The brain is constantly looking for a reason to tell you to sleep more and choose the path of least resistance. Having your clothes laid out can make it that much easier to put them on so you can get on with your day. You want to make this as easy as possible for your brain, especially in the morning.
- Personal favorite: Use a programmable smart light or bulb with a timer and set your lights to turn on when you want to wake up. Studies show that exposure to light has a powerful effect on your circadian rhythm, influencing your sleep and wake times. By simulating the sunrise with the gradual increase in brightness, the smart light can wake you up gently.
- Don't hit the snooze button. When you hit the snooze button, you've already lost. As soon as your alarm goes off get up and get ahead of your day and take life on.
- Write a powerful quote or your "why" on a Post-It Note the night before and put it in a convenient place where you would see it when you wake up in the morning. This can remind you of your core purpose when your brain is telling you to go back to sleep. It will give you the fuel to take control of your brain to force yourself to wake up instead of sliding back into those bedsheets. Often, we get motivated by books, but as soon as we face the actual test (like waking up in the morning), we suffer defeat because we "forgot" why we set the goal in the first place. Don't forget your goal. Don't forget your why. Remember your "why" during the moments that count in life. Here are a couple of examples:
    - I wake up early to show up as my full self for my friends, family, and significant other.
    - My body deserves the best of me, so it's paramount that I feed it what it needs.
    - I wake up early to work out and meditate to manage my emotions and increase positive thoughts to perform better at work.
    - I wake up early to feel better about myself and to live a happy life.
    - Quote: *It's easier to wake up early and work out than it is to look in the mirror each day and not like what you see.* Jayne Cox
    - Quote: *Win the morning, win the day.*

- When you rise in the morning, think about how you're going to feel after the morning routine is over. A sense of accomplishment and control over your day! You will be more productive at work, you will seem to levitate over life's problems, and improve your overall satisfaction throughout the day. All of this can come from the simple task of waking up in the morning. Consciously thinking about how you are going to feel after your morning routine can induce positive emotions of encouragement to put one foot after the other to get your day started.
- Simple, yet can be tough at first: Go to bed earlier!

Establish Your Morning Routine Structures

Thousands of people, including the names I've mentioned, have understood and applied the secret of implementing a morning routine. Because of this, many people have had time to perfect this ritual to obtain optimal mental performance, health, and life satisfaction. Did you notice anything else similar about the names I listed? Let's take a deeper look at their specific activities.

You will see they are quite similar. They are broken up into a couple of main buckets, each accomplishing a particular goal. These include physical fitness, mental and spiritual health, and a time for growth or reflection. Each of these buckets will keep you physically fit, mentally sound but also allow you to expand toward the highest vision for yourself. When life seems to throw you around as soon as the day starts, consistently fostering these core structures in life will give you more control of your day and destiny. In the book, *The 5am Club* by Robin Sharma, he discusses the simple 20/20/20 formula that further breaks this out. He says that if you want to "master yourself," you should spend the first hour of your day entirely focused on yourself. This includes four interiors that he describes as the "Mindset, Heartset, Healthset, and Soulset."

Sharma says that these four interiors must be mastered in the morning to ensure you can reach mastery level performance in your life. If one of them is out of alignment, then it can significantly influence the other.

For example, your "Heartset" as Sharma describes, is your emotional life and well-being.

There is no way you can confidently bring your whole self intellectually to work if your emotional life is not in order. Emotions buried and not dealt with will always be expressed and may wreak havoc in parts of your life that you care deeply about. Always remember that emotions repressed become expressed eventually, and most of the time they come out in harmful ways. It's essential to do the hard work of resolving your emotional life so you can bring your full self to life. Addressing this area could be anything from journaling, meditation, and reflection.

Your "Healthset" is your physical health, and without it, you can't do anything or even enjoy the fruits of your success. A morning routine with fitness intertwined can help you levitate over stress, promote better concentration, and unleash feel-good dopamine spikes, which I discussed in Chapter Seven. To bring it all together, "Soulset" is the icing on top. This is your spirituality. Sharma says, "Too often, everyday life pulls us toward the superficial and the material. So, take some time in the quiet moments of the early morning to remember who you truly are." Life can get so busy that sometimes we can't even hear the pulse of our own soul. Your spiritual side could be prayer, meditation, or anything that you feel connects you or grounds you. So, get quiet and be still. As Blaise Pascal famously said, "All of humanity's problems stem from man's inability to sit quietly in a room alone."

We live in a society that constantly promotes movement as success. *Movement is not success.* Intentional stillness and quietness can offer a great deal of insight for yourself. And to do this, it's paramount to take time every day to become centered and grounded in who you are, what you truly desire, and where you want to go.

Like Pascal said, "sit quietly in a room" and remember who you are. Solutions will come, problems will disintegrate, and you will be able to face each day with intentional action and conscious purpose. This grounding can take place every morning before your hectic day starts.

As I mentioned before, implementing new habits, like waking up early in the morning, is not easy, but once you start to experience the enhancements in your life satisfaction, you will never want to go back. Trust me. When you start falling out of your morning routine habits, you will feel it. It might show up in your performance at work, in your relationships, or your overall happiness. You might say to yourself, "I just don't feel like myself." It's because subconsciously, you know what your body needs to live the highest version of yourself; and it takes a little discipline at first.

Here's the truth most people won't tell you—no one can give you discipline. There is no podcast, book, or person on earth that you will meet that will ever provide you with discipline. I may be able to provide you with the latest research, tips, and strategies but at some point, your internal flame can only stay lit from the will and desire from your own heart. Inspirational figures and self-help books like these can help ignite your flame within, but it's your job to help keep it lit. Implementing an effective morning routine will be the same way. Those days when you just don't feel like waking up, remember why you started in the first place.

I can give you all the knowledge and success stories about how a morning routine can change your life, but at the end of the day, it's up to you to try it out and figure out what works best for you to make massive changes in your life. So, as Michael Jordan expressed in the title of his book, the key is to be "Driven from Within." And once you've ignited the flame and know how to keep it, you can use resources around you to master that flame and cultivate it into a healthy fire that will never burn out.

Be Proactive in the Morning, Not Reactive

With so many external things and demands pulling us left and right, one of the most potent ways to truly take control of your life is a consistent morning routine. Because no matter what happened the day before or what may happen in the future, you always return to yourself. The core of who you are. You consistently return to the pillars of life that will keep you energized, aligned, disciplined, and healthy. And as you continue to intertwine this new habit into your day, your full self, including your discipline and healthy habits, will spill over to every other area of your life. You will feel more dynamic, productive, and, most importantly, content, and happy because you will begin to internalize that you don't have to allow life to beat you up day-to-day. You don't have to be the result of circumstances in life. You have the ability to show up as your full self and let your creative talents, personality, and joy shine through you.

Endeavor to be proactive in life, not reactive. If you're reactive in this always-on society, you may always feel as though you are behind the curve. And you may feel like you have no control over your life. This is because you're dependent upon external circumstances to tell you who you should be, what you should do, and where you should go, instead of turning inward and listening to yourself. So, do yourself a favor for the sake of your health, relationships, and overall well-being—don't unconsciously pick up your phone and start scrolling. Take some time for you. Stay conscious and be self-directed as soon as you arise to start your day. And it can all start with a simple morning routine to catapult your entire life journey. This is where radical self-care becomes nicely integrated into your daily life.

RADICAL SELF-CARE EXERCISE:
The Abundant Morning

Now it's your turn to develop a morning routine to get your day started on the *right side of the bed*. If you start your mornings with mental, physical, and spiritual wellness at the forefront of your day, you will be adequately prepared to leap over stress for a full and productive day. Implement, what I like to call, *The Abundant Morning* to ensure your life fosters expansion, strength, health, love, and splendor. Your readiness for the day fosters your expectancy for the good you desire. Use *The Abundant Morning* to kickstart your day on the right foot.

To make this easy for you, you can use the chart below to break up your morning into three specific core areas: physical fitness, mental and spiritual wellness, and knowledge growth. The chart will show you why each of these areas are necessary to your life, and you can use the last column titled "Your Action Plan" to write in what you are going to do in each of these three core areas. Planning this out the night before so you can tackle your morning with less conscious thinking and cognitive bandwidth makes it that much easier to move from task to task. Pretty soon it will become a habit, and you will not have to think about what comes next. It will become natural.

	Benefits	Examples	Tips	Your Action Plan
Physical Fitness (at least 30 min)	Increased focus Can reduce stress hormones, such as cortisol Helps your brain think faster Improves overall mood Can set the tone for healthier food decisions Improves mental resilience	Yoga Running, walking Swimming Strength building Dance classes Jumping rope Spin class Biking	Lay out your workout clothes the night before or you can even sleep in them. Workout with a friend or join a workout class! Studies show that working with a friend increases your chances of consistency and motivation.	
Mental and Spiritual Wellness (at least 20 min)	Helps achieve mental clarity Increased focus You feel aligned to a higher purpose Helps to set positive intentions for your day Strengthen immune system Superior ability to handle stress	Meditation Prayer Say affirmations to yourself Reflection Sitting in complete silence Journaling	Find a quiet place away from distractions and use the same place consistently. Use a phone app (listed at the end of Chapter Eight) to help guide you through a meditation session. Light a candle or listen to smoothing music.	
Knowledge Growth (at least 20 min)	Increase decision-making capacity Rewire your brain, build a stronger memory and increase analytical abilities Stimulates creativity Can inspire you to take more risks to achieve your goals	Podcasts Reading self-help books or biographies of inspirational figures Reading articles Watching educational YouTube videos	Pick a book that you've always wanted to read but never had time. Research a topic on the internet that you've always been curious about. It could be a skill or passion project.	

Reminder: Turn on "Do Not Disturb" on All Your Devices

Here is a bonus I personally add to every morning routine that just takes five minutes:

Either before or after you focus on your spiritual wellness (ex. meditation, prayer, sitting in complete silence), I would recommend that you intentionally focus on the following core areas:
1). Focus on at least three things that you are grateful for.
2). Focus on vitality, mental, and physical health.
3). Visualize three goals you desire to achieve.
4). Ask yourself: How can I live the fullest version of myself today?

1. Focus on at least three things that you are grateful for.
As discussed in Chapter Five, focusing on what you are grateful for gives your day a boost. And it frames your mind to focus on what you do have instead of what you don't have. Feelings of gratefulness are the quickest way to raise your energy and open yourself up to experience more of what life has to offer. It doesn't have to be big or grand either.

Are you grateful for your friends and family? Are you thankful for hot water? What about the smell of your favorite fragrance? A warm cup of coffee or tea in the morning? For your job? It's incredible how easy it is to overlook the simple things in life that we take for granted, so it's necessary to come back to center and focus on the simple things that make life enjoyable. It truly is the little things in life that count. Life will never give you more than what you are currently grateful for.

2. Focus on vitality, mental, and physical health.
The next focus area is your well-being and vitality. Without it, you can't be productive, help others, or reach the highest vision of yourself. Focus on what it will feel like to be in your healthiest state and think about how it would feel throughout your body. Intentionally put focus on every part of your body, starting at your toes, up to your knees, hip, chest, shoulders, fingers, back up your arms, and up your spine, all the way up to your head. Focus on health, well-being, and strength as you consciously focus your intentions throughout every part of your body. Remember, your success and happiness depend on the health of your body and mind.

3. Visualize three goals you desire to achieve.
Pick three goals that mean a lot to you. It could be developing more meaningful relationships, purchasing a new house,

obtaining a larger income to take care of the people closest to you, or simply wanting a more fulfilled life. Whatever they are, focus on it. Act as if the goals are already accomplished and fulfilled. Close your eyes and visualize what it will feel like to have that car, have that healthy and strong body, loving relationships, or to just be content with yourself. This is the secret. Because if you can visualize it in your mind and feel within, you can manifest it into your reality. Some psychologists claim as Jack Canfield writes in his book *The Success Principles,* that one hour of visualization is worth seven hours of physical effort. What a claim!

4. **How can I live the fullest version of myself today?**
   Asking yourself this question can help open yourself up to the possibilities and true expansion of life itself. Progression toward your highest self is what your soul yearns for.
   Now ask yourself: What does that look like for you? How would you feel? What would you give? What would you accomplish? Would you have more compassion for yourself? Would you have more empathy for others? Would you chase your dreams and finally take action on a particular idea? Would you call your family and friends more? Would you do more kind gestures for the people closest to you? Would you call someone to forgive them to release the tension fostered in your heart? Would you have more compassion for yourself?

   Your reality is based upon your expectations. Your expectations toward life lead you to each emotion, interaction, and action that you take in life. Whether your expectations toward life be positive or negative, they will influence your predictions of what you hope or believe can happen in your life. They can either set you up for success and joy or dismay and discontent. So, expect the best in your life and watch it unfold in accordance with your expectations. Asking yourself this question positions you to develop greater levels of self-awareness to choose thoughts, emotions, and actions that serve you and serve others around you.

Use hashtags #RadicalSelfCare and #SuccessStartsWithin on social media and share with others to inspire them to join you on your path toward activating your potential.

CHAPTER TEN

POWER OF THE COMPANY YOU KEEP (WITHIN)

Associate yourself with people of good quality, for it is better to be alone than to be in bad company.
Booker T. Washington

We Are One

I debated myself for months about adding this chapter into a book mainly focused on internal qualities needed to foster a successful and healthy life. Although this book focuses on strategies to help foster a better you so that you can obtain greater levels of success and well-being in your life, we can't escape the significance of how others close to us unconsciously influence who we are and who we become.

This includes not only your significant other but also your friends, family, coworkers, and business associates. As I've stated and it's worth repeating in this chapter; *you* are essentially the average of the five people you surround yourself with. And as our global society continues to be more technologically intertwined, we will become even more interdependent on each other. Your radical self-care journey toward the life you envision for yourself will be heavily influenced by whom you expose yourself to on a daily basis.

Our social relationships can influence every area of our lives—from our diets, income, values, character, and even our future self. As I touched on in Chapter Three, our social relationships are unconsciously conditioning ourselves internally, thus influencing the external results in our lives. And because humans are naturally communicative species, meaning we quite literally need people in our lives to survive, it is necessary to be mindful of who we expose ourselves to. We can no longer see ourselves as separate from one another. This old paradigm of life does not serve us *any longer*. Sciences such as quantum physics are concluding that we are, in fact, all one. And that separation between ourselves is a figment of our imaginations.

In essence, what you do to others is what you do to yourself and vice versa. Let's examine this at a more practical level. You ever notice how good it makes you feel when you give someone else a compliment or give a gift to someone? When we elevate others, we also lift our spirits simultaneously. Although radical self-care is about self, a large part of that focuses on staying mindful of the company you keep around you. The people you surround yourself with have a significant effect on your well-being, success, and even life expectancy. Let me show you why developing your success within should always include the quality of your social relationships. Your life depends on it, literally.

We cannot survive by ourselves. It's simply not possible. One of the worst punishments you can give a human being is solitary confinement, common among jails and prisons. It involves physical isolation, which means that person has little to no interaction with other people.

In an article written in the *Journal of the American Academy of Psychiatry and the Law*, it states that solitary confinement can be as distressing as physical torture. Over time, the inmates can experience depression, social withdrawal, hallucinations that affect their senses, and problems with attention, concentration, and memory. This is an extreme example, but it's evident being alone with minimal positive human interaction can have huge effects on our mental and physical well-being. This innate desire to be around other humans is so ingrained into us that we need each other for our psychological survival. Emotional connectivity with each other continues to remain a core part of being human.

The Secret to a Meaningful and Successful Life

There was a recent study on millennials to understand what their primary life goals were. The study concluded that over 80 percent of the tested subjects said that a major life goal was to get rich. It explains that another 50 percent of those same young adults stated that another major life goal was to become famous. Based on the data presented, researchers further explained that many of us have been conditioned that these are the things we "must" go after to live a fulfilling and happy life. We've been consistently told to climb the organizational ranks, push hard to achieve, and make a certain income. This has been the definition of success and happiness.

And let me very clear, there is nothing wrong with setting these goals for ourselves, but it's necessary to understand that each of these has its place in our lives. As you continue to advance toward your goals and your ideas are realized, you will understand that success means nothing if you can't share it with others. And a majority of our fulfilment and happiness will stem from the people we help and the relationships we cultivate. In fact, one of the world's longest studies of adult life has actually backed up this claim.

Robert Waldinger, a psychiatrist from Harvard University, has been a part of one of the most extended studies of adult life ever conducted. Since 1938, his colleagues and predecessors have tracked the lives of 724 men for over eighty-five years to answer one simple question:

What makes a meaningful and healthy life?

The Harvard Study of Adult Development has been tracking the lives of two groups of men since World War II. Year after year, the study included medical exams, drawing blood, scanning their brains, and interviewing their children. From all the data collected, what did they learn about what makes a happy and healthy life? Well, it turns out that the lessons are not about being famous or attaining a certain amount of income. They concluded that the clearest message from all this data was that: "Good relationships keep us happier and healthier. Period." Meaningful relationships actually keep us healthy and happy. Many of us put so much time into our careers, how we look, our goals, and yearning to become "someone" that we neglect one of life's most important gifts of all—our relationships.

As I mentioned before, humans are sociable by nature, so even if you believe that you're an introvert you still may yearn for connection. Waldinger says, "It turns out that people who are more socially connected to family, to friends, to community, are happier, they're physically healthier, and they live longer than people who are less well connected." This study shows that individuals who are more isolated and experience loneliness, feel less happy. It also indicates that their health declines earlier in midlife, their brain functioning declines, and they even live shorter lives than people who are not lonely. Meaningful relationships protect the health of our bodies and mental capacities of our brains. Meaningful social connections keep us alive longer.

What does this mean? It's important not to focus solely on material things and achievements to sustain happiness and well-being. It's essential to develop meaningful relationships with family, friends, and community. Focus on the friends, family, and build a community that you trust and care about; this will keep you happier and healthier. Cultivating and investing time into your relationships are necessary ingredients for a full life. Not only that, but when you build a community of people you trust, and they trust you, you can accomplish your goals faster!

Here's a great analogy that can make this clear for you. One of my good friends and Chief Program Officer for Positively Caviar, Inc., Shayma Sulaiman, thinks of her closest friends as plants. She cares for them. Waters them. Nourishes them and cherishes them because she knows when she does, the plants are able to grow to reach their fullest potential. Correspondingly, it becomes a pleasing sight for her eyes, psychologically, reducing stress, and purifying the air she breaths. The plant and her are both pleased and content by her efforts. Same thing for our relationships. When we take care of them and cherish them, they are motivated and encouraged to become their fullest potential. Trust, mutual respect, and companionship are all naturally expressed in the relationship because of its care and value. Thus, increasing our health and satisfaction in life. The good life is built off good and meaningful relationships.

This Harvard study is a perfect example that the definition of a successful and happy life needs to be reimagined. When you think about the highest vision for yourself—whether it be a certain amount of income, a successful business, or even buying a particular house—don't ignore your relationships. Your friends, family, and acquaintances play a pivotal role in your life.

As the Harvard study concluded, your relationships literally influence the quality of your life and how long you live. We need to look at our relationships a little bit differently because, based upon these scientific studies, the people we share our lives with, whether negative or positive, influence our well-being and even our life expectancy. When you share your life with another, they are actually biting off a chunk of your destiny.

If you truly want to live a long, healthy, and successful life, it's best to keep relationships at the top of your priority list as you continue to build the life your soul desires.

RADICAL SELF-CARE TIP:
Present Relationships (PR)

One of the greatest gifts you can give another person is your presence. Humans yearn for communion, consideration, communication, and connection. It's something that our souls need to live the highest vision of ourselves. As our twenty-first century lifestyle becomes more attention-grabbing and distracted, it's very easy for us to lose focus and attention when conversing and connecting with friends, family, and coworkers. Not being fully present with the people we are talking to can create pitfalls in trust, emotional connection, business outcomes, and our overall well-being.

**In today's age, we yearn for connection
but don't properly practice it.**

Think about it: In the past week, how many of your conversations were interrupted by you or the other person unconsciously picking up their phone? Being disrupted by an email, text message, or social media notification? Or it could even be related to you thinking about something you have to do or forgot to do, which causes you not to be emotionally present with the other individual. As our brains continue to adapt to this environment, we've almost become unconscious to this type of behavior. It is significantly playing a role in developing meaningful connections and having deep conversations with loved ones and business associates.

How do you feel when you are talking to someone, and they pick up their phone when you are sharing something important? Or how do you feel when they don't make eye contact with you? This type of connection is something humans innately crave because we want to feel listened to, accepted, and understood by others. This is how humans build trust and respect. And our new society is making it that much harder to truly connect with others, which can contribute to loneliness, emptiness, and a sense of separateness. We don't realize how these subtle moments in our lives actually play a pivotal role in our overall health, success, and fulfillment in life.

The next time you talk to someone, give them your complete undivided attention and consciously *be there* during the conversation. Don't think about what you have to do, the email you have to write, the notification you have to respond to—just be there with that person and listen. Make eye contact. Be present. Be attentive. Watch their gestures. Listen to their tone of voice. When humans feel connected and emotional trust has been established by focusing on their gesturers and tone of voice, researchers call this "neural resonance." This basically means you can sense the emotions of another, which can increase emotional bonding, trust, and empathy. You could even say, neurologically, the other person has become more attracted to you.

Whether it be a loved one, friend, a business associate, a grocery store worker, or someone you just met, consciously practicing this simple tip every day can do wonders for your relationships. And ironically when you do this for another, it compounds and enhances the quality of your life simultaneously.

So, every time you feel like you or someone else's cup is low, try giving Present Relationships, or PR for short, a try. You could even say to your partner or to your friend, "give me some PR."

While you pour your attention and presence into others, your cup starts to fill up and overflow as well.

Develop Your Sixth Sense

Now let's dive a bit deeper as to how other people influence us and how you can develop more awareness so you can navigate your relationships more constructively and competently. Have you ever met someone and instantly felt the energy of that person, but they might not have even uttered a word? You can't quite put your finger on it, but instinctively you know you may not be able to trust this individual. Or have you ever walked into a room and instantly sensed the energy, either positive or negative? Many of us have used the idiom, "I could cut the atmosphere with a knife." Meaning a tense situation or conversation has happened in the room.

This can be said, as some people call it, "reading the room." Have you ever had a conversation with someone, and afterward, you felt emotionally drained or uneasy? Or how about you were having a great day and all of sudden you spend time with someone and all they do is complain and tell you all of their problems constantly? They're a chronic complainer and they don't seem to have the desire to really solve their issues. Over time this can be draining to anyone who comes around them. Now I want you to hold on to that thought, now let's look at the other side of this.

Have you ever been around someone who makes you instantly happy when you see them? You can't quite put your finger on it, but when you part ways with that person you feel good about life and even yourself. Your energy is uplifted, and you feel good about your future. Or, how about you're having an "off day," and in the very minute you speak or see that particular person in your life, you feel instantly better. Well, let me tell you something, these types of people in your life are literately adding years to your life!

The negative people you may encounter in your life who leave you mentally and emotionally drained are doing quite the opposite. Negative people will come into our lives; that's inevitable. That's not the issue. The issue is allowing these types of people to stay in your life without consciously knowing how they make you feel day-to-day. The negative emotions you could be feeling can very likely be deriving from someone close to you. Try to remain consciously aware of the state of your internal emotions and where they may be arising from. Otherwise, you may continue to be negatively influenced by someone close to you and may not even realize it.

Do what I like to call "emotional and mental check-ins" with yourself while you are spending time with certain people in your life to become aware of how you feel when you are around them. See, many of us don't even realize the substantial impact people can have on our internal emotions and mental state—whether we like it or not. Doing check-ins can cause you to gain inner awareness of how you feel and discover why and how you started to feel a particular way. In this case, you want to ensure that the company you keep around you is uplifting you and encouraging you to become a better you. Once you uncover these emotions and how you feel around certain people, this will be your baseline or guiding scale for who you may need to limit or continue seeing regularly. If you notice your energy or emotions slide down to the negative side while you are with certain people in your life, then you should try your best to limit your interactions with them as best as possible.

On the other hand, if you are with someone and you feel uplifted, positive, and expansive when you are around them, then I would highly advise you to keep these people in your circle at all costs. These types of people are good for the soul and play an essential role in your overall well-being and success in life. Now I should add that it's necessary to keep people around you that also challenge you, or as some people say, "give it to you straight." They may make you uncomfortable at times, but experiencing these emotions is actually good for you. There is simply no growth in keeping people around you who only tell you what you want to hear. You want to strike the right balance between positive and trustworthy people who can give you the truth and their honest opinion when needed—whether it be about your professional career or life decisions. Ultimately, this allows you to grow and expand toward your goals to reach your best self, personally and professionally.

Scientific studies have concluded that humans emit their own electromagnetic frequency, whether it be positive or negative. The universe is made up of vibrational frequencies and based upon our internal emotions and thoughts, we have the power to influence or determine what type of frequency or energy we wish to emit from ourselves. If this sounds too metaphysical for you, then you should know that in 1994, a panel of scientists at the National Institute of Health chose the scientific name "biofield" to describe this field of energy and information that surrounds the human body. And in the examples I described previously, humans have the incredible power to innately pick up on these frequencies—be it walking into a room full of tension or meeting someone for the first time and feeling as though you cannot trust them even though they might not have said a word. These are innate skills that can be cultivated and can guide you to meaningful, trustworthy relationships.

Some people call it their intuition, a hunch, a sixth sense, or some say, "I just have a feeling." Whatever we choose to name it just understand that people affect people, and we can feel it. To bring this closer to home, I'm reminded of a quote that goes a little something like this: "In religion we call it spirits. In science we call it energy. In the streets we call it vibes. All I'm saying is trust it." This is perfectly said. Being mindful and intentional about the type of people you continue to keep around you is a necessary skill. As you continue to develop this muscle or internal awareness, you will begin to obtain greater levels of discernment to know who you need to keep in your life, limit, or even cut off. This type of muscle pays dividends in business relationships, choosing a partner, or even the friendships you choose to continue to foster in your life.

Warren Buffett, one of the wealthiest people on the planet, once said you should be looking for "three things, generally, in a person. Intelligence, energy, and integrity. And if they don't have the last one, don't even bother with the first two." Finding and keeping people around you can trust and who have integrity is one of the most important things you can do for your health and success in life.

So, as it turns out, the popular quote has it exactly right, "life **is** way too short for bad vibes." And I mean that quite literally. If you continue to hang around negative people, your life can literally become even shorter. Remember, your life expectancy is influenced by the people you keep in your life. Simply put, *who you associate yourself with regularly can add or subtract years from your life*. This is how important it is to be mindful of the relationships you cultivate on a day-to-day basis.

Now, this doesn't mean just running away from every negative person you encounter. That's nearly impossible. However, when they do come around, you need to respond appropriately and, as I like to call it, "protect your energy." Know the people in your life who can potentially undermine your health and success and know the people who can increase it! By consciously remaining aware of this, you can make better decisions of what relationships you should pour into and which ones you need to let go of slowly. You should never pour your energy into others who are not helping to refill your cup. To put it bluntly, don't give your time and energy to those who don't provide you with any in return.

It's Always Been an Inside Job

There are always two sides to every coin. Let me explain. In any relationship in our lives—whether it be friends, significant others, or even business associates—how you are treated is significantly influenced by how you treat the other person. If you want to be around happy people, smile more. If you want people to support your goals, support the goals of another. If you long for a deep and meaningful connection, try doing something nice for a family member or friend—be the energy that you want to attract in your life.

When this conscious decision is acted upon, something strange begins to happen. You start placing yourself in situations and around people who tend to elevate your life. And the more you do this, the more people of the same frequency you are emitting will continue to be attracted to you. This is where the saying "birds of a feather flocked together" comes nicely into play. The more you continue to emit the energy you wish to receive, the more it comes right back to you ten-fold.

In reality, every relationship is actually an inside job, first. How you treat yourself internally manifests outwardly to influence every person you meet and interact with. This is because what you believe internally is what you see, attract, and do externally. The type of relationship you have with the people closest to you is an exact reflection of the relationship you have with yourself. This is why our relationships are actually an inside job. Our relationships are a mirror to the relationship we have with ourselves.

For example, do you know someone in your life with plenty of friends and with seemingly amazing meaningful relationships in their life? Or maybe you've met someone who smiles and is happy all the time or willing to always help someone in need? Well, relationship experts will tell you very candidly that the reason why their relationships thrive, and they are able to give more and do more for another is because of the relationship they have with themselves. These types of people have learned to develop a love for their innermost being or core intrinsic self, and it's outwardly expressed through every thought, action, and gesture given to the people closest to them.

Now let's go on the other side. Do you know someone who doesn't have many friends or who may go from one relationship to another without making any of them last? They may constantly argue or fight with the people closest to them. Most of the time, this isn't because they are outwardly mean or a bad person on purpose. However, it can simply be because of underlying insecurities stemming from past traumas or negative experiences that the person has not internally dealt with yet.

Naturally, this is outwardly expressed in every relationship they encounter. Again, as I touched upon in Chapter One, when you marginalize your love, compassion, and care for yourself, you naturally marginalize the people around you. In this case, many of these people have poor and unhealthy relationships with themselves. Most of them look to others to define them and unconsciously yearn for others to "complete" them. In reality, true happiness and your identity can only be found and cultivated internally. So, if you want to change your relationships in your life, it's fundamental to invest and care for yourself first. Your reality is always a reflection of your inner experience with yourself.

In Earl Nightingale's *Lead the Field*, he says that most people take "the attitude that if only people would be nice to them, they would be nice in return. They're like the person sitting in front of the cold stove waiting for the heat. Until he puts in the fuel, there won't be any heat. It's up to him to act first." Many of our relationships would change if only we take the first step to change our internal relationship with ourselves. You should not rely on some external circumstance or thing to magically make your relationships more meaningful, loving, and closer. This can only start with you. Many people seem to think caring friendships and relationships just happen on their own when, in reality, in many cases it first begins with a conscious choice made by you.

Ask yourself when you are around your closest friends and family, coworkers, or even business associates, if you are investing time, energy, and love into them? Are you uplifting them? Challenging them to be their very best? Sharing knowledge or experiences to benefit them? Encouraging them or providing advice? Are you helping them to accomplish their goals? If not, you should begin to. Because when they are feeling their best, then your relationship with them tends to improve and naturally enhances your life.

It will then become a mutually enjoyable relationship between both of you and a feedback loop of positive human interaction that occurs every time you are around them. Thus, it not only improves your relationship with the other person but also your emotional health, fulfillment, and even life expectancy.

I should add that it's important to exercise caution to not overly give to people who are not ready to receive. This type of discernment comes with time and practice. And I am sure you know of a few people in your life that you give your time and energy to but it's not being reciprocated. I think we all can. Developing this inner knowing is critical to ensure you are not spending your time and energy on others who are taking advantage of you. Under most circumstances, the care and consideration should be coming from both sides for a mutually beneficial relationship.

Find Joy Within to Improve Your Relationships

Here is the truth: We need to develop our internal joy within ourselves; otherwise, we feel compelled to seek it from someone or something else. As a result, we continue to unconsciously yearn for confirmation, completeness, and happiness from external things or people. True happiness, success, and well-being in life can only be cultivated within. And once this happens, your life will begin to unfold with unlimited possibilities and love. Because you are not constantly searching for things outside of yourself like money, cars, or even people to make you happy and complete, you already feel complete and grateful for what you have. This is one of the most powerful states to live in because you are not dependent on anything outside of yourself to make you happy.

Ironically, when you reach this state, the goodness of life compounds and begins to fall in on you. As Michael Beckwith has said, "You have to like yourself when you're by yourself." Meaning, when you are by yourself, it's essential to be comfortable with your thoughts and embrace them. Embrace your thoughts to fully embrace who you are so you can provide to others around you more abundantly. He then goes on to say, "Then you can be with others; otherwise, you're pulling on others to make you happy."

Radical self-care is a journey that can transform every aspect of your life, including your relationships and, most importantly, the relationship with yourself. And our relationships represent a large percentage of the success, well-being, and fulfillment that we all innately yearn for. So, by all means, keep your relationships at the top of your list when you think about what true success looks like for you in your life. Because once you focus on the *company you keep around you and the company you keep within*, your life will become more meaningful and joyful. As the Harvard study concluded, an abundant and prosperous life is built off of meaningful and healthy relationships, and the best way to enhance your relationships is to improve the relationship with yourself. And one of the greatest ways to elevate the relationship with yourself is through radical self-care.

RADICAL SELF-CARE EXERCISE:
Who's Feeding or Draining Your Energy?

The company you keep around you is who you will stay like or will become in the future. They will either keep you stagnant or help you flourish to reach your highest self. Remember, birds of a feather always flock together. It's not by accident. If you want to:

- Increase your income, hang out with people who have more money than you.
- Become a better speaker, join Toastmasters.
- Have a closer relationship with your significant other, be around people who are in successful long-term relationships or marriages.
- Become more happy and joyful, hang around the happiest people you know.

It sounds simple but most people don't intentionally do this. These people are doing something different than most, and you can learn from them by just being around them. You'd be surprised how much you can learn from someone by just being in the presence of that person.

Here's the exercise:

Pull out your phone and scroll through the last ten text messages and calls you have made or people who have reached out to you. Even scroll through your social media accounts and DMs and find the five to ten people you communicate the most with. Take out a pen and write down each of their names. Next to each of their names, write down if you believe they are primarily positive or negative people in your life. You can either write a "P" for positive or "N" for negative. Or you can use a "+" or "−" respectively. Whatever works for you.

As you think about these people, I want you to use the following questions to help you determine if you should limit or spend more time around these people in your life:

- Do I feel uplifted when I am around them?
- Are they inspiring me or are they expiring me?
- Are they helping me to achieve my highest self?
- Are they aligned with my morals and values?
- Are they supportive and caring?
- Do they exhibit attributes that I wish to adopt within myself?
- Are they challenging me to become a better me?
- Do they provide critical feedback to help me grow?
- Are they goal-orientated?
- Are they in a place that I hope to be in my life?

If you have identified this person as positive, continue to consciously make time to hang around them more often. They are enhancing and expanding your life. Quite literally, as discussed, they are adding years to your life.

If a person you've listed is negative, then you may need to limit how much time you spend with them. If they are family members, that's okay; just be mindful of how their presence makes you feel internally and be cautious about spending too much time with them to ensure it does not negatively affect you. You can even use the Guard Your Mind (GYM) technique I discussed in Chapter Two to help with this.

If everyone on your list is negative and is draining your energy, then make it priority to find positive people to engage with. Not sure where to find these people? Consider meetup.com, search LinkedIn for people who share common goals or values or check Eventbrite.com to find events or casual gatherings with people who share your interests.

Use hashtags #RadicalSelfCare and #SuccessStartsWithin on social media and share with others to inspire them to join you on your path toward activating your potential.

CHAPTER ELEVEN

NOW IT'S UP TO YOU

If you can't fly, run; if you can't run, walk; if you can't walk, crawl; but by all means keep moving.
Rev. Dr. Martin Luther King Jr.

Address It

Throughout this book, I've given you strategies and principles that have been proven to radically improve the quality of your life. Scientists, philosophers, and great thinkers have continued to stretch and search for the secrets for a healthy, happy, and successful life, and many of those lessons are in this book. Now it's up to you. Knowledge is only potential power. Your real power comes from you taking the initiative to effectively apply these principles every day throughout your life. Daily action is necessary for any improvement in life.

Simply reading self-help books, hoping for things to happen, listening to podcasts, or watching motivational videos on YouTube is a great start. Still, if you don't take any action to step outside of your comfort zone to realize the life you desire, your results and quality of life will continue to feel stagnant. You need forward momentum, and for that to happen, the first step is required. And as we continue to be overwhelmed with a digital sensory overload of information constantly hacking our attention to pull our thoughts toward things that may not serve us—it's not going to get any easier.

One of the biggest things I've learned from my wife is her ability to address situations in her life head-on. Throughout her life, no matter what tested her, she's persistently stared her personal and professional problems directly in the face. This type of mindset allowed her to develop a muscle of perseverance and drive that inspires me every day. Even when she falls, fails, or is disappointed with herself, she continues to get up. In fact, during conversations in the early years of our relationship, she used to say two simple words that continue to shape every part of my life to this day: *Address it.*

Many times in life, we know a problem exists, or something feels off, but we seem to think it's going to fix itself, or we believe we can hope or wish it away. As I mentioned before, when you hear a bad noise coming from your car, it's important to fix it right away; otherwise, waiting could result in something much worse. The same thing goes for the success in your life. If you become aware of something that is simply not going right in your life—whether it be your physical health, your relationships, or a problem on the job or with your business—it's up to you to find the resources or people to help you avoid further negative consequences that may not serve you in the long run. It's likely that someone has already solved the issue you may be experiencing. Luckily this book can be your resource! And the sooner you address it, the sooner your life gets better.

Use your emotions as a guiding light to determine if you are on the right path or not. Feelings never lie. If you feel good, then you are heading in the right direction. If you feel bad, self-limited, or experience negative emotions, then a change might need to occur. It could come from habits that may not be serving you, who you surround yourself with, or a self-limiting belief. Which, by the way, you have complete control over, but when challenged, many of us don't have the knowledge to take the intelligent action needed to make ourselves feel and be better.

And even when we know what we need to do to live a happier and healthier life, we don't always act on the knowledge consumed. It's a battle between what we should be doing vs. what we actually do. As I've said previously, just because "we know better, doesn't mean we do better."

Steven Kotler in his book *Stealing Fire* says, "We'll think more, talk more, and stress more. We'll wait until after we feel better to go for that walk in the sun, rather than going for that walk in order to feel better. We'll wait until after we get that job offer to pump our fists and stand tall, instead of the other way around." This statement speaks upon scientific research, which proves that sunlight can increase our moods and how "power poses" before interviews or when we are feeling nervous can lower cortisol and increase confidence improving our chances of obtaining a particular goal like a job offer.

Don't just sit around expecting your life to get any better, especially when you now have tools to improve your life. Any change can feel like a struggle at times, but at the end of the day, just as Michael Beckwith has said, "Pain pushes you until the vision pulls you." So, the challenge then becomes how long do you want to continue to soak in discontentment until a higher vision of yourself pulls you toward your desired life.

Change the Target

There needs to be a new definition for what success and happiness look like. It's time that we re-engineer the traditional success symbols that consumerism and society force us to chase. A BMW, a big house, or how many likes you get on Instagram are false symbols of success. Please don't get me wrong, though; there is nothing wrong with having or attaining these things. It's okay to have desires but don't let those external desires have you. It's evident that true happiness has never come from material things. They can come and go. They are fleeting and always have the potential of being taken away.

Achieving an external goal may provide a sense of accomplishment or relief, but once it fades, most of time it doesn't provide you with lasting fulfillment. Our state of mind should not be solely dependent upon external things; otherwise, our internal happiness can be governed by them when they are not present. Instead, we should be seeking well-being and peace of mind, not external validation. We must change the target of what we are aiming for to obtain sustainable success.

In fact, research by Shawn Achor, author of *The Happiness Advantage*, has confirmed that only about 10 percent of our happiness stems from the external world, while 90 percent is based on how our brains process the world. This suggests that our internal processes, perception, and attitude substantially impact our overall happiness in life. This is how two people could have the same job; one person is fulfilled, and the other is miserable. In other words, we determine our happiness and success in life.

There are tons of unhappy rich people and celebrities. But there are also many extremely happy, wealthy, and successful people. So, be mindful of how you use material items to measure your success in life. True well-being and happiness, which is the ultimate measure of a successful life, is cultivated within. Once you begin to find peace and well-being within you, you want nothing more than to share it with everyone you know. It excites you to support, care for, and help everyone you know. You've let go of grudges, jealousy, and envy because inside your heart, you want nothing more than to express your inner joy to everyone you meet.

Real success and inner wealth are found in having peace of mind, a healthy body, self-awareness, a clear conscious, meaningful relationships, and helping others to realize their dreams. But the only way to reach this lofty mountain peak is to modify our target of what we are aiming for so we can reach the right summit. And that target should be commitment to *self-mastery*. This is what real success looks like. Instead of seeking external validation, we should be seeking to cultivate internal peace, a calm poise, and well-being. As the saying goes, "It's better to travel well than to arrive."

You've devised strategies to challenge your negative self-talk, made time to cultivate your inner joy daily, know how to deal with negative people, and gained a sense of calm fearlessness during uncertain situations. This is when true mastery is reached. At this level, success, peace, and contentment begin to fall in on you with ease. Your peace and joy cultivated within will vibrationally match and will be reflected in your external experience. Thus, you will begin to attract exactly what you are cultivating within.

If peace lives within your heart, guess what type of people will be attracted to you? If you truly feel that you are wealthy and worthy of success, guess what type of actions you will take toward your dreams, knowing this to be true? And if you are happy and joyful, guess what type of situations and experiences you will attract into your life? A successful, happy, and fulfilled life is an inside job. When you continue to take care of yourself internally, your external world will start to change. You will have more energy. You will give more. You will love more. And you will feel true bliss day-to-day knowing that you don't need anything outside of yourself to truly make you happy.

Am I saying life will be easy and challenge-free? Absolutely not! You will have days that don't go as well as you would like them to, but here's the key: you now have the tools to cultivate your inner well-being and, even when challenges do arise, you can continuously activate latent potential. None of the strategies in the book will make your life perfect, but they *will* help you manage the life you currently have to catapult you toward better circumstances and results.

Many of us go through life wishing, praying, and hoping our lives match our internal desires. For faster progress and a sustainable journey, we must change the target of a successful life from the accumulation of external material items and titles to *inner well-being*. Once you truly care for yourself, then all of your problems, frustrations, stress, and goals will start to feel like a graceful journey. It will become a journey that you will enjoy and learn from, not rush. When you get into this space and realize life is about how you respond to it and not the actual event itself, it won't feel like a struggle or a fight. You will begin to feel as though you are *moving with life, not against it.*

A Relaxed Mind for Success

When you make radical self-care a priority in your life and put yourself first, you will be full of insight and creativity that you didn't even know you had. Indeed, it is true from a traditional sense that long hours of hard work can produce the success you desire, but it's clear a more balanced and sustainable approach is needed for the long haul. The new science discussed in this book confirms that a relaxed mind and a peaceful attitude can increase creative insights, productivity, and problem-solving functions in the brain much more effectively. Whether it be through meditation or exercising, these methods can lead to cutting-edge innovation and better ideas to help you solve challenging problems, thus increasing your odds of success in your professional career or personal life.

One famous example of this is 3M, a corporation famously known for their development of the Post-It Notes, which encourages employees to use up to 15 percent of their working hours to pursue their own ideas. They call it the 15-percent rule. The Post-It Note was developed because of this same rule, which allowed scientist Art Fry to step away from the day-to-day work grind to let his mind rest to draw from its creative source. Even Google modeled 3M's approach and created the 20-percent rule, giving rise to Gmail and Google Earth. If you recall in Chapter Eight, I discussed how major corporations like Google, Nike, and Apple are investing in meditation and mindfulness rooms to foster wellness, increase performance, and improve creativity. It seems we are all coming to understand the importance of stepping away from the hustle and allowing the powers of a relaxed mind to improve health and human ingenuity.

Meditation, yoga, healthy habits, and physical fitness are all great examples of radical self-care that can increase your performance and health and help you achieve a more relaxed mind to foster creativity and better ideas in your life. Working smartly gives your mind and body the ability to be at peace to stimulate higher-brain function and improve your creativity and intelligence, thereby increasing your odds of your desired outcomes. It's necessary to integrate ways to invest in ourselves and use our bodies effectively to achieve optimal health and accomplish our goals simultaneously. Nonstop aggressive hard work without replenishing your mind, body, and soul will only take you so far. It's just simply not sustainable. Here's how I like to think of it: the better you become at taking care of yourself, the more capable your body becomes in receiving more creative ideas that will boost your life satisfaction, increase your income, enhance your family's quality of life, and the contributions you provide to the world.

When you continue to regularly take care of yourself, you will be able to take on challenges without your unconscious limiting beliefs driving you. You will have the mental clarity to evade distractions increasing your productivity and influencing your overall fulfillment throughout the day. You will develop a sense of mental stability, courage, and patience that yields you the ability to persist despite challenges. You will experience fewer setbacks, and even when they do occur, you will not be discouraged by them. It's necessary to take care of yourself first to ensure there are no blockages in your creative potential. Once you do this, your ideas, joy, and success will be streamlined and realized.

This is because you've created a stable enough platform within your mind and body to allow yourself to use those crucial core domains (pattern of thinking, mindset, and beliefs) discussed in Chapter One more effectively to consciously achieve your desires.

Go Within to Develop Your Gifts

Our purpose in life is to develop our gifts of intentionality to be effective co-creators of our lives. And in order to develop our gifts and reach the success we yearn for, we must create a stable foundation for our bodies through continuous radical self-care. This is the essence of the human soul, and if we do not feel we can create and control our destinies, we feel stuck, depressed, or in a rut. It's simply in our fundamental nature to create and manifest our desires with the God-given talents that we've been blessed with. If we feel as though we are not fully expressing ourselves, we can feel cheated out of life when we wake up in the morning. And as we are being seduced by the endless loop of our attention-grabbing, media-obsessed, twenty-first-century society that we live in, our levels of focus, intentionality, and concentration are slowly shortening, forcing us not to spend enough time focusing on what our souls unconsciously yearn for. We spend so much of our time focused externally that we tend to sacrifice the core needs of our mind, body, and soul.

In a world where *everything feels like emergency*, it can be very easy to lose sight of our true nature, forget our own identities, and even the love and care we require. Cultivating radical self-care is necessary so that we can effectively self-actualize in our lives. And one of the most powerful things you can do is spend time on yourself to ensure your cup is full so that you can abundantly pour it into others. Building your success within by using radical self-care is more than just focusing on yourself—it's about diving deep into your soul to ensure you are evolving and unfolding to become a deliberate creator of your life. So along with scheduling that massage or journaling, make sure you add monitoring your self-talk, questioning your own beliefs, discovering your why, meditation, and cultivating the relationship with yourself to elevate the relationships closest to you.

Although glamorized, life is not about striving harder and putting in long hours to achieve the success we yearn for. Trust me, I am a firm believer in persistent action but not at the expense of our bodies' health and closest relationships. The more we go *within*, the stronger and more resilient we become—mentally, physically, psychologically, emotionally, and spiritually. Thus, yielding us the ability to become more effective and efficient in carrying out our goals, dreams, and life purpose.

The key to a happy and successful life is not overworking or living in a constant state of unnecessary busyness trying to fit more into your day.

It's about healing from the inside out so you can use your mind and body more efficiently to increase creativity, tackle challenges easier, foster greater levels of joy, and streamline your success. This, in turn, allows you to increase your contributions and love that you have toward your family, friends, and the world.

You're no longer waiting for your future achievements to feel empowered. Or postponing your joy until you achieve your goals. Or losing your peace of mind in the hustle of pursuing your dreams. Or constantly seeking external acceptance to feel love.

Once you are here, you are no longer sacrificing your present well-being to activate your potential.

You're cultivating these inner qualities and conditions in the *here* and *now* and taking them **with you** along your journey to success.

When you focus on your internal needs first and integrate the practices in this book, you will start to feel whole and in flow with who you *really* are because you've invested in one of the most critical assets—yourself! This makes you a joyous conscious creator of your destiny to unleash the true creative potential that can be cultivated within. It's a prerequisite to take care of your inner self if you want to achieve the highest vision of yourself externally. *For if you don't go within, then you go without.* And when you make your internal peace, happiness, and well-being a priority in life, all of your external goals have a way of working themselves out anyway. This is because well-being always precedes true success. This is the irony of life. And it can all begin with *radical self-care.*

So, when you think about enhancing the quality of your life, be sure you are replenishing your inner soul so you can truly master life from the *inside out.*

The Key

We misplace our true power, love, and success.

When we externalize our power, love, and success, it forces us to think that we are separate from what we already are. This mentality reinforces an identity that we must go out and get what's already within us. When in reality, we've always been what we're searching for.

If we think our true identity is separate from us, we place our power outside ourselves. Therefore, we feel lost, powerless, and stuck. Just as sour apples spring from an unhealthy tree, our roots, or in this context, our identity needs to be correctly identified so that we may spring healthy fruit into every facet of our lives.

You are love. You are success. You are joy.

This is your true identity. And when you live from this identity, from within, your life will effortlessly flow for you in your relationships, health, and wealth instead of feeling like you are at the mercy of circumstances in your life. Everything responds to you at the level of your recognition of this great truth.

You are the key.

Chazz Scott

AUTHOR COMMENTS

Thank you for your reading this book. I hope it provides you with inspiration and a better understanding of how to increase the quality of your life. If the book has helped you in some way, I'd love to hear about it. Please feel free to write a review on Amazon, as honest reviews help other readers find the right book for their needs. You can also feel free to send me an email at chazz@chazzscott.com. I realize that scientific literature changes over time, and references in this book may need to be updated. However, if you believe I've made a mistake in the book or didn't give credit to someone where it's due, please email me so I can correct this as soon as possible.

ACKNOWLEDGMENTS

Success Starts Within couldn't have been written without some amazing people in my life. Thank you to my mom, dad, and grandparents for continuing to be my guiding lights. I wouldn't be the person I am today without their love, strength, faith, and tenacity. Thank you to my amazing wife for your constant support, love, and guidance. I am grateful to the entire team at Central Recovery Press for selecting my manuscript for publication and guiding me along the way as a first-time author. Thank you to my fantastic editors, Valerie Killeen and Nancy Schenck. Also, thank you to Jennifer Mutz, for your expert marketing skills and to sales manager, John Davis.

In addition, as a first-time author, I received a ton of support along the way from my editor and book coach Marisa Solis. I can honestly say without her vision and expert editing skills, you would not be reading this book today. Thank you for believing in my book. While fifty-seven publishers and agents rejected the original manuscript, you continued rooting me on and providing guidance along the way. Also, thank you to Vanessa Campos for your guidance and counsel in this new world of publishing. Many thanks to my friends Austin, Nikki, and Shayma, who helped me tailor my book exercises and messaging. Your feedback has been instrumental.

Lastly, thanks to everyone who reads this book and takes a positive step in the direction toward their highest self. I'm thankful that you allowed this book to be a part of your journey toward well-being and success.

SEMINAR AND SPEAKER SERVICES

Book Chazz for your next event: https://www.chazzscott.com/speaking.

REFERENCES

Chapter One
The Intersection of Wellness and Success

K. M. Sheldon and T. Kasser, "Coherence and congruence: two aspects of personality integration," *Journal of Personality and Social Psychology*, (1995): 68(3), 531–43. https://doi.org/10.1037/0022-3514.68.3.531.

Radical Self-Care, Indiana State University. (December 1, 2020). Retrieved October 11, 2021, from https://www.indstate.edu/student-affairs/msp/self-care.

Chapter Two
Guard Your Mind

A. Hafenbrack, Z. Kinias, and S. Barsade, "Debiasing the mind through meditation: mindfulness and the sunk cost bias," *Academy of Management Proceedings*, (2013): (1) 11582. https://doi.org/10.5465/ambpp.2013.11582abstract.

B. C. Neilan, B. M. Meaker, B. H. Plush, B. M. Field, B. E. Somerville, and B. S. Shaikh, "Reading can help reduce stress," the *Telegraph*, (March 30, 2021). Retrieved July 20, 2021, from https://www.telegraph.co.uk/news/health/news/5070874/Reading-can-help-reduce-stress.html.

E. Commodari and M. Guarnera, "Attention and reading skills," *Perceptual and Motor Skills*, (2005): 100(2), 375–86. https://doi.org/10.2466/pms.100.2.375-386.

J. D. Creswell, L. E. Pacilio, E. K. Lindsay, and K. W. Brown, "Brief mindfulness meditation training alters psychological and neuroendocrine responses to social evaluative stress," *Psychoneuroendocrinology*, (2014): 44, 1–12. https://doi.org/10.1016/j.psyneuen.2014.02.007.

N. Morgan, "How to master yourself, your unconscious, and the people around you," *Forbes*, 3, (March 19, 2013). Retrieved July 19, 2021, from https://www.forbes.com/sites/nickmorgan/2013/03/07/how-to-master-yourself-your-unconscious-and-the-people-around-you-3/?sh=7c8336496762.

R. Bernstein, "The mind and mental health: how stress affects the brain," (March 16, 2021), Touro University WorldWide. Retrieved July 20, 2021, from https://www.tuw.edu/health/how-stress-affects-the-brain.

R. L. Leahy, *The Worry Cure: Seven Steps to Stop Worry from Stopping You* (New York: Random House, 2021).

Chapter Three
Understand Mental Conditioning

"Abundance of information narrows our collective attention span," *ScienceDaily*, (April 15, 2019). Retrieved July 7, 2021, from https://www.sciencedaily.com/releases/2019/04/190415081959.htm.

Conditioning, Britannica.com, (2021). Retrieved June 29, 2021, from https://www.britannica.com/science/conditioning.

Conscious, Dictionary.com, (2021). Retrieved June 29, 2021, from https://www.dictionary.com/browse/conscious.

Dopamine Jackpot! Sapolsky on the Science of Pleasure, YouTube, (March 2, 2011). https://www.youtube.com/watch?v=axrywDP9Ii0&ab_channel=FORA.tv.

G. Rizzolatti and L. Craighero, "The mirror-neuron system," *Annual Review of Neuroscience*, (2004): 27(1), 169–92. https://doi.org/10.1146/annurev.neuro.27.070203.144230.

"High levels of exercise linked to nine years of less aging at the cellular level: new research shows a major advantage for those who are highly active," *ScienceDaily*, (May 10, 2017). Retrieved July 15, 2021, from https://www.sciencedaily.com/releases/2017/05/170510115211.htm.

I. Shalev, T. Moffitt, and A. Caspi, "Violence exposure during childhood is associated with telomere erosion: a longitudinal study," *Comprehensive Psychiatry*, (2013): 54(1), e10. https://doi.org/10.1016/j.comppsych.2012.07.044.

L. A. Tucker, "Physical activity and telomere length in US men and women: An NHANES investigation," *Preventive Medicine*, (2017): 100, 145–51. https://doi.org/10.1016/j.ypmed.2017.04.027.

M. Mendioroz, "Telomere length correlates with subtelomeric DNA methylation in long-term mindfulness practitioners," *Scientific Reports*, (March 12, 2020). Retrieved July 15, 2021, from https://www.nature.com/articles/s41598-020-61241-6?error=cookies_not_supported&code=a4fb5933-6e28-4584-8d7d-a5da7ded5a7d#:%7E:text=In%20fact%2C%20intensive%20meditation%20training,candidate%20biomarker%20of%20human%20aging.

Microsoft, "Attention spans," (2015). http://dl.motamem.org/microsoft-attention-spans-research-report.pdf.

S. Leroy, "Why is it so hard to do my work? The challenge of attention residue when switching between work tasks," *Organizational Behavior and Human Decision Processes*, (2009): 109(2), 168–81. https://doi.org/10.1016/j.obhdp.2009.04.002.

S. Rogers, "Your mobile attention span is now so short you won't finish this article," *VentureBeat*, (July 11, 2016). Retrieved July 7, 2021, from https://venturebeat.com/2016/07/11/your-mobile-attention-span-is-now-so-short-you-wont-finish-this-article.

T. Freire, "The anti-aging impact of meditation," *Wall Street International*, (January 19, 2018). Retrieved July 15, 2021, from https://wsimag.com/wellness/35256-the-anti-aging-impact-of-meditation.

Unconscious, Dictionary.com, (2021). Retrieved June 29, 2021, from https://www.dictionary.com/browse/unconscious.

Using the Power of Habits to Work Smarter, HelpingYourEngineerYourFuture, (2021). Retrieved September 14, 2021, from http://www.helpingyouengineeryourfuture.com/habits-work-smarter.htm.

Chapter Four
Affirm Your Self-Talk

A. R. Peden, M. K. Rayens, L. A. Hall, and L. H. Beebe, L. H., "Preventing depression in high-risk college women: a report of an 18-month follow-up," *Journal of American College Health*, (2001): 49(6), 299–306. https://doi.org/10.1080/07448480109596316.

J. Murdock, "Humans have more than 6,000 thoughts per day psychologists discover," *Newsweek*, (July 15, 2020). Retrieved August 29, 2021, from https://www.newsweek.com/humans-6000-thoughts-every-day-1517963.

Joe Dispenza, *You Are the Placebo: Making Your Mind Matter* (Carlsbad, CA: Hay House, Inc., 2015).

M. A. Killingsworth and D. T. Gilbert, "A wandering mind is an unhappy mind," *Science*, (2010): 330(6006), 932. https://doi.org/10.1126/science.1192439.

Chapter Five
Discover Your Why

"What is "hitting the wall" during a marathon and how can you avoid it?" *Runner's World*, (April 2, 2019). Retrieved July 28, 2021, from https://www.runnersworld.com/uk/training/marathon/a774858/how-to-avoid-the-wall-and-cope-if-you-hit-it/.

"Why gratitude is good," Greater Good, (2010). https://greatergood.berkeley.edu/article/item/why_gratitude_is_good.

Chapter Six
Work Toward Ascension

A. Mackenzie, *The Time Trap: The Classic Book on Time Management* (fourth edition), (New York: AMACOM Books, 2009).

D. Gillaspie, "You'll never accomplish goals you don't really care about," *Entrepreneur*, (January 20, 2017). Retrieved July 23, 2021, from https://www.entrepreneur.com/article/254371.

H. J. Spiers, "Keeping the goal in mind: prefrontal contributions to spatial navigation," *Neuropsychologia*, (2008): 46(7), 2106–108. https://doi.org/10.1016/j.neuropsychologia.2008.01.028.

J. Hoomans, "35,000 decisions: the great choices of strategic leaders," (March 20, 2015), Robert Wesleyan College. Retrieved July 23, 2021, from https://go.roberts.edu/leadingedge/the-great-choices-of-strategic-leaders.

J. Murdock, "Humans have more than 6,000 thoughts per day psychologists discover," *Newsweek*, (July 15, 2020). Retrieved August 29, 2021, from https://www.newsweek.com/humans-6000-thoughts-every-day-1517963.

R. J. Compton, "The interface between emotion and attention: a review of evidence from psychology and neuroscience," *Behavioral and Cognitive Neuroscience Reviews*, (2003): 2(2), 115–29. https://doi.org/10.1177/1534582303002002003.

Chapter Seven
Schedule Regular Exercise

B. Gutmann, A. Mierau, T. Hülsdünker, C. Hildebrand, A. Przyklenk, W. Hollmann, and H. K. Strüder, "Effects of physical exercise on individual resting state eeg alpha peak frequency," *Neural Plasticity*, (2015): 1–6. https://doi.org/10.1155/2015/717312.

B. Winter, C. Breitenstein, F. C. Mooren, K. Voelker, M. Fobker, A. Lechtermann, K. Krueger, A. Fromme, C. Korsukewitz, A. Floel, and S. Knecht, "High impact running improves learning," *Neurobiology of Learning and Memory*, (2007): 87(4), 597–609. https://doi.org/10.1016/j.nlm.2006.11.003.

C. W. Cotman and C. Engesser-Cesar, "Exercise enhances and protects brain function," *Exercise and Sport Sciences Reviews*, (2002): 30(2), 75–79. https://doi.org/10.1097/00003677-200204000-00006.

California Department of Education, "State study proves physically fit kids perform better academically," (December 10, 2002). https://americansportsinstitute.org/wp-content/uploads/pdf/PhysicallyFitKids.pdf.

"Exercise: The magic bullet for depression and substance abuse?" Sandstone Care, (May 17, 2017). Retrieved July 26, 2021, from https://www.sandstonecare.com/blog/exercise-depression-substance-abuse.

G. Mammen and G. Faulkner, "Physical activity and the prevention of depression," *American Journal of Preventive Medicine*, (2013): 45(5), 649–57. https://doi.org/10.1016/j.amepre.2013.08.001.

J. Ratey, "The ADHD exercise solution," (March 17, 2020). *ADDitude*. Retrieved July 26, 2021, from https://www.additudemag.com/the-adhd-exercise-solution/.

J. J. Ratey, *Spark: The Revolutionary New Science of Exercise and the Brain*, (Boston: Little, Brown and Company, 2021).

K. G. Orphanides, "Runner's high: your body makes its own cannabis when you run" (April 20, 2017), *Wired UK*. Retrieved July 26, 2021, from https://www.wired.co.uk/article/your-body-makes-its-own-cannabis-when-you-run.

"Moderate exercise not only treats, but prevents depression," *ScienceDaily*, (October 28, 2013). Retrieved July 23, 2021, from https://www.sciencedaily.com/releases/2013/10/131028163003.htm.

M. Y. Li, M. M. Huang, S. Z. Li, J. Tao, G. H. Zheng, and L. D. Chen, "The effects of aerobic exercise on the structure and function of DMN-related brain regions: a systematic review," *International Journal of Neuroscience*, (2016): 127(7), 634–49. https://doi.org/10.1080/00207454.2016.1212855.

New York Times, "Fight Depression on Your Treadmill," (April 3, 2001). Retrieved July 23, 2021, from https://www.nytimes.com/2001/04/03/health/fight-depression-on-your-treadmill.html.

Chapter Eight
Maintain a Meditation Practice

K. Williams, "Mobile users spent $195 million in meditation apps last year, up 52% over 2018," (January 31, 2020), Sensor Tower Blog. Retrieved August 1, 2021, from https://sensortower.com/blog/meditation-apps-2019-revenue-downloads.

M. A. Killingsworth and D. T. Gilbert, "A wandering mind is an unhappy mind," *Science*, (2010): 330(6006), 932. https://doi.org/10.1126/science.1192439.

M. Curtin, "Neuroscience reveals 50-year-olds can have the brains of 25-year-olds if they do this 1 thing," (January 5, 2021), Inc.com. Retrieved August 1, 2021, from https://www.inc.com/melanie-curtin/neuroscience-shows-that-50-year-olds-can-have-brains-of-25-year-olds-if-they-do-this.html.

M. Levin, Why google, nike, and apple love mindfulness training, and how you can easily love it too," (January 5, 2021). Inc.Com. Retrieved August 1, 2021, from https://www.inc.com/marissa-levin/why-google-nike-and-apple-love-mindfulness-training-and-how-you-can-easily-love-.html.

Chapter Nine
Jumpstart Life with a Morning Routine

R. Alahmad, "Always connected how smartphones and study: how addicted are we to facebook mobile?" (2021), SlideShare. Retrieved August 29, 2021, from https://www.slideshare.net/roonitta/study-how-addicted-are-we-to-facebook-mobile/4-Always_Connected_How_Smartphones_And.

Chapter Ten
Power of the Company You Keep (Within)

M. R. Waldman and C. Manning, *NeuroWisdom: The New Brain Science of Money, Happiness, and Success*, (New York: Diversion Books, 2017).

Chapter Eleven
Now It's Up to You

S. Achor, "When will I be happy?" HuffPost. (September 20, 2011). Retrieved August 12, 2021, from https://www.huffpost.com/entry/pursuit-of-happiness_b_904740.

CPSIA information can be obtained
at www.ICGtesting.com
Printed in the USA
JSHW022139130723
44720JS00001B/2